"A. L. James's brilliant and uncompromising book presents a rigorous and unheard-of way of interrogating the music of Ornette Coleman. It takes its cue from a remark made by Charlie Haden, which becomes the point of departure for a highly speculative journey towards a definition – in logical, topological, and musicological terms – of what it means to 'follow' in music. In the best tradition of continental theory, A. L. James lends a psychoanalytical and philosophical ear to the most banal and yet mysterious – the most enigmatically obvious – details in a musician's discourse about his music".

Peter Szendy, David Herlihy Professor of Comparative Literature and Humanities at Brown University

"In this brilliant technical analysis, A. L. James's harmolodic work of love *follows* Ornette Coleman in precisely the way he demanded of his fellow musicians, by tracking the movement of the sonic *àgalma* that both encapsulates and displaces the solitude of the Idea in the space of free difference".

Scott Wilson, author of *Scott Walker and the Song of the One-All-Alone* (Bloomsbury) and *Stop Making Sense: Music from the Perspective of the Real* (Routledge)

Ornette Coleman, Psychoanalysis, Discourse

Ornette Coleman, Psychoanalysis, Discourse develops tools from psychoanalysis for the analysis of Ornette Coleman's discourse.

In this psychoanalytic, philosophical and musical meditation on what it means *to follow*, A. L. James presents an analysis of Ornette Coleman's discourse that is a kind of listening for listening – an attempt to discern in and between the lines of Coleman's speech, the implication of new ways to listen, new ways to experience Coleman's music as movement and space – as *Movements in Harmolodic Space*. Each chapter of this book is oriented with respect to fragments from Coleman's discourse, dealing with a piece, or collection of pieces, from Coleman's work, with particular attention to the implication of relations and relationality. Insofar as Coleman's discourse about his work also contains allusions to fields beyond music, it develops tools that draw elements and structures from these fields together, finding in their relation echoes and parallels.

Ornette Coleman, Psychoanalysis, Discourse will be of great interest to psychoanalysts, musicians, and musicologists. It will be relevant for academics and scholars of psychoanalytic and Lacanian studies, music, and cultural studies.

A.L. James is an artist and writer from London.

The Lines of the Symbolic in Psychoanalysis Series
Series Editor: Ian Parker, *Manchester Psychoanalytic Matrix*

Psychoanalytic clinical and theoretical work is always embedded in specific linguistic and cultural contexts and carries their traces, traces which this series attends to in its focus on multiple contradictory and antagonistic "lines of the Symbolic". This series takes its cue from Lacan's psychoanalytic work on three registers of human experience, the Symbolic, the Imaginary and the Real, and employs this distinctive understanding of cultural, communication and embodiment to link with other traditions of cultural, clinical and theoretical practice beyond the Lacanian symbolic universe. The Lines of the Symbolic in Psychoanalysis Series provides a reflexive reworking of theoretical and practical issues, translating psychoanalytic writing from different contexts, grounding that work in the specific histories and politics that provide the conditions of possibility for its descriptions and interventions to function. The series makes connections between different cultural and disciplinary sites in which psychoanalysis operates, questioning the idea that there could be one single correct reading and application of Lacan. Its authors trace their own path, their own line through the Symbolic, situating psychoanalysis in relation to debates which intersect with Lacanian work, explicating it, extending it and challenging it.

Philosophy After Lacan
Politics, Science, and Art
Edited by Alireza Taheri, Chris Vanderwees, and Reza Naderi

Critical Essays on the Drive
Lacanian Theory and Practice
Edited by Dan Collins and Eve Watson

A Social Ontology of Psychosis
Genea-logical Treatise on Lacan's Conception of Psychosis
Diego Enrique Londoño-Paredes

Ornette Coleman, Psychoanalysis, Discourse
Movements in Harmolodic Space
A.L. James

For more information about the series, please visit: https://www.routledge.com/The-Lines-of-the
-Symbolic-in-Psychoanalysis-Series/book-series/KARNLOS

Ornette Coleman, Psychoanalysis, Discourse

Movements in Harmolodic Space

A.L. James

LONDON AND NEW YORK

Designed cover image: Getty | FrankRamspott

First published 2025
by Routledge
4 Park Square, Milton Park, Abingdon, Oxon OX14 4RN

and by Routledge
605 Third Avenue, New York, NY 10158

Routledge is an imprint of the Taylor & Francis Group, an informa business

© 2025 A.L. James

The right of A.L. James to be identified as author of this work has been asserted in accordance with sections 77 and 78 of the Copyright, Designs and Patents Act 1988.

All rights reserved. No part of this book may be reprinted or reproduced or utilised in any form or by any electronic, mechanical, or other means, now known or hereafter invented, including photocopying and recording, or in any information storage or retrieval system, without permission in writing from the publishers.

Trademark notice: Product or corporate names may be trademarks or registered trademarks, and are used only for identification and explanation without intent to infringe.

British Library Cataloguing-in-Publication Data
A catalogue record for this book is available from the British Library

ISBN: 9781032534886 (hbk)
ISBN: 9781032534848 (pbk)
ISBN: 9781003412304 (ebk)

DOI: 10.4324/9781003412304

Typeset in Times New Roman
by Deanta Global Publishing Services, Chennai, India

Contents

	Acknowledgements	*xii*
	Series preface	*xiii*
	Preface	*xv*

1 What does it mean to follow?   1

I want you just to follow me 1
What does it mean to follow? 2
The Squid Piece 3
Discourse 5
  Discourse as Other 5
  Quilting 6
Space 8
  Relations 9
  Topology 10
Notes 11

2 Transference   13

Transference: the development of a term 15
  The transference of a name 15
  Transference and the signifier 16
  Freudian identification 17
  Freudian transference 17
  Transference as completion 18
  Metaphor as transference 19
Transference – first sense 19
  General reflections on transference 20

viii   Contents

Transference – second sense 20
  Transference and transposition 21
Analogous transferences 22
Summary of approach 22
Notes 23

3   "No one knew where to go"   25

Hamilton's solution 26
  Vectors 26
Ornette's solution 29
  Thirds and tonics 29
  Tonic and situating vectors 31
Problems 34
  First problem: "tonic" 34
  Second problem: tonal orientation 35
  Tonic relation 36
  Ornette's solution: summary of problems 37
  Third problem: two "wheres" 38
  Analysis and synthesis 39
  An order of coordination 40
What does it mean to follow? 41
  Concluding remarks 42
Notes 42

4   Invisible   45

Introductory analysis 45
Transposition 47
  The transference of a relation 47
  Equivalence quotients 48
  From points to relations 49
Invisibility 50
  Relations and invisibility 50
  A lost or hidden object 50
  Univocal applications 51
Free direction 53
  Three directions 53
  Free vectors 54
  Free 55
What does it mean to follow? 56
A law governing manifestations? 57

That's it, that's it! 57
Only a half-step away 59
What does it mean to follow – revisited 61
Notes 63

5   Lonely Woman (solitude)   65

A space of solitude 66
Isolated points 67
An interval that will have everything in it 67
Interval 68
The transference of a name 68
Transference of a relation 69
Everything in it 70
"Everything" 70
"In" 71
"Having everything in it" 71
Pitch sole 71
Carries a complete idea 72
Phrase ideas 72
Disconnection 73
Movement 74
Har-mo-lodic Movement 75
A cure for solitude 76
Loss of a relation, loss of an Idea 77
Lack of a relation, lack of an Idea 78
What does it mean to follow? 79
Notes 81

6   Lonely Woman (no relation)   82

The tension in all love conflicts 82
Cherokee 83
Schuller's "Lonely Woman" 85
Two "tensions" 85
Analysis of "Lonely Woman" 86
"Lonely Woman" – phrase 1 87
"Lonely Woman" – phrase 2 88
"Lonely Woman" – phrase 3a and 3b 88
"Lonely Woman" – phrase 4 89
"Lonely Woman" – phrase 5 89
Analysis of transcription 89

x   Contents

A natural, freer time 91
  Spread rhythm 92
  Netted rhythm 92
  Breathing in space 93
  Hasn't any relation 95
What does it mean to follow? 98
Notes 99

7   *Skies of America*   101

The sensation of unison 101
  Hamiltonian unison 102
Sharp or flat in tune 103
  Tuning neighbourhoods 104
  Transference of a pitch name 105
The notation of unison 105
  Higher by name 106
  Higher by sound 106
  Transference of an Idea name 107
A different unison for the same notes 108
  The same four notes 108
  A different unison for the same notes 109
  Transference of a letter name 111
The harmolodic clef – 8 112
  Harmolodic reading 112
  It doesn't change the sound you're making 112
  Transference of a sound name 114
Unison 114
  One-sound 114
  From one-point-sound to one-relation-sound 115
One's own logic 116
  Its own law 116
The sound of one's own voice 117
  I would know it was you 117
  The magic mouthpiece 117
  Phantom centre sound 118
  The sound of one's own voice 119
What does it mean to follow? 120
Notes 121

8 Conclusion   123

You go where I go 123
Convergent movements 124
A transpositional logic 125
I don't want them to follow me 126
Notes 128

Appendix   *129*
Bibliography   *131*
Index   *146*

Acknowledgements

Very special thanks are due to Robert Adlington and Mladen Dolar for their support and inspiration, as well as to Bernard Burgoyne, Peter Szendy, Saloni Singhania, Susannah Frearson and series editor, Ian Parker. To those musicians and critics who kindly offered their time to speak about their experiences playing, talking and thinking with Ornette Coleman, the author is deeply grateful. They are Karl Berger, Daniel Carter, Charles Ellerbe, John Giordano, Thierry Jousse, Matt Lavelle, Al McDowell, Dave Moss, Bern Nix, Victor Schonfield, Ed Schuller, George Schuller, Ingrid Sertso and Federico Ughi. The research for this book was also supported with funding from SEMPRE, the Society for Music Analysis, and the University of Nottingham.

Series preface

What has Lacanian psychoanalysis to say about music? This groundbreaking book provides some answers and poses questions about our assumptions regarding what counts in the real – how it strikes us, moves us – our imaginary relation to the kinds of enjoyment and disturbance that we attempt to make sense of and convey to others, and the symbolic structuring of the world. A.L. James creates for us a realm of study, carefully defining its coordinates and spelling out what forms of technical apparatus we will need in a detailed reading of quite specific phenomena, of what constitutes the way other musicians, and then aficionados (and let's also say fans, and now readers intrigued by psychoanalysis), "follow" jazz trumpeter and saxophonist Ornette Coleman. What does the injunction to "follow" mean, and what follows from that?

This is not psychoanalysis as psychobiography, not the reductive "interpretation" of what Ornette Coleman and his followers were up to, but a close reading of the text, in this case of music, for which we need a guide. Conventional psychobiography attempts to account for what is pleasing or jarring in cultural productions by making reference to the childhood or the internal mental operations of the subject under study. In this way, there is a misjudged appeal to what is "real" in otherwise invisible personal history, and "interpretation" – which is not at all the kind of interpretation Lacanian psychoanalysis is interested in – delves into and pretends to disclose hidden motivations. What is real about music, in this case, is thereby tamed, rendered "meaningful". Music "appreciation" of different kinds complements that kind of mastery of what is real about music with what usually amounts to a banal and intuitive "wine-tasting"-style judgement of what succeeds and what fails. That approach to music relies on a number of culturally shared interpretative motifs that are profoundly and misleadingly imaginary.

In contrast, this study tracing movements in "harmolodic space" stays true to a Lacanian psychoanalytic focus on the signifiers that structure and then seem to give meaning to what we experience of music. This is a book about the symbolic, and, in the process of tracing the symbolic coordinates of Ornette Coleman's work, it expands the remit of psychoanalysis in a rigorous and innovative way. Music is structured, symbolic and draws us into symbolic forms, intimate, personal and sometimes alarming. Ornette Coleman is not "easy listening", and this book is not easy reading. You will learn and think, and return to the music the better for it.

Psychoanalytic clinical and theoretical work circulates through multiple intersecting antagonistic symbolic universes. This series opens connections between different cultural sites in which Lacanian work has developed in distinctive ways, in forms of work that question the idea that there could be a single correct reading and application. The *Lines of the Symbolic in Psychoanalysis* series provides a reflexive reworking of psychoanalysis that transmits Lacanian writing from around the world, steering a course between the temptations of a metalanguage and imaginary reduction, between the claim to provide a god's eye view of psychoanalysis and the idea that psychoanalysis must everywhere be the same. And the elaboration of psychoanalysis in the symbolic here grounds its theory and practice in the history and politics of the work in a variety of interventions that touch the real.

Ian Parker
Manchester Psychoanalytic Matrix

Preface

A very unusual ear

This is a book about the musician, composer and thinker, Ornette Coleman. Ornette's name – and Ornette is one of the few musicians known by his first name – is associated with the origin of what is sometimes called "free jazz" – a term that may evoke attempts to escape the constraints of too-rigid conceptions of improvised musical time and space, with their focus on making melodies fit predetermined chord progressions, what Ornette called "set patterns" – in favour of something more spontaneous, open, *free*. However, Ornette has called into question this word, "free", offering *complete*.[1] So, perhaps we could start this book about Ornette Coleman by saying that this is a book about *complete jazz*, except that Ornette, like many Black American musicians, was ambivalent about this designation, "jazz", linking it to what he called "the caste system in sound", with all of its implied hierarchies and denigrations.[2]

In fact, Ornette would invent a new term – *harmolodics* – to refer to his music, a portmanteau articulation of two musical expressions – *har*(mony) and (mel)*ody*, or (mel)*odics* – with a third expression – *mo*(vement) – at their junction – *har-mo-lodics*. This enigmatic term has been the cause of much perplexity and feverish interpretation, with Ornette's own attempts to explain the term – most formally in "Prime Time for Harmolodics", the article he wrote for *DownBeat* in 1983 – only serving to intensify the mystery. In the liner notes to the recording of *Skies of America* released in 1972, Ornette promised a theoretical text on harmolodics, called *The Harmolodic Theory*, which would perhaps answer all our questions about this enigmatic term, but this text, alas, has never appeared.[3]

So, how does one approach this difficult work, how does one attempt something like an interpretation of Ornette's discourse, without seeking to conceal or disguise the enigmas and complexities that are perhaps intimately connected to its appeal? How does one listen to this discourse, with implications of what it could mean to listen itself, without silencing what is attempting to make itself heard in these complexities, at once so resistant to, and productive of, an effect of sense? Oriented by something Ornette said to the bassist Charlie Haden sometime in the late 1950s

xvi Preface

– "you follow me, and you go where I go" – this book finds an answer to these questions, and to the question of what it means *to follow*, in tools offered by psychoanalysis – in particular the notion of *transference*, with its intimate connection to harmolodic thought but also its way of listening, of attending to, discourse, not in order to analyse Ornette, or to offer some kind of speculative diagnosis, but to develop new ways to listen to Ornette's music as space and as movement through that space – as *Movements in Harmolodic Space*.

And, in fact, there is evidence that Ornette may have had a direct interest in psychoanalysis and the mechanisms of the unconscious, for each of the titles to the tracks on his 1962 album *Ornette!* are derived from the titles Brill gave to his translations of four of Freud's texts: "W.R.U." (*Wit and Its Relation to the Unconscious*), "T.&T." (*Totem and Taboo*), "C.&D." (*Civilization and Its Discontents*) and "R.P.D.D" (*The Relation of the Poet to Daydreaming*). We are only in a position to speculate about the depth of Ornette's engagement with the ideas found within the texts to which these titles allude, but what better terrain than Ornette's discourse could there be for a form of analysis that takes as its object precisely these points of enigma we have just encountered that repeat and insist in the discourse of the analysand – the form of analysis represented by psychoanalysis, a science, perhaps, albeit a controversial one, of nothing less than freedom?

The artist, Seth Price, has proposed four canonical reasons why artists make art – *craft*, the ability to "make cool stuff"; *money*, the lure of the unregulated field of art-money relations; *scene*, the sense that the contemporary art world is a great party; and, first of all, *freedom*, the ability to do what one wants.[4] What attracted this author to "improvisation" – whatever we might mean by this term – was precisely this promise of freedom, this promise of access to a space of licence somehow beyond the realm of musical rules and even laws. If these hopes did not long survive the encounter with really-existing improvisation, showing themselves to be little more than fantasies, there remained the sense that conventional approaches to musical freedom *were* limited, *were* unnecessarily constrained by contingent regulation masquerading as universal law.

The first time this author heard Ornette Coleman, it was a track with the most beautiful Ornettian title – "Law Years" – from the 1969 album *Science Fiction*, and it was immediately and stunningly clear that this music was a solution to the problem of freedom with which the author had been struggling, a solution in which freedom seemed to overlap, nonetheless, with a headlong sense of momentum and imperative. So, if this music was a product of Ornette's "very unusual ear",[5] as his collaborator Don Cherry once described it, what *law* governed this ear, what was *the law of the ear* that produced such imperative freedom, a freedom marked by such an effect of imperative momentum? The existence of this book can be traced to this moment, standing transfixed in front of a set of speakers, and it is also why it is possible to say that, in some sense, this book chose its author rather than simply the other way around.

Background

Ornette Coleman was born in Fort Worth, Texas, perhaps on 19 March 1930 – there is some uncertainty about the exact date of Ornette's birth.[6] He received his first alto saxophone sometime around 1944–1945, at approximately 14 or 15 years of age and, lacking a teacher, taught himself to play.[7] According to stories he has himself told of his early development, Ornette misunderstood the construction of the alto, mistaking particular notes of the musical alphabet for others, and although he would be forced later to realise his mistake when humiliated by a school bandleader, such events would punctuate and even contribute to the development of his distinctive voice.[8]

On his work as a professional musician in venues across Fort Worth, then later as an itinerant musician playing blues and dance music, as well as in sessions with more adventurous musicians, Ornette would suffer abuse and even violence in part as a result of the originality of his ideas, at first influenced by the work of musicians such as Charlie Parker and later as an attempt to go beyond its limitations.[9] At the time of recording his first album, *Something Else!!!!*, Ornette was not an established figure on the jazz scene, although known to many as a musician whose idiosyncratic approach signalled an inability to "pay his dues", to demonstrate his fluency in an approach to improvisation oriented with respect to harmonic coordinates. In Ornette's own words, "they said that I didn't know the changes and was out of tune",[10] a criticism echoed by Walter Norris, the pianist on Ornette's first album, *Something Else!!!!*, in a story told by the drummer, Ed Blackwell.

> I remember Walter Norris saying to me, "Ornette doesn't seem to know his own tunes". What he meant was that he got all the correct changes, but Ornette's horn didn't fit the changes.[11]

Norris' remark, which equates knowledge of a tune not with knowledge of the melody, which Ornette had himself composed, but with the "changes", makes sense against the background of a contemporary practice of composing new melodies for the temporal-harmonic frameworks – "changes" – of popular songs. Charlie Parker's "Moose the Mooche", for instance, appropriated the harmonic progression of "I Got Rhythm", George Gershwin's song from the musical *Girl Crazy*, whilst jettisoning the original melody. The improvisation would then, in virtuosic fashion, "make the changes" – improvise melodies, often at high speed, to fit these pre-established temporal-harmonic frameworks. Whilst musicians such as Parker extended what it meant to "make the changes", widening the palette of notes heard to fit the harmony, it was certainly possible *not* to make the changes, and, indeed, Ornette reports instances where he attended jam sessions only for a rhythm section to fall silent when he began to play.[12]

These are themes that would emerge in many other contexts, in relation to many other aspects of Ornette's music. There is a story from 1959, the year Ornette would be received as a special guest by the Lennox School of Jazz, a year in which, in some respects, Ornette's fortunes had at last begun to change. However, by no means were all of the faculty well-disposed to the sounds Ornette was making. In fact, the trombonist Bob Brookmeyer, furious at the positive reception being afforded Ornette, would resign his faculty position, his parting shot – "Damn it, tune up!" – focussing on a feature of Ornette's playing that also concerns, in its own way, this question of alignment we have been discussing.[13] Even a musician as sympathetic to Ornette as pianist Paul Bley would later joke that, having hired Ornette for his residency at the Five Spot in 1958 – a decision that would eventually cost Bley the residency itself – they would spend most of the day practising, with three-quarters of that time trying to get Ornette to play at 440 (the frequency to which the "A" above "middle C" is to be tuned in standard tuning).[14] And, later, the critic Ekkehard Jost, who would subject Ornette's sound to a series of measurements "with the aid of electro-acoustic processes", would suggest that the problem of Ornette's tuning was a function of the limited opportunities that Ornette at that time had to play, which would be rectified in subsequent years when these opportunities became more frequent.[15]

However, this is already to cede ground where something much more interesting is at stake. In an interview some years after the stories we have been discussing, Ornette's own reflections on the early development of his sound would cast a new light on this apparent problem of tuning, revealing an ear unusually tuned to the splits and apparent paradoxes constituting an experience of musical identity:

> I realised that you could play sharp or flat in tune. That came very early in my saxophone interest. I used to play one note all day, and I used to try to find how many different sounds I could get out of the mouthpiece (I'm still looking for the magic mouthpiece) … I'd hear so many different tones and sounds.[16]

So, the stories we have already alluded to here – of melodies that do not go the way of harmonic pathways, of sounds that depart from expected timbres and tunings – each in their own way touch on the questions at the heart of this book: of movement, of direction and of space. For if Ornette's melodies, tunings, timbres – and we could add rhythms, timings, tonalities – are going somewhere other than we might expect them to go, *where* are they going? In the direction of which point, and through or to what nature of space, do they move? These are the questions to which we will return again and again in this text in an attempt to answer the question of what it means to follow, of what it means to go, to move, where Ornette goes.

Layout of the book

This book is laid out in the following way. Chapter 1 is an introductory chapter, introducing the main questions addressed in the text, as well as an overview of the approach we develop in this book to the analysis of *discourse* and *space.* Chapter 2 then offers an account of the notion of *transference* – a key idea in this text, for reasons we are about to explore. Each chapter from Chapter 3 to 7 is then oriented with respect to a fragment or fragments of Ornette's discourse dealing with a piece, or collection of pieces, from Ornette's work. These are first dealt with on their own terms, with each chapter then drawing through the consequences of prior chapters in relation to new material. Finally, the appendices offer some background to some of the spatial questions we explore in Chapter 6.

The approach we take in this text, which puts the accent on discourse, orienting each chapter with respect to a fragment of Ornette's speech or writing about his music, has some consequences in terms of both the choice of tools and how these are elaborated throughout the text, yielding a text that is at times a little unorthodox. At a first level, there are what could be considered "background" tools: tools from psychoanalysis for an analysis of discourse, including the key notions of *quilting* and transference, as well as tools for the analysis of space, including the *relation*. These tools apply throughout the book. However, there are also tools that emerge as a consequence of close attention to Ornette's discourse – what might be called "foreground" tools – and these are developed in the course of the analytical chapters; the notions of analysis and synthesis and "free vectors" are instances of these.

Source material

Much of the written or spoken material that forms the object of our analysis is drawn from interviews published in music journals, liner notes and longer texts on Ornette's work, such as John Litweiler's,[17] and from the author's own transcriptions of Ornette's interviews with, for instance, Gunther Schuller.[18] The author also travelled to the United States in 2015 to interview a number of musicians who had worked, or spent time discussing music, with Ornette: Charles Ellerbe, Al McDowell and Bern Nix, all of whom appeared on Ornette's *Virgin Beauty* and *In All Languages*; Karl Berger and Ingrid Sertso, two musicians who set up the Creative Music Foundation with Ornette in the early 1970s; John Giordano, who conducted and, in a sense, re-arranged the version of *Skies of America* that appeared in Shirley Clarke's film about Ornette, *Made in America*; Ed Schuller and George Schuller, sons of Ornette's friend, Gunther Schuller, both of whom played, or experienced distinctive auditions, with Ornette; and musicians such as Matt Lavelle, Dave Moss and Federico Ughi, all of whom had spent extended periods studying and playing with Ornette at his New York apartment. Finally, the author travelled to Paris to interview the critic Thierry Jousse, who had arranged for Derrida to meet Ornette in 1997, and who was present at their meeting. Whilst material from all of these interviews may not appear in the book, they were nonetheless all invaluable as contextualisation for the author's own thoughts.

In addition, we transcribed numerous compositions and improvisations from Ornette's recorded work between *Something Else!!!!* in 1958 and *Skies of America* in 1972, only some of which appear in this book. Any transcription involves xx Preface

interpretation – how the specific temporal configuration of frequencies is to be conceived as, for instance, pitch and durations – and, where possible, there has been an attempt to offer the most open form of interpretation of the sounds heard, pending what is implied at the level of our analysis of Ornette's discourse. Thus, for instance, we frequently represent pitches without durational and metrical interpretation. It is perhaps impossible to reduce interpretation to nothing, however, and, in this respect, Ornette's discourse has priority over any preliminary interpretation implied by the transcription. If we also give priority to the analysis of Ornette's composition, this is not only because of Ornette's own insistence that he be considered a composer and not (only) an improviser but also insofar as the composition marks a singular point in Ornette's process prior to any concrete, collective articulation in the form, for instance, of a group improvisation. The relations that make up the composition, constituting its specific character, are Ornette's own in a way the relations internal to a collective improvisation are not.

Notes

1 Mandel, "Driven to Abstraction", 39.
2 Amongst the promotional material that came with the 1995 album *Tone Dialling* was a puzzle that, when pieced together, revealed the following message: "*Remove the caste system from sound*". For a discussion of this idea, see Coleman, interview by Shoemaker; Mandel, "Driven to Abstraction".
3 In "A question of scale", his 2005 interview with Andy Hamilton for *The Wire* magazine, Ornette suggested that the book was to appear "soon".
4 Price, *Fuck Seth Price*, 34–40.
5 Liner notes to *Something Else!!!!*.
6 Litweiler, *Harmolodic Life*, 21.
7 Litweiler, *Harmolodic Life*, 25.
8 Litweiler, *Harmolodic Life*, 25.
9 Litweiler, *Harmolodic Life*, 21–40.
10 Hentoff, Liner Notes to *Something Else!!!!*.
11 Litweiler, *Harmolodic Life*, 57.
12 "On the Creation of Free Jazz": 2.18–2.19.
13 Litweiler, *Harmolodic Life*, 70.
14 Litweiler, *Harmolodic Life*, 62.
15 Jost, *Free Jazz*, 53.
16 Litweiler, *Harmolodic Life*, 25.
17 Litweiler, *Harmolodic Life*.
18 Coleman, interview by Schuller.

Chapter 1

What does it mean to follow?

I want you just to follow me

There is a story told by Charlie Haden that recounts his encounter as a young, 21-year-old bassist from Shenandoah, Iowa, with a sound that would change the course of his life, making of him a new listener. At the inception of what was to become Haden's new vocation as listener and interpreter of this sound so close, it seemed to him, to the human voice, the room lit up, and he would spend the following days searching for the man responsible for this most human of sounds emanating from the wide open mouth of a white, plastic saxophone:

> One Monday night I went over to a club called the Haig, and Gerry Mulligan and Chet Baker were playing there. And while they were playing a man came in the back door, an African American with a horn alto case, and asked if he could play. And, apparently, they said, yes, and he came up, took out a plastic horn and started to play, and the whole room lit up for me. It was like the heavens opened up.[1]

Haden would ask his friend, the drummer Lenny McBrowne, about the source of this extraordinary sound he had heard, about the saxophone with the sound of a human voice. Convinced of its provenance, McBrowne would introduce Haden to Ornette Coleman, and together the two would travel in Ornette's little Studebaker, so the story goes, to Ornette's apartment, a space Haden found overflowing with transcripts of Ornette's beautiful melodies. Here they would play together some of Ornette's music for the first time:

> He picked up a piece of music and said, let's play this. I was so scared, but we played. He said, now, I wrote some changes out here when I wrote the melody, but when we start to improvise, I want you just to follow me, and you go where I go. And I said, man, finally I've been given permission to do what I want to do.[2]

"I want you just to follow me", says Ornette to Charlie Haden at one of their first meetings, sometime in the late 1950s, "and you go where I go". But what does it

DOI: 10.4324/9781003412304-1

2 What does it mean to follow?

mean to *follow*, and what, in particular, does it mean to follow Ornette? If, as a starting point, we take the second part of Ornette's formulation – "you go where I go"– to be an *answer* to our question regarding the first, so that "to follow" *means* "to go where I go", the question, "what does it mean to follow?" becomes, simply, w*hat does it mean to go where Ornette goes?*, entailing not only the question, where is Ornette going?, but what is a "where"? and what does it mean to "go"? These questions are at the heart of this book and evoke a field of effects that will orient us with respect to the many expressions from Ornette's discourse that we will draw into relation to our central question, the question of what it means to follow – effects of *where* – of *endpoints*, *direction* and of *space* – as well as effects of *going* – of *motion*, of *movement* – of *Movements in Harmolodic Space*.

What does it mean to follow?

The question of what it means to follow is, of course, already a question of real significance for the analyst of music, for how can the analyst be sure that their analytic attempts to follow, to "go where the other goes", are not in danger of *producing their own object*, such that what is heard is, in fact, an effect of the hearing, not the neutral reception of something immanent to the sounds themselves? How does one follow, in other words, without unwittingly becoming the one who leads? The approach we take in this book is an attempt to offer an answer to this question – one made possible by Ornette's willingness, rare amongst artists, perhaps, to speak and write at length about his music.

Rather than assume that a "direct" approach to Ornette's music is possible, with pertinent features immanent to it and accessible to a sufficiently sensitive analyst, we seek a singularly Ornettian conception of the space of Ornette's music, and movement through that space, by interposing between analysis and text a psychoanalytically informed analysis of Ornette's spoken and written discourse. This analysis then forms the basis of our analytic approach to Ornette's music. In this way, we use tools from psychoanalysis to develop a way of listening that is a kind of *listening for listening*, an approach that aims to discern in and between the lines of Ornette's spoken and written discourse new ways to listen, new ways to experience Ornette's music as movement and space. What we want from psychoanalysis, above all, is its *ear*, its particular way of attending to discourse, which would then imply new ways of listening, of attending to music.

In this sense, rather than attempt to develop a *general* theory of musical experience, reliant, perhaps, on rules and norms the grasp of which would constitute the condition for a notion of musical "competence", our aim is to develop a *singular* theory – a theory based on the singularity of Ornette's discourse and the ways of listening it may imply. This situates the approach we take at a distance from those attempting to develop, for instance, a general theory of musical "movement", including work in the field of musical "expectation" or anticipation,[3] image schema and gesture,[4] that seeks to ground the generality of experience in, for instance, the norms and laws of Gestalt theory, style, Darwinian evolution or the primacy of

What does it mean to follow? 3

a particular mapping from, say, the body or the laws governing physical forces. Instead, starting with Ornette's "unusual ear", as his collaborator Don Cherry once called it – its *irregularity*, its *irreducibility to the norm* – we assume the non-existence of a general rule governing musical experience, the non-existence of a norm or law that counts for every ear, with its implication that those ears for which such laws or norms don't count can somehow be discounted.

One danger of such an approach is the implication that our analysis of Ornette's discourse about his music simply constitutes a direct transcription of Ornette's experience of his music, as if it were possible to reduce the gap between "words" and "things" to nothing. Whilst we neither claim that there is *no* relation between Ornette's discourse and his experience, this book is not an analysis of Ornette Coleman – nor, certainly, is it a *psychoanalysis* of Ornette Coleman – but, rather, an analysis of the implications in Ornette's discourse of new ways to listen, new ways to experience his music as space and as movement through that space. And, perhaps, the production of *other ways of hearing*, of new ways to listen, with their capacity, as we discover in Chapter 5, to *cure solitude*, is as harmolodic as anything else we are here about to say.

The Squid Piece

The roots of the approach we take in this text are to be found in a project we undertook on a piece by the writer and artist Gregory Whitehead. In a preamble to a performance released in 2001, Whitehead describes the genesis of the piece, which he calls "the squid piece", in an experience of "random overhearing", in which a "scrap of language", a fragment of something spoken – a *voice* – which he describes as "disconnected to discourse", floats out, taking control of his mind;

> It's about those little scraps of language, particularly in cities … that you hear in the market or in a random overhearing, and they just literally take over your consciousness for the course of the day. You cannot delete that particular scrap, and it just has your name on it, and it has decided it is going to control your mind […] I overheard this conversation where somebody said, "so you wanna talk about squid?" And the way it was said was so bizarre, so disconnected to discourse. It was just a voice that kind of floated out, and rather than have it rattle around as this kind of interminable loop for the rest of the day, I decided I had to just make a piece out of it. And it's based really on […] you know, in a way […] turning the squid into calamari, and then letting it be squid again, and then back to calamari.[5]

What was particularly striking about Whitehead's characterisation of this experience was the peculiar formulation he gives to its spatial character, its being "disconnected to discourse". To what extent did such a formulation, we wondered, in which "to" appears where we might expect a "from" – disconnected *to*, rather than disconnected *from*, discourse – imply not so much the absence of a connection

4   What does it mean to follow?

but, rather, a disconnection that is "disavowed" – not recognised consciously but present – *avowed* – nonetheless, at the level of this peculiarity of discourse? This led us to a number of further, related questions. For, if "disconnected to" implies less the absence of connection than a connection that is disavowed, what does this disavowal have to do with the particular effect of dominating control experienced with respect to this alien scrap, its ability to "take over your consciousness"? And, if these two factors – disavowal and domination – are intimately linked – if the effect of domination is contingent, that is, on the subjective disavowal of a connection – what does this imply about the subject's complicity in their own subjection, in the scrap's "decision" to "control your mind"?[6]

Where, with Whitehead's work, the analysis was focused on one text – the preamble to a performance of the piece, describing its genesis – in this project, we deal with numerous fragments from Ornette's discourse, each implying a particular approach to his work. As a consequence, there is an increase in complexity, as we deal with not only the implications for our approach internal to a particular text but also the implications that arise when these fragments are drawn into relation. In addition, in this project we introduce some new tools from mathematics – in particular tools from topology – including the notion of *relation* – to give a clearer formulation to the dimension of space Whitehead's allusion to disconnection implies. More broadly, however, both these projects have in common an attention to the question of music as "cure". Whilst in the case of Whitehead's piece, the notion that music could have curative effects emerges in relation to the loosening of the hold the alien "scrap" has on his consciousness; here cure is situated in relation to Ornette's notion of "sound medicine", and, in particular, to the question of a cure for solitude, which we discuss in Chapter 5. In both instances, whilst psychoanalysis has offered coordinates for thinking through these different notions of cure, we have endeavoured to approach them on their own terms, without the assumption of any necessary relation between them or to the broader notions of cure in a psychoanalytic sense.[7]

It will be clear, then, that our aim is not to add to the growing fraternity of literature offering a biographical or historical account of Ornette's life and work; an accurate and detailed account of Ornette's life and work, as well as attention to oral-historical testimony, has been indispensable for this book. However, we contend that tools other than, or in addition to, historical tools are needed in order to make sense of Ornette's music and thought.[8] Although it occupies a highly significant position in Ornette's discourse, neither do we propose to offer an overarching definition of "harmolodics", the neologism which Ornette coined to name his approach and which one might be tempted to take as a signifier of a unified or coherent Ornettian system.[9] And if we propose a psychoanalytic orientation, nor do we aim to use psychoanalytic concepts to explain music, on the one hand, or music to explain psychoanalytic concepts, on the other.[10] Rather, this book takes Ornette's discourse as a point of departure, using tools developed from psychoanalysis to pay attention not only to what is said but also to what is implied at the level of the gaps and inconsistencies, shifts and transferences, that constitute what is said about a singularly *Ornettian* constitution of such spaces and movement through them. Insofar as Ornette's discourse about his work also contains allusions to fields beyond the field of music, it seeks to develop tools that are able to draw elements and structures from these fields together, finding in their relation to one another echoes and parallels that evoke a field of problems that go beyond the field of music.

In the rest of this chapter, we introduce some of the tools we use, correlative to features of a Lacanian Discourse Analysis,[11] to develop a psychoanalytically informed way of listening to Ornette's spoken and written discourse that is a kind of listening for listening– a way of listening for implications of ways to listen and what these might imply about music as space and as movement through that space.[12] These are: an analysis of discourse in which discourse appears as an *Other's discourse*; *relations*; and elements from *neighbourhood topology*. Whilst they cover a broad field, these tools can be collected under two main themes: first, an approach to the analysis of discourse in which *transference* and *quilting* play a key, structuring function; and, second, an approach to space as characterised by particular forms of relation, which may also constitute the *vehicle*, the means of movement, through that space. In the text that follows, both quilting and transference appear as tools in relation to both Ornette's music and his spoken and written discourse about that music; we find, in other words, quilting functions and transferential shifts both internal to the space of his music and internal to the space of his discourse about his music. And, in a sense, one of the key problems this text explores is the consequences that follow – in particular at the level of what it means to follow – when points of quilting – points that perform a unifying, spatialising function in relation to discourse – are subject to transferential shifts in both the related senses of transference which we elaborate in the next chapter. The notion of *transference*, with its correlative notion of *signifier*, will be explored in more detail in the next chapter.

Discourse

Discourse as Other

In the early 1950s, discourse is conceived, for Lacan, in terms of the *discourse of the Other*,[13] implying the effects on the speaker of speech from another scene – something, perhaps, overheard or read between the lines in another's speech – which, although repressed, then manifests itself at the level of his own discourse in the form of symptomatic acts or linguistic formations. The notion of "discourse analysis" this implies enables us to answer the question: what does it mean to *listen* to Ornette? If Ornette's own words about his music are to be taken seriously as an attempt to articulate something about the relations governing its constitution, as well as those that relate these musical relations to relations outside his music, how does one give proper attention to these words without treating these words as identical with a notion of authorial intention, on the one hand, or attempting to make them a complete and consistent system, on the other? In this sense, if we give authority to Ornette's discourse, working through its problematic implications, it is not to

6 What does it mean to follow?

ask Ornette what his music means, but what his discourse, including its gaps and inconsistencies, implies about his music as space and movement through that space.

We do not draw the whole of Ornette's discourse into a single, unified statement. Rather, beginning with fragments from Ornette's discourse about his work – phrases, short passages, single expressions – we think through the consequences of their immediate articulation for musical analysis. With particular music-analytical tools then developed from an analysis of Ornette's discourse, we turn to Ornette's music, with attention first to the specific music to which this discourse initially refers; Ornette's music now appears with a particular Ornettian spatial structure and character, and resonates in the wider space of concerns that constitute Ornette's own work and thought. If such fragments imply consequences first for the specific music to which they refer, it is nonetheless possible to think through their consequences for other Ornettian contexts. Here we are not attempting to provide an analytic key to the whole, derived from one of its parts, but, by transferring the thought articulated in a part of Ornette's discourse to other spaces, to think *with* Ornette, even if to think with him is to think his thought to a point Ornette has not yet transferred it.

This approach, which begins with fragments, attempting to think through consequences as constituted on the basis of their own terms, thus allows tensions and disjunctions to form and manifest both between fragments, as well as internal to the fragments themselves, insofar as any fragment is itself a relation of fragments. Rather than a problem to be dissolved or concealed, however, these tensions then become the spark for new consequences, which can themselves be transferred to new contexts and relations. In a sense, then, our mode of "discourse analysis", rather than an approach that seeks to catch Ornette out, drawing attention to the points at which it is inconsistent, or at which it somehow fails, simply proposes to *take Ornette at his word*, avoiding the impulse to minimise the tensions and difficulties at the level of the specific articulations he offers in service of a deeper, unifying meaning. This allows a much richer and more interesting discourse to emerge, the gaps and inconsistencies of which may manifest a knowledge that goes beyond what is conscious.

Quilting

When Jacques Lacan introduced the notion of *point de capiton*, or "quilting point" in his seminar on psychosis, it was to denote a particular point of stability or "quilting" in a space of signifiers characterised by a shifting relation between signifier and signified. Were we to analyse the scene as a musical score, he says, referring to the function of the signifier "fear" in *Athaliah*, the play by Racine, we would see that it is the point – which he refers to as a "spatialising device" – at which signifier and signified are knotted together:

> Everything radiates out from and is organised around this signifier, similar to those little lines of force that an upholstery button forms on the surface of a

material. It's the point of convergence that enables everything that happens in the discourse to be situated retroactively and retrospectively.[14]

Lacan's notion of a "quilting point" thus implies a number of features:

- It performs a *situating function*.
- The effects of situation it produces emerge *retroactively*.
- It constitutes a *point of convergence*, insofar as everything "radiates out from and is organised around this signifier".
- It is a *spatialising device*.

Quilting is important to this text for a number of reasons. First, if a quilting point is a point of convergence – of *intersection* – this already implies an intimate connection between quilting and what it means to follow, insofar as to follow means *to go where I go*, to move, in other words, such that this movement *converges to a common point*. Second, these movements to a common point of convergence produce effects that are effects of *situation*, which is to say, of *being somewhere*, directly correlative to the "where" of following – the "where" of the point to which both "you" and "I" go, to which the movements of "you" and "I" converge. In Chapter 3, we discuss retroactive effects of situation in terms of the constitution of *situating vectors*, linked to the ancient distinction between *analysis* and *synthesis*. Third, if these effects of situation emerge *retroactively* – contingent, that is, on the appearance of a context of later points, which "act back" on points that come before – this implies another sense of what it means to follow, insofar as retroaction complicates the *order* that pertains to the emergence of effects of situation. And, fourth, if quilting points are *spatialising*, if they imply, in other words, a convergent *space*, this offers another sense of the "somewhere" following – "going where the other goes" – implies.

   Each of the four aspects of quilting implied by Lacan's account, and their relation to the question of what it means to follow, are explored in detail in the text that follows. However, in addition to these, we note two further features, with consequences for the approach we take to Ornette's discourse. First, those points of convergence in Ornette's discourse to which we give particular attention – those signifiers that in Ornette's discursive universe have particular weight and density – are signifiers that imply *relations*. If points of convergence in Ornette's discourse imply convergent relations, in other words, these relations converge to points that themselves imply a particular form or feature of relations. These key signifiers are then the points around which our chapters are oriented. Second, these points of convergence, implying something about the form or nature of relations, *are signifiers that have been subject to some significant shift at the level of meaning* for which the notion of *transference* allows us to account – we are thinking here of the signifiers *tonic, interval, idea, free, solitude, no relation, movement* and *unison*. And, as we have already stated, one of the central questions this text seeks to explore is what happens when points of quilting, of stabilisation in a space of discourse, are subject to transferential shifts, in both senses we elaborate in the next chapter.

8   What does it mean to follow?

When it comes to the question of linking the notion of quilting point to music, however, we may pay attention to a very suggestive remark made by the music theorist, Steven Rings, about the nature of tonal hearing, with the experience of convergence it implies. If convergent structures are to be found in both works that are tonal and atonal,[15] what distinguishes tonal hearing, says Rings, may be the experience of what he calls tonal *qualia* – the effect of perceived "scale-degree-ness" – which seems to inhabit a pitch as an effect of *situation* – of its "being somewhere" – with respect to a tonic point of convergence. In the absence of such effects, says Rings, listeners lack orientation; the listener is struck, says Rings, by what he calls the pitch's "tonal anonymity".[16] In this sense, the presence or absence of such "qualia" might be taken as a feature enabling us to distinguish convergent musical structures that perform a quilting function from those that do not. Convergence would thus emerge, in other words, as a necessary condition of an experience of quilting, yet insufficient without the effects of situation produced by the relation to a common point such convergent structures imply. We return to the dimensions of convergence and qualia in Chapter 3 in the context of a discussion of *tonic* and *situating vectors*, as well as in our later discussion of Ornette's notion of *Idea*, for which we propose a generalisation in Chapter 5, including to the dimension of time and temporal relations.

And, of course, musicians did not have to wait for the work of Jacques Lacan for an account of the retroactive effect of what comes after on what comes before. Already in 1911, in his Theory of Harmony, Arnold Schoenberg had, for instance, discerned the ordered nature of such effects in the emergence of tonal significations from the interrelation of an ordered set of chords. "If we set down one of these chords independently, taken out of its context", he says, "then we cannot determine whether it belongs to one key or another. It can just as well belong to [C major as to G major]". Rather, "which way it is to be reckoned" – its particular tonal significance – "depends on what goes before and what comes after. A triad c-e-g can be I in C major or IV in G. The succeeding chords determine whether it is one or the other".[17] Whilst Schoenberg focusses on the interrelation of an ordered set of chords, it is clear that such a retroactive structure could be generalised to many, if not all, aspects of music relations, such that we could speak of the retroactive effect of a tonic on the notes of a tonality, constituting them as "3rds" or "5ths" or "2nds", or of the root on the other notes of a chord, or of the later notes of a melody on the notes that come before, determining their particular function within the melodic structure, or of a metrical "1" with respect to the points of a rhythm, determining their particular weight and significance, and so on.

Space

A spatial approach to Ornette's music is implied by the *where* of "following", which is at the heart of this book, but also, more specifically, by the answer Ornette gives to a closely related problem, which we discuss in detail in Chapter 3, of "knowing where to go". If "no one knew where to go or what to do to show that he knew where he was going", Ornette's answer refers directly to *space*, and in particular to the performance of a shared space. What we also find everywhere in Ornette's discourse, however, are relations to fields other than music, but whose importance for an understanding of his music seem to be, for Ornette, real and clear, and whose relation to his music can be situated at the level of spatial structure. In this section, we introduce some of the mathematical tools we use – in particular, the notions of *relation* and *neighbourhood* – to give a clearer formulation to those features of Ornette's discourse that imply space and movement through that space.[18]

Relations

"Relation" is a term with a number of more and less formal senses in and outside of mathematics, with the more formal mathematical definition characterising the relation as a "subset of the Cartesian product" – the subset of, for instance, ordered pairs that the relation relates. Whilst the more and less formal senses imply one another, when we use the term it is most often in a somewhat less formal sense, to indicate that there are points, x and y, and a third term, a relation, that links one to the other; x "is the mother of" y, y "is higher than" z, and so on. However, the more formal sense of relation does reveal an intimate link between relations and *order*; a binary relation, for instance, implies a collection of *ordered pairs* (x, y), which is to say that relations imply a distinction between *antecedent* and *consequent*, *what leads* and *what follows*, with direct consequences for the question this book seeks to address.[19] We discuss particular forms of relation in the context of the analytical chapters that follow.

Relations are important to this text for a number of reasons. First amongst them is that the relation – in particular, the *vector*, which the Irish mathematician William Rowan Hamilton introduces in his lectures on quaternions – draws together the dimensions of *movement, order* and *space*, which the question of what it means to follow implies. For, if a Hamiltonian vector is what "moves a movable point" from one coordinate to another, from antecedent to consequent, from what leads to *what follows*, it also implies a *space* through which such ordered movement moves. Hamilton's vector is closely related to the musical notion of *interval* – the "gap" between pitches in a pitch space – with the means Hamilton proposes for the production of vectors precisely the arithmetic music analyst Allen Forte[20] proposes for the production of musical intervals – what Hamilton calls "analysis" by means of subtraction, which produces the relational vehicle that, in "synthesis", moves a movable point from A to B, antecedent to consequent, initial to end point.

However, relations are important to this book for another reason, which is the importance that Ornette gives to the notion of *transposition*, a notion which, as we will see, complicates the question of what it means to follow. Transposition – a key aspect of harmolodic thought – implies a particular kind of shift, a shift *from points to relations* – from pitch to interval, in the more limited musical sense – the consequences of which are at the heart of this book. We link this shift to two notions of *transference*, which the notion of transposition draws together – transference

10 What does it mean to follow?

as the *movement of a relation*, on the one hand, and transference as *meaning shift*, on the other. However, transposition in the harmolodic sense is not, we propose, only to be taken in its more limited musical sense but rather indicates a relational affinity linking spaces of any kind – musical and otherwise – such that this affinity constitutes the necessary and sufficient condition for an experience of identity.[21] Such relational affinities are at the heart of this book and at the heart of Ornette's work, insofar as Ornette's discourse implies a practice governed by a logic that is transpositional.

The search for allusions to relations in Ornette's discourse is, for these reasons, one significant characteristic of our approach to his discourse, together with an attempt to think through the particular spatiality and ordered movement through such spaces such relations imply. Each of the chapters from Chapters 3 to 7 thus gives attention to relations in particular ways, with Chapter 3, "'No one knew where to go'", introducing a Hamiltonian approach to intervallic and *tonic relations*; Chapter 4, "Invisible", introducing *free relations*; Chapters 5 and 6, *solitude relations* and *non-relations* in relation to "Lonely Woman"; and Chapter 7, "Skies of America", introducing the key Ornettian notion of "unison", conceived as a *unison relation*.

Topology

Such relations can give character to *space*; a *metric* or *distance function* on a set of points characterises a metric space, an *order relation* on a set of points characterises an ordered space, or a space with an *order topology*, and so on.[22] This is one of the approaches Hausdorff offers in his 1914 text on set theory, in which the foundations of general topology are proposed. For instance, a metric forms the basis for the notion of *metric space*, which can be thought in terms of a function (a form of relation), says Hausdorff, in the sense that the metric function assigns to each pair of points of a set a real number, which is the distance between the two points. However, it is perhaps also important to mention here a distinction between relations in this sense and what might be called "spatial relations", which have to do with the particular interrelation of *neighbourhoods* defining a space, as proposed by Hausdorff in the form of his topological axioms.[23]

Hausdorff defines a *neighbourhood* of a point, x, in a metric space as the set of points less than a given positive distance from x. As such, the distance functions as a radius, ϱ, with a neighbourhood of x a line segment in one dimension, a circle in two dimensions and a sphere in three dimensions, each with x as their centre point. Neighbourhoods – particular kinds of point sets and their interrelation – then become the basis for the neighbourhood axioms characterising the properties of a topological space. However, the validity of the topological axioms is not limited to these "spherical neighbourhoods" in one-, two- and three-dimensional metric spaces, says Hausdorff. He gives the example of an ordered set in which distance cannot be defined; a neighbourhood of x is then any "intermediate range" ("Mittelstrecke") E_b^a containing the element x – that is, for $a < x < b$ the set of elements, y, for which $a < y < b$"[24] [our translation]. Whilst distance cannot generally be defined, these neighbourhoods, Hausdorff says, nonetheless meet his neighbourhood axioms.[25] In Chapter 5 of this book, neighbourhoods form the basis for the definition of *isolated points*, *disconnection* and *disconnected space*; in Chapter 4, we introduce a simple pitch neighbourhood; and in Chapter 7, we develop a "tuning neighbourhood" using Hausdorff's ordered-set neighbourhood.[26] Details relevant to these neighbourhoods will be introduced in the context of these chapters.

We now turn to an account of *transference*, with quilting a key notion in our approach to the analysis of discourse.

Notes

1 Haden, "Charlie Haden on the Creation of Free Jazz": 1.16–1.49.
2 "On the Creation of Free Jazz": 3.16–3.34.
3 See Meyer, *Emotion and Meaning in Music*; Narmour, *The Analysis and Cognition of Basic Melodic Structures*; Huron, *Sweet Anticipation*.
4 See Larson, *Musical Forces: Motion, Metaphor, and Meaning in Music*; Hatten, "A Theory of Musical Gestures"; Gritten and King, *Music and Gesture*; *New Perspectives on Music and Gesture*.
5 Whitehead, "Intro: The Squid Piece".
6 The idea of a repetitive, dominating "earworm" has of course been explored in Peter Szendy's very elegant *Hits: Philosophy in the Jukebox*.
7 Of course, the question of what constitutes a "psychoanalytic cure" is itself an open question.
8 For book or chapter-length texts with a historical orientation, see, for instance, Litweiler, *A Harmolodic Life*; Mandel, *Miles, Ornette, Cecil*; Spellman, *Four Lives*; Wilmer, *As Serious As Your Life*; Golia, *The Territory and the Adventure*. For other texts with a broad, introductory and/or historical orientation, see McRae, *Ornette Coleman*; Rockwell, *All American Music*, 185–197.
9 For attempts to explain harmolodics as a system, see Wilson, *Ornette Coleman: His Life and Music*; Rush, *Free Jazz, Harmolodics and Ornette Coleman*. For an important early attempt to give Ornette's music a theoretical articulation, see Jost, *Free Jazz*, 44–65. Jost's chapter was influential for many subsequent studies, such as Cogswell, "Melodic organisation"; Block, "Organised Sound"; Sasaki, "Two Types of Modulation"; Mazzola, *Flow, Gestures and Spaces in Free Jazz*.
10 For instances of recent texts on music and psychoanalysis, see Fink, *Repeating Ourselves*; Klein, *Music and the Crisis of the Modern Subject*; Régnault, "Psychoanalysis and Music"; Schwarz, *Listening Subjects*; *An Introduction to Electronic Art*; Smith, *Desire in Chromatic Harmony*; Smith and Overy, *Listening to the Unconscious: Adventures in Popular Music and Psychoanalysis*.
11 Parker, "Lacanian Discourse Analysis in Psychology".
12 In the context of musicology and related fields, discourse has been approached from two broad perspectives – discourse *about* music, on the one hand, and music *as* discourse, on the other. For the former, see Nattiez, *Music and Discourse*, as well as work influenced by Lakoff and Johnson's "cross-modal metaphors", which function, even if not explicitly as such, as the "discourse analysis" of metaphors in speech and writing about music. For instances of the latter, see Agawu's *Music as Discourse*, McKerrell's and Way's *Music as Multimodal Discourse*, as well as work on music and structural semantics, topics and narrative, such as Monelle's *Structural Semantics and*

12 What does it mean to follow?

Instrumental Music and Klein's and Reyland's *Music and Narrative since 1900*. For approaches that draw on Zizek's development of Laclau's and Mouffe's ideology critique, see Brodsky's *From 1989, or European Music and the Modernist Unconscious*; and Harper-Scott, *The Quilting Points of Musical Modernism*.

13 Lacan, *Ecrits*, 61.

14 *The Psychoses*, 268.

15 Rings, *Tonality and Transformation*, 114.

16 Rings, *Tonality and Transformation*, 43.

17 Schoenberg, *Theory of Harmony*, 156.

18 For existing approaches to music as space, see, for instance, Tymoczko, *The Geometry of Music*, work on Neo-Riemannian transformation, such as Cohn's *Audacious Euphony: Chromaticism and the Triad's Second* Nature; and work on algebraic topology and topos theory – for instance, Tymoczko's "Why Topology?" and Mazzola's, *The Topos of Music*. For a discussion of space in relation to tonality, see Lerdahl, *Tonal Pitch Space*, and for an introduction to music and set theory, see Schuijer, *Analysing Atonal Music: Pitch-Class Set Theory and Its Contexts*.

19 If retroaction is often presented in temporal terms, the order that pertains to a particular relation would allow a generalisation of the notion of "retroaction" beyond the domain of temporal order; "retro" – "backwards" – "action" is now any action that inverts the order that pertains to a particular relation, *whether or not that order is the order that pertains to time*. As such, on the one hand, the past can now act "retroactively" on the present, insofar as this action inverts the order that pertains to a relation relating the present to the past, and, on the other, we can speak of "retroaction" with respect to relations where any necessary implications of time are absent.

20 Forte, *The Structure of Atonal Music*, 209.

21 If relations can *move*, be transferred, so as to be manifest by a distinct set of points, relations become the basis for a "non-retinal" point of affinity linking spaces that might, in terms of the particular qualities of their manifesting points, appear to have nothing in common. Although we do not propose any direct historical connection, it is for this reason that it is possible to link Ornette's harmolodic practice to a practice that is "conceptual", insofar as conceptuality implies a shift from a notion of identity (the identity of an artwork) conceived in terms of points (the particular materials chosen to manifest an "idea") to identity conceived in terms of relations (the particular constellation of relations which characterise the idea a particular artistic manifestation manifests). See Osborne, "Contemporary Art is Post-Conceptual Art".

22 For an introduction to topology, see Borisovich et al. *Introduction to Topology*, 11–13.

23 Hausdorff, *Grundzüge der Mengenlehre*.

24 *Grundzüge der Mengenlehre*, 214. Unfortunately, the first edition of Hausdorff's text has not yet been translated into English.

25 "Wir werden uns später mehrfach überzeugen, daß die Gültigkeit der Umgebungsaxiome keineswegs ein Privileg der sphärischen Umgebungen ist. Hier genüge ein Beispiel, das zugleich zeigt, wie man die geordneten Mengen nach demselben Formalismus wie die Punktmengen behandeln kann: ist E eine geordnete, der Einfachheit wegen offene Menge (d. h. ohne erstes und letztes Element), so verstehe man unter einer Umgebung von x jede das Element x enthaltende Mittelstrecke E_a^b d. h. für $a < x < b$ die Menge der Elemente y, für die $a < y < b$. Diese Umgebungen erfüllen unsere Axiome, während sich Entfernungen im allgemeinen nicht definieren lassen".

26 For previous uses of musical neighbourhoods, see Mazzola, *Flow, Gestures and Spaces in Free Jazz*.

Chapter 2

Transference

In "What Causes Structure to Find a Place in Love?", Bernard Burgoyne has sought to address the question of the relation between psychoanalysis and science – a question which, as Burgoyne shows, concerned Freud himself – and, in particular, between psychoanalysis and mathematics. Burgoyne draws on the work of the Hungarian psychoanalyst Imre Hermann, who, in a series of texts published between the end of the Second World War and the mid-1960s, proposed to find structural problems in the everyday problems of conflicts in love the analysis of which had already been undertaken in the field of mathematics. If the fields of love and of mathematics are usually taken to be separate domains, Hermann finds between them a structural *parallel* – a thesis the strongest form of which could be articulated thus:

> All structures in the domain of sexual love have translations in the domain of mathematics equally, all mathematical structures correspond ("homologously") to some structural domain within the field of love.[1]

The existence of such parallels – or "homologies" – says Burgoyne, means that one can "do love" by means of mathematics, and mathematics by means of love.[2] However, if the structures at work in the field of love find their parallel in those of mathematics, if the structures of each are homologous – they "say the same thing" – what structures are to be supposed on each side? What terrain is common to the structure of the unconscious and the structure of mathematics? Burgoyne finds an answer in the development of a notion, given an early articulation by philosopher of the Scottish Enlightenment Dugald Stewart in his work on the processes underlying shifts of meaning.[3] This process, which is given the name *transference*, has a structure, which, says Burgoyne, is that of "giving to the connotation of a term some content that originally belonged elsewhere. Its subject is that of shifts of meaning".[4] Burgoyne shows how Stewart's theory of transference is taken up by Freud in a text on the elementary structures of the human mind,[5] as well as by the Irish mathematician William Rowan Hamilton, who sought to make the theory of transference a foundation for all mathematics. It was then later taken up by the mathematician Abraham Robinson, whose transference theorems are those

DOI: 10.4324/9781003412304-2

asserting that "any statement of a specified type which is true for one particular structure or class, is true also for some other structure or class of structures".[6]

For someone familiar with Ornette's work, it is possible to discern a profound relation between the ideas uncovered in Burgoyne's article and those to be found in Ornette's discourse, a kind of fundamental consonance at the level of the problems they address, which makes their relation appear with the force of something like necessity. This, we propose, is for two main reasons. First, what Ornette has sometimes called "harmolodics" – the theoretical articulation he has given to his own music – is, in some respects, *itself a theory of meaning shifts* – whether they are the shifts implied by transposition, a key aspect in Ornette's musical discourse, "reinterpretation" in its more tonal sense or by homophonic "mishearings" made possible by consonances relating the sounds of one language contingently to another. Second, the movement of Ornette's work from the earliest recorded pieces in 1958 to the 1972 recording of *Skies of America* – the historical range covered by this book – *is a movement towards parallelism*; if in the early 1960s, as Charlie Haden notes, "the harmony in the horns was real harmony", later, and certainly by the time of the searing textures of *Skies of America* in which the London Symphony Orchestra articulates *tutti* transposed versions of the same melody – what Ornette will call melodic *unisons* – "the harmony was all parallel".[7] Whilst such "parallelisms" are most evident in the transpositional logic of *Skies of America* and elsewhere, it is also possible to discern relations of parallel in the connections Ornette has made between the space of his music and those spaces implied by the impasses of love, of language, of race; if one can "do love" by means of mathematics, as Burgoyne proposes, one can also, Ornette seems to suggest, "do love" by means of music (and vice versa). These relations are in the foreground in the later chapters of this book on "Lonely Woman" and *Skies of America*.

In this sense, transference is not simply another tool to analyse Ornette's discourse; rather, Ornette's discourse is, we suggest, *itself already an intense meditation on the nature of transference*. Ornette's is a *transferential* discourse, a discourse both on, and permeated by, the shifts for which the notion of transference attempts to account. The notion of transference is thus not simply to be "applied" to Ornette's discourse; rather, throughout this book, we stage an encounter between the lineage of thought that Burgoyne uncovers and harmolodic thought. Harmolodic thought is, we propose, an intervention in the development of the notion of transference, a new coordinate in the history of this idea. The reader is encouraged to trace these connections in the text that follows. However, if it is possible to discern real parallels between the theoretical concerns at the heart of harmolodics and those to be found in the development of the notion of transference, this would imply that transference as an analytical tool emerges from *within* harmolodics, as something implicit to it, and not something simply imposed from outside. In this sense, to give priority to the structure of transference in our analysis of Ornette's discourse is to attempt something like a *harmolodic reading of harmolodics*, to answer the question of what harmolodic thought is *for harmolodics*, not for some, perhaps arbitrary, theoretical coordinates with which the analyst is identified.

At one level at least, then, our analysis of discourse is a kind of *tracking of transferences* – a search for shifts in Ornette's discourse at the level of meaning, and for the elements that "ground" such shifts, as well as an attention to the dimension of "parallel", which Ornette's collaborator, Charlie Haden, identified as a key, emergent aspect of harmolodic harmony in the late 1960s. And this tracking of transferential shifts in Ornette's discourse overlaps with another of our tools – the search for quilting points – signifiers that function as points of convergence, of intersection – in Ornette's texts; those signifiers dominant in Ornette's discourse, in other words, seem to be those that (1) imply relations, and (2) *have been subject to some significant shift at the level of meaning*, for which the notion of a transferential shift allows us to account. We are thinking here of signifiers such as *tonic, free, interval, movement* and *unison*. These key signifiers in Ornette's universe are then the points around which our chapters are oriented.

Transference: the development of a term

It is not clear whether Freud read Stewart's text[8] in which the notion of transference was given an early articulation as a theory of meaning shifts, but we know that he did read John Stuart Mill's *System of Logic*, where Stewart's ideas were not only discussed but quoted directly, and even given some development in terms of Mill's theory of specialisation and generalisation.[9] Surveying the field of uses to which the notion of transference is now put, it is clear that this signifier has *itself* been subject to the kinds of shifts for which Stewart's theory of transference was designed to account, and it would be to misunderstand the very import of Stewart's theory to assume the existence of something common to all of these uses, simply because they share a name. However, there is something common to *some* of these uses, we contend, a common structure; this structure – the structure of transference – is what constitutes a central coordinate in our approach to Ornette's discourse. We give an account of this structure below, after a short survey of the contexts in which this structure is to be discerned.

The transference of a name

In his essay on the beautiful, opposing his theory to the assumption to be found in the Encylopedie entry, *Beau*, that there must be a property in common to all objects that share the name "beautiful", the Scottish philosopher Dugald Stewart instead proposed the following more modest condition:

> I shall begin by supposing that the letters A, B, C, D, E, denote a series of objects; that A possesses some one quality in common with B, B a quality in common with C, C a quality in common with D, D a quality in common with E; – while, at the same time, no quality is to be found which belongs in common

to any *three* objects in the series. Is it not conceivable that the affinity between A and B may produce a transference of the name of the first to the second, and that, in consequence of the other affinities which connect the remaining objects together, the same name may pass in succession from B to C, from C to D; and from D to E? In this manner, a common appellation will arise between A and E, although the two objects may in their nature and properties be so widely distant from each other, that no stretch of the imagination can conceive how the thoughts were led from the former to the latter.[10]

These "distant" applications are possible because Stewart's law – the law that governs the "transference of the name" from one object to another – is not that in order for a name to be transferred to some new object, this object must have some one thing in common with *all* objects that share that name, with that quality constituting the condition for the transfer of that name, but merely that it have some property in common with *one* other object that shares that name; one, in other words, is enough. As a consequence of this more restricted version of the law stipulating a quality in common, there is no guarantee that the quality in common allowing the transference of the same name will always be the *same quality*, hence the difficulty encountered by the imagination in attempting to make sense of such shifts.

Transference and the signifier

Stewart's account of meaning shifts forms the basis of a definition of the signifier offered by Bernard Burgoyne. A signifier is, he says,

> a phrase or fragment of a phrase to which is connected a class of meanings which are themselves attached to each other by laws of shifts of meaning.[11]

In set theory, the notion of a *class* was developed as a means to constitute collections of elements on the basis of an arbitrary condition for membership, without thereby invoking Russell's paradox.[12] One can thus refer to a class of green cars, warm climates and so on. However, if, as Stewart suggests in his theory on the laws governing shifts of meaning, there is no necessity of a property common to all objects that share a name, in what sense do they constitute such a class, and what would constitute its condition for membership? The answer must be that all objects that share a name have in common *their having something in common with at least one other member of that class*. In this sense, the "quality in common" – the "being the same" at the level of some contingent property – between a point and one other point of the class itself constitutes the "common property", which then constitutes the condition for class inclusion.

Thus, a signifier – a phrase or collection of phrases – can change meaning, can establish connections to new meanings, insofar as something in common exists between one meaning and another to which a signifier is now to be transferred, without it being necessary that a single quality in common grounds *all* of the shifts constituting as a class the meanings connected to that particular signifier. Meanings, in this conception, thus form what might be called a *transference class*; rather than a particular property in common, as the Encyclopedists assumed, the condition for membership of such a class, the property all members of that class have in common, is an experience of "partial" commonality with respect to at least one other member of that class, with one enough to satisfy the condition for inclusion in that class.

Freudian identification

We use "partial" here in the sense implied by Freud's notion of *partial identification*. Suppose that a little girl, says Freud, develops the same painful symptom as her mother – for instance, the same tormenting cough. If this identification comes from the Oedipus complex, he says, it signifies a hostile desire on the girl's part to take her mother's place with respect to the father, producing a realisation of this desire under the influence of a sense of guilt: "You wanted to be your mother, and now you *are*, anyhow so far as your suffering is concerned".[13] In this case, says Freud, the identification is "partial" and "extremely limited"; it pertains not to the whole of an object, taking the whole as its model, but rather borrows from the other only a single trait (einziger Zug).[14] A "partial identification" in other words, is "partial" not because it has only some of the properties of a relation of identification; it is "fully" a relation of identification – rather the "partiality" is on the side of the object. A partial identification is partial because it relates only the *part* by means of a relation of identity, of being the same, rather than the whole, of an object to the part of another object.

Freudian transference

In the postscript to Freud's account of his analysis of a young woman referred to as Dora, given in the "Fragment of an Analysis of a Case of Hysteria", Freud characterises transference in terms of a metaphor of printing; transferences, he says, are *facsimiles, new editions*, of the impulses and phantasies aroused during, and made conscious by, the progress of the treatment. Sometimes these transferences have a content that differs in no way from the original model, except with respect to this substitution, in which case they can be considered "new impressions" or "reprints", and, at other times, these contents have been subjected to a moderating influence, which he terms "sublimation". In this instance, they will no longer be new impressions, near facsimiles of some past constellation on which they are modelled, but "revised editions".[15]

These transferences have a peculiarity, says Freud, which is that they replace some earlier person by the person of the analyst; a whole series of psychic experiences are revived not as belonging to the past but as applying to the person of the analyst in the present.[16] When, in a dream she recounts, Dora gives herself the warning that she had better leave the treatment, just as she had formerly left Herr K's house, Freud berates himself for not having detected a significant shift in their

18 Transference

relations, a transference from Herr K – a key figure in Dora's erotic impasses – to himself. Have you noticed, he could have asked, anything that leads you to suspect me of intentions similar to those of Herr K, or have you been struck by anything about me which has caught your fancy, as happened previously with Herr K? Then her attention would have been turned to some "detail" of their relation, or in his person or circumstances, under which would be hidden something "analogous" concerning Herr K. It was because of this something in common – what he calls an "unknown quantity" – that she had transferred her cruel impulses, her revengeful motives, from Herr K onto Freud, "acting out" a vengeful desertion of the treatment in place of a revenge against Herr K for his desertion of her.[17]

Transference as completion

In *The Meaning of Meaning*, the text written by I. A. Richards in collaboration with C. K. Ogden, the authors attempted to delineate a new, general theory of meaning and reference, based, in part, on the theories of signs developed by C. S. Peirce, containing within it a nascent theory of what they call *expectation*, proposed some twenty years before the publication of Meyer's *Emotion and Meaning in Music*, and related directly to the notion of transference we have been developing.[18] A *context*, say Richards and Ogden in *The Meaning of Meaning*, "is a set of entities (things or events) related in a certain way" – and this "set" – what they call a *context* – is recurrent; each of its elements has a character (being a particular kind of thing, rather than another) such that other sets of entities occur having the same character and related by the same relation, with these recurrences approaching identity; they occur "nearly uniformly".[19] The existence of such recurrent contexts forms the basis of expectation, for the recurrent quality of contexts is such that the recurrence of merely a part is sufficient to call up the whole, the rest of the context to which this part is connected and which thereby constitutes its "completion". In the somewhat archaic terms Ogden and Richards used at the time, borrowing from the vocabulary of contemporary psychology,

> The expectation is the excitation of part of an engram complex which is called up by a stimulus similar to a part only of the original stimulus situation.[20]

This is related to the question of what they call "interpretation", for a peculiarity of interpretation, they say, is that when a context has affected us in the past, the recurrence of merely a part of that context – what they propose to call a "sign" – will cause us to react in the way we reacted before; "a sign is always a stimulus similar to some part of the original stimulus and sufficient to call up the engram formed by that stimulus".[21] As such, a part is a "sign" of the whole. It is thus possible to see that what Richards calls "expectation" – the process in which the whole of a context is expected to recur, "completing" the appearance of just a part – also has the structure of a transference; what Richards calls "completion" is, in other words, the transfer to a present element, x', of those contextual elements, A, to which a past element, x, is connected, contingent on the experience of a "similarity", a "partial identification", between x and x' – the stimulus is *similar* to a "part only" of the original situation.

Metaphor as transference

This structure is also to be found in the account Richards later gives of *metaphor* in his *The Philosophy of Rhetoric*. Richards' account of metaphor is, in a sense, a theory of *perception*, which generalises the notion of metaphor to cover not only all cases where a word, to use a phrase from Johnson, "gives us two ideas for one", where, in other words, different uses of a word are compounded into one, such that we speak of something "as though it were another", but also all processes normal, he says, to perceptual experience, where we think or feel of one thing in terms of another – as when, looking at a building, it strikes us as having a face and confronting us with a peculiar expression.[22] Richards proposes to introduce two new technical terms – *vehicle* and *tenor* – to aid in the distinction between the two halves of a metaphor, the two ideas that any metaphor gives us, sometimes referred to unsatisfactorily as "the original idea" and "the borrowed one", or "what is really being said or thought of" and "what it is being compared to" and so on.[23] The relation between vehicle and tenor is governed, according to Richards, by what we have called "Stewart's law"; the metaphorical transfer is contingent on some element in common between the points from and to which a name is to be transferred. Richards calls this element common to tenor and vehicle, thus enabling the shift from one to another, the *ground* of the metaphor.[24]

Transference – first sense

Given these coordinates, for each of the instances of transference given above it is possible to discern a general structure; transference – the transfer of some element– is contingent on a "partial identity" – the experience of something, a certain element or "quality", in Stewart's terms, in common between one element to which something is already connected, and another element to which it is to be transferred. That the existence of such a "partial identity", an element, a "quality in common", is the condition for a transference is what could be called Stewart's law; Stewart's law states simply that there can be a transference if there is a common quality somewhere to be found between the elements from and to which another element is to be transferred. In the case of Stewart's transference, the "transfer of a name" from one "object", A, to another "object", B, is contingent on the experience of a quality in common between objects A and B; in the case of Freudian transference, the transfer of hostilities, of "cruel impulses", from Herr K to Freud, is contingent on some "similarity" – what Freud calls an "unknown quantity" – linking, for Dora, Herr K to Freud. And in the case of the little girl who identifies with her mother by means of a tormenting cough, we could say, this partial identification – the "single trait" – is the condition of two transferences– both the fantasised transfer of the relation that constitutes her mother's place with respect to the object of

20 Transference

her love, her father, as well as the Stewartian "transference of a name", represented here, perhaps, by the signifier "mother" – now she is "mother", we could say, at least insofar as her suffering is concerned. In the case of "completion" offered by Ogden and Richards, completion – the "transference of the context" – is contingent on a similarity – a partial identity – between some point, x, and a past point, x', contained in that context. And, in the case of metaphor, the transference of a term is contingent on the experience of an element in common between vehicle and tenor, which *grounds* this transfer.

General reflections on transference

* To say that transferential shifts are governed by laws – by Stewart's law – is not to say, of course, that shifts that do not obey this law cannot happen. Rather, to suggest that shifts are law-governed is merely to say that Stewart's law constitutes *the condition for an experience of lawfulness* – shifts that are experienced as not obeying this law, in other words, can happen but will simply be experienced as "unlawful".
* From the perspective of Stewart's law governing transferential shifts, which element satisfies the condition for transference, which element constitutes the "common quality" is, in some sense, *a matter of indifference*; there is nothing in Stewart's law to distinguish one quality in common from any other, a "proper" commonality from one that is "improper"; it states only that there must be one.
* However, that the specific nature of the element in common is a matter of indifference from the perspective of Stewart's law does not mean that the specific character of this element will be without significance in the context of some specific transference. On the contrary, this book is, in a sense, an investigation of the effects – of veiling, of direction – that emerge when the element in common satisfying Stewart's law is a *relation*, with the shift from points to relations and back again characterising its movement and structure.

Transference – second sense

However, there is something that it would be easy to overlook or gloss over in this account of transference we have offered. For, when we look more closely, it becomes clear that Burgoyne's account of the development of the notion of transference implies at least two somewhat distinct senses, the relation between which is not immediately clear. On the one hand, there is transference as *meaning shift* – this is the sense most closely linked to Stewart's "transference of a name", as well as the general structure of transference we have proposed. On the other hand, however, there is transference as *parallelism*, what Burgoyne refers to as "translation". What, then, is the relation between these two senses? What, in other words, does transference as meaning shift have to do with transference as "translation" or "parallelism", with those affinities at the level of structure, which mean that, as

Burgoyne suggests, structures in the field of love and mathematics "say the same thing"?

In Chapter 4, we introduce the notion of a "transference of a relation", which appears in William Rowan Hamilton's work on algebraic time. Unless we conceive this transference as contingent on an experience of commonality – that there is, for instance, something in common between some point manifesting a relation and another manifesting point to which this relation is then transferred – Hamilton's notion of a "transference of a relation", producing a simple form of "parallelism", thus marks a point of divergence with respect to the account we have just offered, constituting something closer to a "partial identification"– a point of identity, of being the same, at the level of the *relation* manifest by two distinct sets of points. However, it is also possible to see that insofar as transference in the first sense implies meaning *shift* – a *change* at the level of the meaning to which Stewart's transferred signifier is connected – such transference necessarily implies, and relies on, transference in its second sense, transference as "parallelism" – what Hamilton calls the "transference of a relation". We will explore this in more detail in Chapter 4.

Transference and transposition

In fact, the two distinct dimensions of transference we have discussed – of structural parallel, on the one hand, and of the transfer of an element on the basis of something in common, on the other – come together in a notion central to Ornette's thought, the musical notion of *transposition*. In a musical sense, transposition implies the transfer of an element (for a music analyst, perhaps, some minimal letter-name, such as "a") on the basis of a commonality at the level of the *relation*; the "interval", in musical terms, becomes the "element in common", both allowing the "transference of a name" as well as producing the structural affinity that ensures that some motif and its transposition (its realisation by another set of pitches) are in "parallel". However, we propose that harmolodic discourse implies a generalisation of the more limited musical sense of transposition – or rather, in harmolodic discourse, transposition in its more limited musical sense, is to be considered the *particularisation* of a more general structure, which includes both the musical sense and, for instance, attempts to re-enact structural impasses in our relations of love, to *transpose* them into new contexts, realising them by means of new, distinct points. This is perhaps correlative to the fact that, for Ornette, harmolodics is not simply a question of music – other art forms can be harmolodic, as implied, perhaps, by his "harmolodic ballet", *Architecture in Motion*, and perhaps even a *dinner* can be harmolodic, as the writer Steve Lake discovered when he was invited to interview Ornette at a restaurant at which Ornette ordered for himself *two versions of each course* – in effect, two "parallel" dinners.[25] This more general sense of "transposition", correlative to what Burgoyne calls "translation", is implicit in the chapters on "Lonely Woman", in which Ornette makes a direct link between music and love relations, as well as *Skies of America*, in which the harmolodic notion of

22 Transference

Unison offers itself as a new name for this field of structural affinities, a new name for "parallel" relations in love, music and elsewhere.[26]

Analogous transferences

However, there is something final to add to this elaboration that has to do with something Stewart says at the end of his discussion of what he calls "transitive applications", governed as they are by Stewart's law. Although by far the greater part of the transitive or derivative applications of words depend on casual and unaccountable caprices of the feelings or of the fancy, he says, there are certain cases in which they open a very interesting field of philosophical speculation. We will quote the passage that follows in full:

> Such are those, in which an analogous transference of the corresponding term may be remarked universally or very generally in other languages, and which, of course, the uniformity of the result must be ascribed to the essential principles of the human frame. Even in such cases, however, it will by no means be always found, on examination, that the various applications of the same term have arisen from any common quality, or qualities, in the objects to which they relate. In the greater number of instances, they may be traced to some natural and universal association of ideas, founded in the common condition of the human race; and an attempt to investigate by what particular process this uniform result has been brought about, on so great a variety of occasions, whilst it has no tendency to involve us in the abstraction of the schools, can scarcely fail to throw some new light on the history of the human mind.[27]

"Some natural and universal association of ideas, founded in the common condition of the human race" – this passage has had a profound effect on the way we have approached Ornette's discourse. For, if the notion of transferential shifts is a key tool in our analysis of Ornette's discourse – if our "discourse analysis" is, at least in part, a tracking of transferences, as well as the consequences these transferences imply for an understanding of Ornette's music – there are points at which we have discovered in completely other fields (rather than languages, as Stewart suggests), with which Ornette may not have been at all acquainted, correlative shifts, correlative transferences, and at these points, we have let our discussion switch to these analogous trajectories in the development of a term. We are thinking, for instance, of the notion of "freedom" in relation to *vectors*, which we discuss in Chapter 4, as well as the initial development of the notion of vectors in the work of William Rowan Hamilton, which we discuss in Chapter 3.

Summary of approach

There was thus an initial period of searching Ornette's discourse for key signifiers – repetitions and insistences that would constitute points of quilting in Ornette's discourse. Here, a number of signifiers came to the fore – amongst them "unison", "interval", "free", "tonic", "movement" – implying *relations*, on the one hand, and subject to a transferential shift at the level of meaning, on the other, with an analysis of these points of quilting entailing the analysis of the *ground* for such shifts, the specific "qualities in common", making such shifts possible. We gave priority to discourse that referred directly to Ornette's music, statements that would constitute the basis for an analytic approach. For instance, Ornette's statement regarding "Invisible", the first piece on his first album, *Something Else!!!!*, that "the melodic direction is pretty free" offered us a number of potential clues and analytic avenues to pursue. If these relational signifiers imply particular spatial qualities, as well as movement through that space, we were then in a position to relate our analysis of the specific pieces to which Ornette referred to some topological notions. For instance, there is a careful connection to be made between the topological notion of an "isolated point" and what Ornette refers to as the loneliness of the "Lonely Woman". We discuss this in Chapter 5. As Ornette's discourse shifted our attention to relations other than specifically musical relations, but with respect to which musical relations were to be considered in a kind of parallel – we are thinking here of Ornette's statements regarding "Lonely Woman" in his interview with Jacques Derrida – there was a question, first, of how such statements were to be analysed, and, second, how such analyses were to be related to our analyses of the music to which these statements referred. We will explore these questions in more detail in the chapters that follow.

We turn now, then, to the work of analysis itself, with each subsequent chapter oriented with respect to a fragment, or fragments, from Ornette's discourse. We start with a fragment that bears directly on the question of *where to go* – of movement, of direction and of space – a question very close to the one at the heart of this book, of what it means to follow, of what it means to go where the other goes.

Notes

1 Burgoyne, "What Causes Structure?", 237.
2 Burgoyne, *Secrets of Space*.
3 Stewart, *Philosophical Essays*.
4 "What Causes Structure?".
5 Freud, *On Aphasia*.
6 "What Causes Structure?", 250.
7 Haden, interview by Ethan Iverson.
8 Stewart, *Philosophical Essays*.
9 See Freud, *On Aphasia*, 78.
10 Stewart, Philosophical *Essays*, 217.
11 Burgoyne, *Topology: Secrets of Space*.
12 Russell's paradox or "antinomy" is the following: if conditions are arbitrary – if, in other words, anything can constitute the condition for membership of a set – this must include the following condition; the members of a set X are all those sets that do not contain themselves as members. This generates the paradox to which Russell refers, for if X is a member of itself, it is, according to the condition that constitutes the set, excluded from membership, but if it is so excluded, then, according to the same constituting condition, it must also be included – it must also be a member of itself. This

paradox disappears, however, if a *class* is distinguished from a *set*, as a class, X, of all sets that do not contain themselves as members does not implicate X (as X is now a class and not a set).

13 "Group Psychology", 106.
14 Ibid., 107.
15 Freud, "A Case of Hysteria", 116.
16 "A Case of Hysteria", 116.
17 "A Case of Hysteria", 118–119.
18 I could find no mention of Ogden and Richards' text in Meyer's *Emotion and Meaning in Music*.
19 Ogden and Richards, *The Meaning of Meaning*, 58.
20 *The Meaning of Meaning*, 52.
21 *The Meaning of Meaning*, 53.
22 Richards, *The Philosophy of Rhetoric*, 116–117.
23 Richards, *The Philosophy of Rhetoric*, 96.
24 Richards, *The Philosophy of Rhetoric*, 117.
25 Lake, "Prime Time and Motion", 33.
26 Whilst the account of musical transference offered here includes metaphor, enabling us to connect transference to the field influenced by the work of Lakoff and Johnson, including more recent work on analogy, this broader focus on transference, we suggest, allows us to draw together metaphor, analogy and metonymy, notions from psychoanalysis, as well as broader shifts at the level of meaning that might be passed over in a more narrow focus on metaphor, or in an approach that attempts to make metaphor the central term. And transference, as articulated in Stewart's work, is, in a sense, indifferent to the terms it relates – it is, at least in some respects, simply a "technical" law, governing how, not what, two things are related, allowing us to discover implications of transferences in Ornette's discourse that might be missed where the centrality of the body is given in advance. For approaches to music and metaphor, see, for instance, Goodman, *Languages of Art*; Scruton, "Understanding Music"; Hatten, "Metaphor in Music"; Cook, *Analysing Musical Multimedia*; Ayrey, "Debussy's Significant Connections"; and Smith, *Desire in Chromatic Harmony*. For metaphor as "cross-domain mapping" in the sense given to metaphor by Lakoff and Johnson, see Johnson, *The Body in the Mind*; Lakoff, *Women, Fire and Dangerous Things*; Feld, "Flow Like a Waterfall"; and Larson, *Musical Forces: Motion, Metaphor, and Meaning in Music*. For an extension of these themes in relation to analogy, see Zbikowski, "Music, Analogy, and Metaphor".
27 Stewart, *Philosophical Essays*, 226.

Chapter 3

"No one knew where to go"

In *A Harmolodic Life*, the book on Ornette Coleman's work and life by John Litweiler, there appears the fragment of an interview in which Ornette recalls his early experiences with Don Cherry, Charlie Haden and Billy Higgins, the three musicians that would go on to create with him, in 1959, the first of a series of groundbreaking albums, *The Shape of Jazz to Come*. At first, says Ornette, these musicians were interested in "bebop", a name associated with the music of Charlie Parker and his collaborators, but they were soon to become interested in the music that Ornette was attempting to write, music that would, however, present a question – "the most interesting part" – a problem to be resolved: "what do you play after you play the melody?"[1]

> That's where I won them over. Because when I started showing them how they could do that – you see, when you play a melody, you have a set pattern to know just what you can do while the other person is doing certain things. Whereas, in this case, when you play the melody no one knew where to go or what to do to show that he knew where he was going. I had already developed playing like that naturally. And when I started showing them how I'd done that – I'd take a chord. So you play the tonic, you play the third, and then found out that they were playing the same space.[2]

If some music – perhaps the music of artists such as Charlie Parker – offered "a set pattern to know just what you can do while the other person is doing certain things", in the case of Ornette's music, there was a problem of direction, of orientation:

> no one knew where to go or what to do to show that he knew where he was going.

To this problem of direction, however, of knowledge with respect to where one is to go, Ornette had already developed a solution, a way of playing that had, he says, developed naturally, and that had to do with the emergence of a shared space:

DOI: 10.4324/9781003412304-3

26 "No one knew where to go"

I'd take a chord. So you play the tonic, you play the third, and then found out that they were playing the same space.

But how are we to make sense of this problem of direction, of this lack of knowledge with respect to "where to go"? What do we mean by *where*? What is a "where", a "somewhere" to which I go, or from which I come? And what does it mean to *go*? What is this movement that takes me from where I am to where I am going? And if some *where* is *unknown*, what would it mean for such a where to be known? What does it mean to *know where*? Then there is the problem of Ornette's solution. "You play the tonic", Ornette says, "and you play the third". But what is a "third", what is a "tonic", and what about a "third" and a "tonic" indicates the presence of a shared space? And if the space that is shared, that is the same, is the space of a chord, what kind of space is this? And, finally, how does the discovery that one shares such a space answer the question of direction, of knowing where to go and what to do to show that one knows where one is going?

We take these problems in turn, dealing first with the problem of *going*, of movement, drawing in the work of William Rowan Hamilton, and in particular the distinction between *analysis* and *synthesis* that appears in his *Lectures on Quaternions* – an approach to movement through space that, as we will see, already implies the articulation of the *known* and the *unknown*. Next, we turn to the question of *space* before investigating Ornette's solution to the problem of "knowing where to go" – a solution in terms of a space that is shared.

And, of course, it is possible to see that the problem to which Ornette appears here to offer a concrete solution – the problem of "knowing where to go" – is a problem close to the one at the heart of this book, of what it means to follow, of what it means to "go where I go". For this reason, we will pay close attention to the solution Ornette offers here, with its mention of apparently prosaic musical features – chords and tonics, and the shared space they imply – before asking how this solution to "knowing where to go" relates to – and, perhaps, in its own way, answers – the question at the heart of this book. Ornette's solution will take us to the heart of some thorny questions regarding his music, to do with the relation to chords, to keys and tonality, to the interrelation of chords to form sequences – questions with answers to which each subsequent chapter will return, and with respect to which they will each constitute a point of complication, of rethinking, causing us to resist any too ready a resolution.

Hamilton's solution

Vectors

In 1848, the Irish mathematician William Rowan Hamilton gave a series of lectures at Trinity College, Dublin, on a new mathematical "calculus", or method, that had for some years occupied his attention and to which he was to give the name the "calculus of quaternions".[3] At the foundation of this new method were the new significations he was proposing to give to the four operations of addition, subtraction, multiplication and division, as the "analysis" and "synthesis" of "ordinal" and "cardinal" relations – the ordinal relation of one point to another, in the case of subtraction and addition, and the cardinal relation of one "ray" to another, in the case of multiplication and division.[4] In the operation he proposed to call "subtraction" – the sign for subtraction, "–", was to be the mark of the *analysis* of one spatial position with respect to another position – "point minus point", the position of one point in space "minus" the position of another point in space, their "geometrical difference".[5] Hamilton called the "unknown and undetermined"[6] point in this operation the "analysand", the symbol, B, which takes the initial place in the relation, before the subtraction sign, and the other "comparatively simple and known"[7] point, A, the "analyser", placed to the right of the subtraction mark: B – A.

The analysis of the position of the unknown point, B, with respect to the known point, A, is an operation that, if performed completely, would tell us not only in what *direction* the analysand is situated with respect to the analyser, but also at what *distance*.[8] Thus, considered "synthetically", as in the operation of addition, this "ordinal analysis" would result in a "rule of transition" telling us not only how to set out – in what direction to travel – but also how far we would need to go after setting out from A in order to reach point B.[9] Thus, if, in analysis by subtraction – B – A = a – with a the name of the step, the interval, the spatial *difference* between point A and B, then, in synthesis by addition – B = a + A – the difference, a, between point A and point B "plus" the initial point A produces the unknown endpoint, B.[10] The result of this operation of analysis – a, the transition or "step" from the analyser to the analysand, a movement which is always to be supposed a straight line – Hamilton called a "vector".

This step (which we shall always suppose to be a *straight line*) may also, in my opinion, be properly called a VECTOR, or more fully, it may also be called "*the vector of the point* B, *from the point* A" because it may be considered as having for its office, function, work, task or business to *transport* or CARRY (in Latin, *vehere*) a *movable point* from the given or initial position A to the sought or final position B.[11]

If we take A and B to be points on a number line, where the position of point A is "3" and the position of point B is "5", the analysis by subtraction of point B with respect to point A produces a vectoral difference, a –

$$B - A = a$$

$$5 - 3 = 2$$

– that, in synthesis by addition, *moves* – "transports", "carries" – a "movable point" from A *in the direction of* B

28 "No one knew where to go"

$$B = a + A$$

$$5 = 2 + 3$$

– a movement that could be represented in the following way (Figure 3.1).

The vector, +*2*, synthesised – *added* – with respect to the point 3, produces the point 5.

In Hamilton's terms, if analysis produces the *vehicle* – the vector – the means of transport, *movement* itself – *going, transport* – is on the side of *synthesis*; it is in synthesis that the "movable point" *moves*, it is in synthesis that the movable point *goes* from A to B, from an initial to an endpoint. Movement is thus, in this sense, *synthetic*, the effect of the synthesis of the product of analysis – the analysis of B with respect to A – with respect to the initial point, A, of that analysis. There is an order that pertains to this synthetic movement, a beginning and an end, an "initial" and "final", a first and last, a before and after, a "where" *from* and *to* which this movement moves. At the level of the order that pertains to vectoral movement, A is the *antecedent* and B is the *consequent*, A is what *leads* and B is what *follows*. This order – the order that pertains to synthetic movement – is inverted in analysis; in order to produce a vector, the vehicle that will transport a movable point *from* A *to* B, from the antecedent to the consequent point of an ordered pair (A, B), one starts with the consequent, one starts with B, which is then, as the "analysand", analysed with respect to the antecedent, the "analyser", A: B − A.

To this ordered "synthetic" pair (A, B) Hamilton maps other distinctions, other pairs: first, the distinction between *where I am to go from*, the initial point of a vectoral movement, and its endpoint, *where I am to go to*; second, the distinction between the *known* and the *unknown*, the "comparatively simple and known point", A, and the "complex" "undetermined" point, B; and third, the distinction, implicit to the notion of analysis, between *analyser* and *analysand*. Taking these various mappings together, we can thus say that the analysis of the unknown analysand, *where to go to*, with respect to the known analyser, *where to go from*, produces the vector *a*, the vehicle, the means of movement, that, in synthesis, *moves* a "movable point" from the known analyser, *where to go from*, to the unknown analysand, *where to go to*.

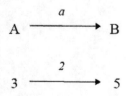

Figure 3.1

The concerns at the heart of the dilemma faced by Ornette's collaborators – of *knowledge*, of *where* and of *going*, of *movement* – thus come together in Hamilton's vector. If *no one knew where to go*, the answer is to be found, says Hamilton, in the ancient distinction between analysis and synthesis, conceived now in terms of the simplest operations of arithmetic; in order to produce the unknown *where to go*, one simply *analyses* the unknown with respect to the known, which produces a vector, a vehicle, a means of movement, that, in *synthesis*, moves "a movable point" from the known "analyser" *where to go from* to the unknown "analysand" *where to go*. "Vector", in other words, as Hamiltonian, draws together:

- *Movement:* if we speak of or represent a vector, this means that something – what Hamilton calls a "movable point" – is *going* – *moving* – somewhere.
- *Knowledge:* where something is going is from the *known* to the *unknown*.
- *Where:* this is *where*, from and to which are the initial and endpoints of the vectoral movement and with the implication of a *space* through which such a movable point moves.
- *Direction:* there is a direction that pertains to this movement, represented by the sign for positive (+), and negative (−), correlative to *order*, implying a distinction between "what leads" and "what follows", a before and after, a *from* and *to*. This enables us to link two senses of *to follow* – "to go where I go", on the one hand, and "to be consequent at the level of order", on the other.

Let us turn again to Ornette's solution.

Ornette's solution

"I'd take a chord", says Ornette. "You play the tonic, you play the third, and then found out they were playing the same space". But, in what sense is this a solution? What is a third? What is a tonic? And what do they have to do with a shared space? And in what sense would the discovery that one is playing the same space answer the question of knowledge with respect to direction, of orientation, of knowing where one is to go?

Thirds and tonics

Each value in a coordinate system can be understood as an expression (direct or indirect) of the being of that point with respect to *0*, the point of origin. In the simplest instance – a one-dimensional line – this relation is direct; "+3" marks the point three unit steps "up" – in the direction of a point greater than it – from the point of origin, and so on. Although it is obscured by the fact that the tonic is referred to by a "natural" number, "1" – "the first degree of the scale" – we could treat the tonic as precisely a "point of origin" in this sense, with all the names – "3rd", "5th" and so on – as marks of *situation*, of "coordination", of *being somewhere* with respect to the tonic, just as the values in a number-line coordinate system are marks of the being of those points with respect to the point of origin – a connection that finds an echo, perhaps, in the fact that a point shares a name with the interval separating that point from the tonic – a "5th" is a 5th interval from the tonic, a "3rd" is a 3rd interval from the tonic, and so on.

In his attempts to define "tonic", the music theorist Steven Rings has suggested, however, that this orienting function of the tonic, the sense in which it functions as a "focal point", situating the points of a space with respect to itself, is not simply a case of the orderly distribution of names, such as "3rd", "5th", and so on, across a sequence of pitches but rather describes a phenomenon of perceptual experience – "the orienting of aural attention in a particular direction", "an act of aural directing which situates the non-tonic pitch classes with respect to the tonic focal point", even when that focal point is acoustically absent.[12] Rings conceives this tonic-directedness in terms of phenomenological *intention* – "the subjective pointing of the ear *from* some subordinate tonal element *to* the tonic",[13] which he represents by means of an "oriented diagraph", a configuration of nodes and arrows all of whose arrows are directed towards a single node.[14]

The situation-effects that emerge as a consequence of such tonic-directedness Rings calls scale-degree *qualia*, the perceptual phenomenon of "scale-degree-ness", "the raw feel of experiencing a sounding pitch as, say, scale degree '3' or scale degree '5'".[15] Rings' theory thus implies two levels, which he represents as the two dimensions of a tonic-oriented space: on the one hand what he calls "pitch chroma" – the pitches, the points, to be oriented; and, on the other, scale-degree *qualia* – the effects of orientation, of situation, which emerge when a pitch chroma is experienced as being with respect to an elective tonic point of orientation. In this sense, the distinction between pitch chroma and scale-degree *qualia* implies a distinction between *coordinated* and *coordinate* – the pitch (chroma) to be situated, to be coordinated, and the fleeting effect of situation, the *qualia* coordinate-effect, to which it is related, emerging as a consequence of its being with respect to the tonic. And one of the aims of Rings' theory is to show how the ear shifts its focal point, its point of focus, in the experience of a piece of music, reorientating the points of a tonal space with respect to a shifting tonic so as to produce new pitch-qualia relations, new effects of situation, as a consequence.

Of course, as Rings shows, the idea that tonality implies tonic-directedness, or that the tonic is a point with respect to which the points of a tonal space are oriented, and in the direction of which they strive, is not at all new. In his treatise on harmony, the music theorist Heinrich Schenker spoke of the meaning of the tonic in terms of what he called the "egoistic drive of the tone", a drive he related to a certain "aspiration" on the part of the tones when situated with respect to this tonic. "This much is obvious", he says: "the significance of the tonic exceeds that of the other scale steps, and they lose in value the farther they go from the tonic". Thus, "a scale-step does not aspire to the place of a VI or II in the system, but, on the contrary, it prefers to be a V at least, if not a I, a real tonic".[16] This allusion to an "egoistic drive", the "aspiration" the degrees of a key feel with respect to the tonic and in relation to which there is a loss, a falling short at the level of *value*, echoes, of course, Freud's account in his essay on narcissism, of the process of *idealisation*. Idealisation, says Freud, names the process whereby a man "has set up an *ideal* in himself by which he measures his actual ego" and onto which he displaces his narcissism. Now this ideal, which Freud calls his "ideal ego", finds itself, like the infantile ego, possessed "of every perfection that is of value".[17]

However, there is another Freudian coordinate we could draw in here. In his text on group psychology, Freud had turned his attention to the question of groups, and, in particular, to the question of what holds a group together. If the individuals in a group are combined into a *unity* [Einheit], Freud says, there must be something that binds them together, and this bond might precisely be the thing that is characteristic of a group. This something, says Freud, is *Eros – love* – the power "which holds together everything in the world".[18] The group is held together by *emotional bonds – love relations* – that bind members to each other and to the leader. Freud introduces a distinction between two forms of emotional bond that characterise group relations: *being in love* and *identification*. Each individual, he says, is bound in "two directions" [zwei Richtungen] by libidinal ties on the one hand to the leader and on the other to the other members of the group.[19] If *identification*, which endeavours to mould a person's ego after the one that has been taken as a model, is one of these "directions" characterising the bonds between members of a group, then *being in love*, representing a "diversion of the instinct from its sexual aim",[20] is the other, characterising the relation of each member of the group with the leader.

In this sense, it is possible to see that a Freudian group, at least at the level of the love relation that binds the members of the group to the leader, is a space with a "tonic" orientation. That is to say, a Freudian group is a space in which all the points of the space – the followers – are related, by means of a relation of love, to a common point: the leader, the one put by means of the idealising love of all of his followers, says Freud, in the position of the "ego ideal".

> A primary group of this kind is a number of individuals who have put one and the same object in the place of their ego ideal and have consequently identified themselves with one another in their ego.[21]

Like the points oriented with respect to the tonic, by means of this idealising love, each of those contained in the group, we could say, is thereby situated as "follower" with respect to a common leader.

Tonic and situating vectors

To draw out the Hamiltonian dimensions of analysis and synthesis with their particular articulation of the relation between the known and the unknown, so intimately connected to the problems experienced by Ornette's early collaborators, we present tonic-oriented movement by means of a *tonic vector*. A tonic vector, like a Hamiltonian vector, is a *vehicle* that moves "a movable point" from a point of a tonic-oriented space *to – in the direction of –* its tonic point of orientation.

32 "No one knew where to go"

By means of a tonic vector, in other words, a "movable point" traverses the interval $(-d)$, separating a point, x, of a tonic-oriented space from y, its tonic point of orientation.[22]

$$x \xrightarrow{\ -d\ } y$$

We could then present the effect of situation that emerges as an effect of this tonic orientation by means of a *situating vector*. If a tonic vector moves "a movable point" from a point of a tonic-oriented space to the tonic, a situating vector moves in the inverse direction from 0, the tonic coordinate – the tonic "degree" – to s, the coordinate – the non-tonic "degree" – that situates a point with respect to that tonic, *such that the situating vector and its endpoint share a name*: a point a "6th" "up" from the tonic is situated by a vector that moves "up" by the interval of a "6th"; a point a "5th" "up" from the tonic is situated by a vector that moves "up" by the interval of a "5th", and so on.

$$s \xleftarrow{\ +d\ } 0$$

The distinction between tonic and situating vectors is correlative to the distinction in Rings' tonal space between *chroma* and *qualia* – between, in other words, the pitches oriented – *coordinated* – with respect to a tonic and the orientations – the *coordinates*, the effects of "scale-degree-ness" or perceptual *qualia* – that emerge as an effect of this orientation. If tonic vectors act on the *coordinated* – the pitch chroma – the situating vectors act on *coordinates* – the scale degrees – moving from tonic degree to degrees other than the tonic. (The significance for our analysis of the notion of situating vector will become clearer in the discussion of Ornette's *Interval* and its correlative *Idea*, which appears in Chapter 5.)

If we conceive these vectors in terms of analysis and synthesis, both tonic and situating vectors are produced by the *analysis* of the end with respect to the initial point – consequent with respect to antecedent, unknown with respect to known, analysand with respect to analyser, where to go to with respect to where to go from, what follows with respect to what leads – which assigns to the points of these pairs the directed interval-distance separating them in a tonic-oriented space. In *synthesis*, by acting on the initial point of these pairs – by *synthesising* the interval-vector produced in analysis with respect to that initial point – "a movable point" *moves*, traversing the interval separating these points in a tonic-oriented space, from antecedent to consequent, known to unknown, analyser to analysand, where to go from to where to go to, what leads to *what follows*. As before, an order pertains to this movement with the relation of antecedence and consequence this implies; at the level of the tonic movement, the tonic is consequent, what follows, whilst at the level of the situating movement, it is the effect of situation (the point to which x is coordinated) that is consequent, which follows with respect to the tonic coordinate (the point to which y is coordinated).

The relation between situating and tonic vectors could then be presented in the following way, where x is the point to be coordinated, producing an effect of situation, s, and y is the point coordinated to the tonic-origin coordinate, 0 (i.e., y "is" the tonic-origin point), as shown in Figure 3.2. Then the analysis of s – the coordinate to which x is coordinated – with respect to 0, the tonic-origin coordinate, produces the situating vector, $+d$, which is the inverse of the tonic vector, $-d$ (as represented by the "directional" difference between the signs for positive and negative), produced by the analysis of y, the point coordinated to the tonic-origin coordinate, with respect to x.

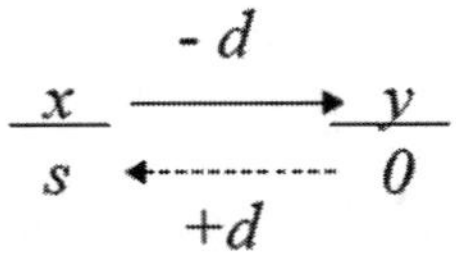

$$
\begin{array}{ccc}
& -d & \\
\underline{x} & \longrightarrow & \underline{y} \\
s & \dashleftarrow & 0 \\
& +d &
\end{array}
$$

Figure 3.2

Returning to the question of a shared space to which Ornette refers, if "third" is the name given to the point insofar as it is experienced as being (somewhere) with respect to another point, it is possible to see that points *share* a space insofar as they are *situated with respect to a common point* – insofar, that is, as the analysis of those points with respect to a common point produces vectors that, in synthesis, move "movable points" from the tonic coordinate to these points, with the name given to this common point, the point with respect to which all the points that share a space are situated, *tonic*. Like the *quilting point* Lacan introduces in his seminar on the psychoses, a tonic is a "point of convergence", a point of intersection, with respect to which all of the points of the space are *situated*, with respect to which they gain their *being somewhere* – their being 3rd, their being 5th and so on.

So, in what sense does Ornette's reference to tonic, with the implication of a space of tonic orientation, constitute a solution to the problem of "knowing where to go"; in what sense does it solve the problem of knowledge regarding movement, going, and the space or the point in the direction of which one moves, one goes? If "where" is conceived in terms of a *space* – "no one knew *to which space* to go" – then Ornette's solution is simply that one goes to the space of a chord, conceived in relation to a tonic. "Where I go" is a chord space with the implication that this space is tonic-oriented. If "where" is conceived, on the other hand, as a *point* – "no one knew *to which point* to go" – then the reference to tonics offers a simple solution, for given the movement that pertains to the tonic vector, what Schenker referred to as the "aspirational" drive to *be* the tonic, internal to a tonic-oriented space, all "movable points" move – are moved by the tonic vector – in the direction of the tonic. All vectors move "movable points", in other words, in the direction of a common point.

34   "No one knew where to go"

With respect to the problem of knowledge – of "knowing where to go" – we now have two solutions. On the one hand, there is Hamilton's solution, given in terms of the ancient distinction between analysis and synthesis, in which analysis of the unknown with respect to the known produces a vector that transports, *moves*, a movable point from the known to the unknown, with the unknown "where I go" now the endpoint of that movement. On the other hand, we have Ornette's solution, given in terms of tonics and tonic-oriented spaces; "where to go" is now the tonic-oriented space of a chord, internal to which all points move in the direction of a common point. Conceiving tonic movement in terms of a tonic vector allows the interrelation of Hamilton and Ornette's solutions, for if tonic movement is produced by means of a vector, the "unknown" is now the tonic, which, when analysed with respect to each of the "known" points of a tonic-oriented space, produces tonic vectors that move "movable points" in the direction of this common, "unknown" tonic point. When we look more closely at these apparently simple solutions, however, a number of significant problems appear.

Problems

First problem: "tonic"

If we look again at what Ornette has said regarding the tonic, there is a certain ambiguity. "I'd take a chord", he says. "So you play the tonic, you play the third, and then found out that they were playing the same space". But to what does this signifier, "tonic", refer? If "3rd" is a point of the chordal space Ornette has taken, does this imply the "transference of the name", "tonic", from "tonal tonic" to "root" of the chord? Is "tonic" a *transference*, in Stewart's sense? Or does Ornette's reference to "tonic" imply that the chord he has taken is the tonic chord of a tonality – chord I in the key of X – and that, in this sense, the "tonic" and "3rd" of the chord simply coincide with the "tonic" and "3rd" of the key? This is a significant problem from the perspective of the question of where to go, for if Ornette's solution implies a movement to a tonic, to which "tonic" is one to go – to a "tonal tonic", a tonic in the usual, tonal sense – or to a "harmonic tonic", as implied by a transference from "tonal tonic" to *root* – or both? This question is, of course, not without consequence for the question of tonality in relation to Ornette's music.

If "tonic" is a transference, and if this transference from tonic to root is *immediate*,[23] there is then the question of what would make this transference possible, of what element, what feature in common, would allow the transfer of the name. It is possible to detect, we suggest, some "qualities in common", along the following lines. Given the names given to the points of the chord – "3rd", "5th" and so on – insofar as they are experienced as being with respect to the root of the chord,

- Both tonic and root perform a situating function with respect to the other points of the space (of the tonality, of the chord), as implied by the names – "3rd", "5th" – marking the being of the points of both a chord and a key with respect to a "harmonic tonic" or "tonal tonic".
- They are both points of intersection, points of *convergence* – all points of the chord, of the key, are situated with respect to this common point.

If we were to persist with this transference on the basis of these common qualities, we would then have a distinction between "tonal tonic" and "harmonic tonic" correlative to the distinction between "tonic" and "root".[24]

Second problem: tonal orientation

The second, closely linked problem is the following: are Ornettian chords, as alluded to in Ornette's solution, *tonally oriented*, are they, in addition to an "internal" tonic orientation, as implied by the transference we have just described, oriented "externally" with respect to a "tonal tonic"? This question is related to something said by the saxophonist Julian "Cannonball" Adderley, who, sceptical but curious about Ornette's music, met Ornette sometime in the early 1960s to discuss his ideas. "Coleman *does* play chords in an improvisation", says Adderley in an article for *DownBeat* describing this meeting, "but does not play 'changes', such as standard II minor seventh, to dominant seventh to I or III chords".[25]

Using the expanded notion of "tonic" an Ornettian transference implies, insofar as it also refers to harmonic "roots", a space of "changes", as described by Adderley, suggests, in fact, three distinct spaces: (a) the space of a *chord* – a tonic-oriented space, in the sense we have developed, insofar as the points of that space are experienced as being with respect to a common point of intersection (the "root" of the chord); (b) the space of a *key*, insofar as the chord is itself experienced as caught up in a wider tonal space constituted with respect to its tonic – the "tonal tonic"; and (c) the space of a harmonic "progression" – conceived as an ordered set of tonally oriented chords. In this simple scheme, each subsequent space, of course, implies the prior space, so (b) tonally oriented chords imply (a) chords, and (c) a sequence of tonally oriented chords implies both (a) and (b). Adderley's "Ornette does play chords but doesn't play changes" could thus mean a number of different things, dependent on how we interpret the signifiers "chords" and "changes". If a chord is a "change" insofar as it has a tonal orientation – insofar as the chord, Fm7, is experienced as IIm7, for instance – then "chords but not changes" implies chords in the absence of such a tonal orientation. If a chord is a "change" only insofar as it is contained in a "sequence" of chords – IIm7 *to* V7 *to* I or III – then this necessarily precludes only such a sequence and not necessarily the tonal orientation for a chord such as Fm7. Briefly, "chords but not changes" thus implies (a) with the possibility of (b), but not (c).

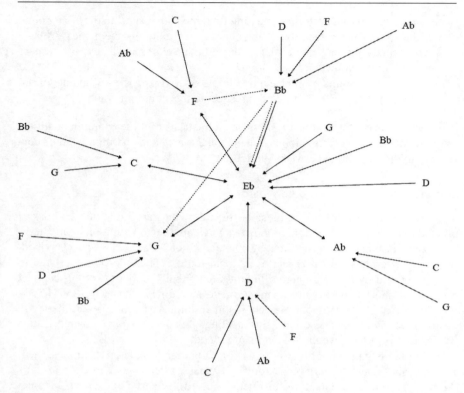

Figure 3.3

Tonic relation

These three levels, (a), (b) and (c), are represented in Figure 3.3, which echoes the oriented diagraphs developed by Rings and shows diatonic chords in the key of Eb.[26] With the exception of the dashed arrows, all of the vectors are tonic vectors, implying the transferential expansion of the notion of "tonic" to include the root of a chord, and, as such, they represent the possibility that "tonic", as we have just discussed, is both a transference from "tonal tonic" to "root" *and* that Ornette's chords are oriented tonally. The centre point of the diagram is the "tonal tonic", Eb, whilst the notes immediately connected to that are either "harmonic tonics" (the roots of the various diatonic chords) or those notes directly in the diatonic chord (G, Bb, D are thus directly connected to the centre point, Eb, as the other notes of an Ebma7 chord). Double-headed arrows from the centre point, Eb, indicate that Eb is both the "tonal tonic" for a "harmonic tonic", as well as contained in the chord for which that note is the "harmonic tonic". Thus, the vector connecting C to the central Eb is double-headed because Eb is both the "tonal tonic" for C and is contained in the diatonic chord of Cm7. The dashed vectors are not tonic vectors but represent the movement implied by the "changes", IIm7 *to* V7 *to* I or III.

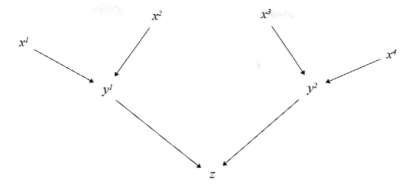

Figure 3.4

As such, each vector in this diagram expresses the relation, "is a tonic for", with a vector linking a point, x, to a point, y, implying that y is a tonic for x. This tonic relation is transitive, which is to say that if Bb, for instance, is a "harmonic tonic" for the notes of the chord of Bb7, and if Eb is a "tonal tonic" for the "harmonic tonic", Bb, then Eb will also be a tonal tonic for the other notes of the Bb7 chord.[27] Given the presence of double-headed vectors, however, it is important to note that transitivity does not cross the centre point (Eb) – so, whilst Eb is a tonic for Bb and (crossing the centre point, moving outwards) Ab is a tonic for Eb, this does not imply that Ab is a tonic for Bb.

A number of further properties would also seem to pertain to this tonic relation. Two points can share a tonic, but the same point cannot *at once* have more than one tonic[28] unless x, y and z link together transitively. If our tonic vectors imply movement – that something, a "movable point", is *going* somewhere, that it is moving in the direction of a tonic consequent – these properties produce a structure such that, no matter where any point is in the structure, and in spite of the immediate point of convergence which is not a point of convergence for *all* of the points of the structure, there is nonetheless a final point of convergence, a point that is a point of convergence for all other points in the structure, and in the direction of which all of the points of the space move. Unlike the other intermediate points of convergence that may emerge in the elaboration of the structure, the final point of tonic convergence is always and necessarily a tonic for all other points of the structure; all other points of the structure, in other words, always and necessarily converge to this common point. Thus, z is a "final tonic" to which all other points of the structure converge, whilst the intermediate tonics, y^1 and y^2, are not (Figure 3.4).

Ornette's solution: summary of problems

In summary, then, does Ornette's solution imply (1) a tonally oriented chord, (2) a chord, with "tonic" as transference to "root", with the implication that the structure of tonic convergence is now to be found *internal* to a chord or (3) both, with

38 "No one knew where to go"

"tonic" as the transferential enlargement of the class of "tonics" to contain the tonic orientation of the points of a chord with respect to a root – a "harmonic tonic" – as well as the orientation of the points of that chord to a wider "tonal tonic", with the third of these possibilities offering an enlarged way of thinking about tonic-oriented spaces, as shown in Figure 3.3? Given these uncertainties, we propose to persist, at least for now, with the most open possibility regarding Ornette's solution, in anticipation of answers to be discovered later, with the most open formulation being the following: "tonic" is a transference from "tonal tonic" to root, but this does not preclude the existence of "tonal tonics"; it merely enlarges the class of things described as "tonic".

Third problem: two "wheres"

The third problem has to do with *where* and can be introduced by means of something Ornette says in the same conversation with Adderley we have been discussing, something about the nature of chords that bears directly on the question of the tonic orientation internal to them. "Chords are just names for sounds, which really need no names at all, as names are sometimes confusing", says Ornette. "For instance", explains Adderley, "F minor seventh is also A flat major sixth".

In the first instance, there is an uncertainty about what to make of the apparent identity of Fm7 and Ab6, the notion that Fm7 *is* Ab6. If Fm7 and Ab6 contain the same pitches, if they are identical at the level of their points but can be distinguished by means of the orientation given to those points, with F the "tonic" in Fm7 and Ab the "tonic" in Ab6, does this imply the insignificance of the tonic relation for Ornette, the insignificance of the only aspect to distinguish one from the other? Or, is the apparent identity of Fm7 and Ab6 an avowal of this very capacity for "modal" reorientation, an avowal of the fact that the tonic is unstable, not given in advance, and that the same set of pitches constituting, for instance, Fm7, can just as easily be reoriented differently with respect to one another so as to produce, say, Ab6?[29]

This second possibility is significant, for if "Fm7 is also Ab6" implies reorientation, that the points of an Fm7 chord are to be reoriented so as to produce an Ab6 chord, and vice versa, this introduces a problem at the level of the knowledge implied by the reference to "tonics", for, in both cases, one knows where to go – one goes to the tonic, insofar as both Fm7 and Ab6 imply spaces with a tonic orientation – but this knowledge at the level of the *coordinate* – the tonic coordinate to which one moves – does not imply knowledge at the level of the point *coordinated* to that coordinate. If one *knows where* – the tonic coordinate – to which to go, in other words, to which tonic is one to go – the tonic of an Fm7 or the tonic of an Ab6? For which point is the tonic coordinate the coordinate?

There are, in effect, two "wheres", two "endpoints" in the direction of which "you" and "I" *go*, of which we move, correlative to the distinction between levels implied by the distinction between tonic and situating vectors. On the one hand, there is "where" as *coordinated*, the specific point coordinated to the tonic coordinate, *0*, and, on the other, there is "where" as *coordinate*, the "*0*" itself, to which a point that "is" the tonic is coordinated. If Adderley's "Fm7 *is* Ab6" implies no necessary relation between coordinated and coordinate, between the point that "is" the tonic – either F or Ab, in this instance – and the coordinate, *0*, to which both, as "the tonic", are coordinated, how does one know where to go, how does one know, even if one "knows" the *coordinate* – that one *goes to 0, the tonic* – "where" to go at the level of the point *coordinated* to that coordinate? Can the relation Hamilton's vector has established between *movement* and *knowledge* help us here?

Analysis and synthesis

One of the earliest articulations given to the distinction between analysis and synthesis appears in the *Mathematical Collection* of Pappus of Alexandria, written around 300 BC. In this text, Pappus defines analysis and synthesis in the following way:

> *Analysis* then takes that which is sought as if it were admitted and passes from it through it successive consequences to something which is admitted as the result of synthesis: for in analysis we assume that which is sought as if it were (already) done and we inquire what it is from which this results, and again what is the antecedent cause of the latter, and so on, until by so retracing our steps we come upon something already known or belonging to the class of first principles, and such a method we call analysis as being solution backwards.
>
> But in *synthesis*, reversing the process, we take as already done that which was last arrived at in the analysis and, by arranging in their natural order as consequences what were before antecedents, and successively connecting them one with another, we arrive finally at the construction of what was sought; and this we call synthesis.[30]

And, in fact, Pappus' definition, which assumes "that which is sought as if it were (already) done", something he relates to the question of "knowledge", of the "known", alerts us to a problem with Hamilton's solution – not, of course, a problem with Hamilton's algebra, which simply restates in vectoral terms some of the basic properties of arithmetic – which has to do with its status as a solution to the problem of the unknown we have been discussing. In terms of Hamilton's vector, this problem could be stated as follows: if the vector, $-d$, plus the "known" point, A, produces the unknown point B, *one must already know* B *in order to produce* B, insofar as $-d$, which produces B when "added" to A, is the product, the effect, the *outcome* of the relation between the known and unknown points A and B. In relation to "Fm7 is also Ab6", the problem is that in order to produce the unknown tonic – the knowledge of which would tell us which orientation pertains to a chord, the orientation implied by Fm7 or the one implied by Ab6 – *one must already know the tonic,* for the tonic vector, which produces the tonic when "synthesised" with respect to some point coordinated with respect to that tonic, is the *product*, the *effect*, of the relation between that "known" point and the "unknown" tonic.

An order of coordination

However, the problem is perhaps even worse than it first appears, for if I know the coordinate to which I move – the tonic coordinate – but do not know the point coordinated to that coordinate, insofar as it is the inverse effect of my relation to this point, insofar as the situating vector is the tonic vector inverted, in other words, this necessarily introduces a problem of knowledge at the level of where I am to go *from* – at the level, that is, of the *coordinate* to which the point from which I go is coordinated. In this sense, it is possible to posit a primordial moment in which where I am going – the tonic – is unknown: it is not known which point is coordinated to this point of tonic origin, and, because where I am is contingent on my being with respect to this common point, where I am, the coordinate to which I am mapped, is also unknown. There is thus an order that pertains to the coordination of elements shown in Figure 3.5, to the solution to the problem of "where I am" and "where I am to go", which we would represent as the ordered set (*x*, 0, *y*, A), describing a movement evoking the "bow-tie" that appears in the account of "teleology" given by Buckminster Fuller, the man Ornette called his "main hero".[32]

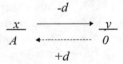

Figure 3.5

At first, there is an impasse. Although Hamiltonian analysis will produce the vector that will move a movable point from *x* to *y*, *I do not know what y is*, and, since −*d*, the vector that will transport a movable point from *x* to *y*, is a *product* of the analysis of *y* with respect to *x*, if *y* is unknown, so is −*d*. Analysis is stuck at the level of pure algebraic possibility – we know *how* to proceed in order to produce a specific vector, −*d*, but not the specific elements, *x* and *y*, with which to proceed in order to produce that specific vector. In other words, as we have said, if −*d* synthesised with respect to *x* produces the unknown point *y*, *one must already know y in order to produce y*, insofar as −*d*, which produces *y* when synthesised with respect to *x*, is the product, the effect, the *outcome* of the relation between the known and unknown points *x* and *y*. At this point, the only solution is to leap, to posit some determinate point as *y*, transforming the unknown *where to go* into the known. Now with A, where I am, the only unknown, and with the set of coordinated points mapped in "parallel" to the set of coordinates, such that the product of analysis at one level can be transferred "inversely" to the other, the analysis of *x* with respect to *y* will produce a difference, +*d*, that will "retroactively" transport a movable point from *0*, the point of origin, to A, the unknown *where I am*, thereby producing the unknown as known. Again, if "Fm7 is Ab6" implies the uncertainty of the tonic, the absence of anything at the level of the pitches themselves, F, Ab, C, Eb, that would allow us to determine the point with respect to which all of the

"No one knew where to go" 41

points are to be oriented – if, in other words, there is no necessary relation between the tonic coordinate and the point mapped to it – then coordination requires a leap; given x, I and the tonic coordinate supposed by the question, *where am I?*, there is no way to overcome the impasse of situation other than by positing a point of orienting origin, a particular pitch to be mapped to the tonic-origin coordinate, thus producing my own situation, my own being somewhere, as its effect.

However, if this is the case, if knowledge is contingent on a leap that posits the unknown as known – if there is, in other words, no necessary relation between the coordinate and the point coordinated to that coordinate other than the relation established by this leap – then there is nothing to stop two listeners from leaping to different conclusions, leaping to two different points of consequences, of end. Returning to Ornette's solution – you play the third, you play the tonic – the third "you" thinks they are playing may, with respect to the tonic to which "I" has leapt, be something other than a third, whilst the tonic which "I" thinks they are playing may, according to the tonic implied by the third "you" thinks they are playing, be something other than a tonic. So, whilst there is something shared at the level of the space "you" and "I" are both playing – they both play spaces orienting the points they are playing with respect to some elective point of convergence – this does not imply that the points that they are coordinating to the coordinates of this space are the same points; the coordinates are shared, in other words, whilst the points coordinated to these coordinates may not be.

What does it mean to follow?

It is thus possible to see that Ornette's solution, with its reference to tonics and tonic-oriented spaces, already entails an answer to our central question, for if a tonic is a point of convergence, the common endpoint of all vectoral vehicles moving "movable points" through a tonic-oriented space, then to be in that space *is already to be "going where the other goes"*, it is already to be moving in the direction of the point to which all other points of the space move. In this space, "knowing where to go" coincides with "knowing where the others go", insofar as the tonic is a point of convergence, a point of intersection for all tonic vectors, the point in the direction of which all tonic vectors move a movable point. If our question regarding the status of "tonic" as transference, from "tonal tonic" to "harmonic tonic" complicates this answer, it is nonetheless possible to see that the structure of convergence that pertains to the tonic is itself reproduced at the level of the wider tonic-oriented space. Although there are now, in other words, immediate points of convergence, there are also "final" points of convergence, which are points of convergence for all the points of the space: all the points of the wider space move in the direction of this "final", convergent, tonic point (Figure 3.3).

With respect to Hamilton's solution, in the absence of any necessary relation between coordinated and coordinate, between a note experienced "as" tonic, and the tonic-origin coordinate, 0, implied by that name, "going where I go" at the level of (tonic) *coordinate* does not necessarily imply "going where I go" at the level of the point *coordinated* to that coordinate. "You", in other words, may follow "me", going where I go at the level of coordinates, whilst *not* following, not going where "I" go,

42 "No one knew where to go"

at the level of the points coordinated to that coordinate. "To follow", in this sense, insofar as "to follow" implies *going to a common point*, entails a leap in which the one who follows becomes, perhaps unknown to themselves, the one who leads, the one who establishes for themselves the point in the direction of which they move, as well as "retroactively" the coordinate for the point from which they have moved.

Concluding remarks

To the question of knowledge with respect to "where to go", this chapter has offered a number of answers, both in relation to Ornette's speech and in relation to its echo in the work of Hamilton. However, these solutions have introduced a number of problems and questions. We are unsure, first, as to the status of "tonic" and whether it implies a transference to the "root" of a chord, and thus either the loss of a wider tonal relation, on the one hand, or the enlargement of the notion of tonic to include "harmonic tonics", on the other. Second, the Hamiltonian solution to the question of knowledge, drawing as it does on the ancient distinction between analysis and synthesis, entails a leap in which the unknown is treated as known; there is, in other words, in the passage from the unknown to the known, a moment of pure contingency in which the unknown is contingently elected, posited as "known", with the consequence that *there is nothing to ensure that two listeners "leap" to the same knowledge*. And, third, there is the question of what the answer we have given to the question of *where to go* – the answer in terms of tonics and tonic-oriented spaces – suggests about the movement *between* spaces, between tonic-oriented chords, for instance. If Ornette "plays chords but doesn't play changes", where "changes" implies a set of chords in a temporal order, what are the consequences of this, in other words, at the level of "sequence", at the level of the movement from one chord to the next? Are such movements implied by Ornette's discourse, and how does one account for them? We will return to these questions in the coming chapters.

And if Ornette's statements regarding tonics seemed to offer a simple solution – one *goes to the tonic* – complicated by problems at the level of knowledge such a solution produces, this answer, as we will see, will be further complicated in what follows. Each of the chapters that follow will offer, in its own way, a kind of complication of this "tonic-knowledge", this knowledge with respect to "where to go", where this "where" is tonic and the space it implies. Where Ornette's solution here has implied *tonic direction* – movement in the direction of a tonic point of convergence – we now turn to the question of *melodic direction* and a direction that, as we will see, immediately introduces a problem at the level of tonic direction, immediately calls the identity of a tonic direction into question, turning the question of where to go – the question at the heart of this book – into a question of *visibility*, of an endpoint to movement that is veiled, invisible.

Notes

1 Litweiler, *A Harmolodic Life*, 54.
2 *A Harmolodic Life*, 54–55.

3 Hamilton, *Lectures on Quaternions*, 2.
4 *Lectures on Quaternions*, 5.
5 *Lectures on Quaternions*, 6.
6 *Lectures on Quaternions*, 7.
7 *Lectures on Quaternions*, 7.
8 *Lectures on Quaternions*, 7.
9 *Lectures on Quaternions*, 7.
10 *Lectures on Quaternions*, 19.
11 *Lectures on Quaternions*, 15.
12 Rings, "Tonic", 6.
13 Rings, *Tonality and Transformation*, 106.
14 See Rings, *Tonality and Transformation*, Chapter 3.
15 Rings, *Tonality and Transformation*, 43.
16 Schenker, *Harmony*, 252.
17 Freud, "On Narcissism", 93–94.
18 Freud, "Group Psychology", 92.
19 "Group Psychology", 95.
20 "Group Psychology", 103.
21 "Group Psychology", 116.
22 In his development of the mathematical notion of vector for the analysis of musical voice leading, the music theorist Dmitri Tymoczko has suggested that the "transformational attitude" – an attitude that underlies Rings' account of a tonic-oriented space – is, in effect, an attempt to understand *vectoral* movement, which Tymoczko characterises as "ways of getting from one point to another" (Tymoczko, "In Quest of Musical Vectors", 256). And, in fact, the formulation Rings gives to the distinction between *interval* and *transformation*, as they appear in David Lewin's transformational theory, closely echoes the distinction between *analysis* and *synthesis* we have just encountered in Hamilton's account of the vector, in which the vector is *produced* by means of analysis and *used to traverse a space* by means of synthesis. Lewin's theory, says Rings, articulates two broad perspectives: "One is intervallic, in which the subject 'measures' the relationship between two musical objects, as passive observer. The other is transformational, in which the subject actively seeks to recreate a given relationship in his or her hearing, traversing the space in question through an imaginative gesture" (*Tonality and Transformation*, 10). However, by drawing together tonic-oriented movement and the account of vectors offered by Hamilton, we diverge from Rings' account in two significant ways. First, we link together the "intervallic" and "transformational" moments, here in the form of analysis and synthesis, in a way that Rings does not, by identifying the relation – the vector – "recreated" in the synthetic moment with the relation – the vector – "created" in the analytic one. The relation produced by analysis, in other words, *is* the relation that acts as vehicle in synthesis. And second, we imply that this tonic-oriented vector is a directed *distance* separating a point of a tonic-oriented space from its tonic point of orientation – a relation that Rings avoids, at least in part, perhaps because it is difficult to determine what specific distances might be for any two points in a "tonal pitch space", given the different ways such distance relations might be calculated. If the relation to Hamilton encourages us to persist with what Rings calls the "distance metaphor", it might be the case that the Hamiltonian articulation of analysis and synthesis implies a more general "analytic" and "synthetic" function, with no necessary relation to distance, which nonetheless retains the sense that the same relation – a "directed distance" or otherwise – emerges as something *produced* in analysis and *used* in synthesis, with the implication, at least in some cases, that this use is the function as *vehicle* allowing us to "synthetically" traverse a space. In any case, by persisting with the implication of distance, we do not seek to propose a new theory of "tonal pitch space" or define what the specific distances might be in such a space. For such accounts

44 "No one knew where to go"

of tonal pitch space, see, for instance, Lerdahl, *Tonal Pitch Space* and Chew, "Toward a Mathematical Model of Tonality".

23 For Stewart's law (see Chapter 2 of this book), only an immediate transference implies a quality in common.

24 Rings has suggested that the structure of tonal convergence, in which all of the points of a tonal space are situated with respect to a common point, can also be found internal to the space of a chord, such that the "root" of a chord functions as a kind of local "tonic", with listeners "hearing down" from harmonic subordinates to the root, aurally orienting the points of a harmonic space with respect to this local point of convergence, producing, perhaps, harmonic-tonic "qualia" as an effect. Rings, *Tonality and Transformation*, 123. However, in a statement about the relation between tenor and alto saxophones, Ornette has taken this implied transference even further, suggesting that "the tenor is the tonic of the alto". Litweiler, *A Harmolodic Life*, 39.

25 Adderley, "Cannonball Looks at Ornette Coleman", 21. In fact, although Adderley quotes Ornette directly immediately before this statement, and at other points in the article in the process of explaining his ideas, the provenance of this insight remains unclear – is it Adderley's supposition regarding Ornette's music, the outcome of his own analysis, or is Adderley reporting something Ornette said to him directly? In the absence of a clear answer to this question, we will proceed, but we will need to treat this statement with some care, situating it with respect to statements Ornette himself has made.

26 *Tonality and Transformation*, Chapter 3. The tonic vectors presented here imply a relation that, like the relation, "is a brother of", is neither symmetrical *nor* not symmetrical; if *a* is the brother of *b*, this does not necessarily imply that *b* is the brother of *a* (she may be his sister), but neither does it imply that *b* is *not* the brother of *a*. This feature is necessary to show that the "tonal tonic" may also be related to a "harmonic tonic" – it may, in other words, also be in the chord for which that "harmonic tonic" is the tonic. We also introduce the stipulation that tonic vectors are exclusive (one at a time), unless points related by means of these vectors link together transitively.

27 To say that a relation is *transitive* means that if $x\,R\,y$ and $y\,R\,z$, then $x\,R\,z$. In this limited context, this is correlative to saying that if the notes D, F and Ab are in the chord of Bb7, and if Bb, the harmonic tonic, is in the key of Eb, then the notes of the chord will also be in the key of Eb.

28 "At once" implies that two different chords that appear in the diagram are two different "moments"; thus, whilst, for instance, the note Ab appears connected to both harmonic tonics, Bb and F (which, in this limited context, means that Ab is contained in both) moments are exclusive of one another: *either* Bb is a harmonic tonic for Ab *or* F is a harmonic tonic for Ab – not both at once. (This is correlative, again in this limited context, to saying that Ab can be experienced as contained in the chord of Bb7 or contained in the chord of F – both are possible, as represented in the diagram, but not at the same time.)

29 By "modal", we simply mean that this reorientation of the points with respect to a new root is analogous to the reorientation of the points of a mode with respect to new orienting points, as in the shift from C Ionian to D Dorian – the points stay the same, but the tonic orientation changes.

30 In Euclid, *The Elements*, 138.

31 Fuller characterises teleology as "the process of OBSERVING consciously, or absorbing subconsciously, from the OUTSIDE INWARD so that one may do from the inside outward". Fuller, *Nine Chains To The Moon*, 44.

Chapter 4

Invisible

When Ornette recorded his first album, *Something Else!!!!*, for Lester Koenig's *Contemporary* label in February and March of 1958, he was interviewed for the liner notes by the writer and critic Nat Hentoff, who asked him about the titles he had chosen, starting with the track that appears first on this album – "Invisible". "Invisible", says Hentoff, "is thus titled because it's rather difficult without concentration to discover the tonal centre of the song". "The key", he says, nonetheless, "is Db", before quoting Ornette directly – "the melodic direction is pretty free", says Ornette. "Actually, these are regular intervals any musician would use anyway, but put together this way, it's very melodious".[1]

"Invisible" thus implies a problem, a difficulty, at the level of the listener's experience of this piece. There is to be assumed a "tonal centre" – a point of tonic convergence implied by the assertion that "the key is Db" – and yet it is "difficult without concentration to discover"; there is an effect of veiling, of "invisibility", such that the centre exists but as veiled, "invisible". At the same time, there is another feature, another dimension, implied by the words that Hentoff quotes directly – there is a "direction" that pertains to the melody, and that "direction", says Ornette, "is pretty free".

These features suggest a number of questions, or problems, to be addressed. First, what does it mean for a tonic – a "tonal centre" – to be veiled, producing an effect of invisibility, such that it is "difficult without concentration to discover"? Second, what is a "melodic direction" and what does it mean for such a direction to be "free"? Third, what might these two problems have to do with one another – what might "freedom" at the level of direction, in other words, have to do with "invisibility", with an effect of veiling? And, fourth, what are the consequences of the answers to these questions at the level of what it means to follow, to go where I go?

Introductory analysis

If we listen to the opening fragments to this piece, "Invisible", it is easy to see how an assertion of Db major might be supported; all of the pitches belong to the Db diatonic collection, with a tonic orientation of Db producing an effect of Db major,

DOI: 10.4324/9781003412304-4

as shown in Figure 4.1, with integers showing pitches as Db scale "degrees" (discussed in the previous chapter as effects of situation – the "being somewhere" of points with respect to a tonic point of orientation).

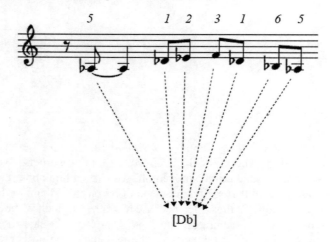

Figure 4.1

Then, in the second phrase, there is a sudden shift to points not in the Db diatonic collection – D, F#, D, B, D. And, if we listen carefully, it is possible to hear in this second phrase, *Y*, this second motif – as well as in subsequent motifs – a *transposed echo* of the first phrase, *X* (indicated as *t+1* in Figure 4.2), an interpretation supported by the movement of the bass, which shifts up a semitone from Db in the first bar to D in the second.

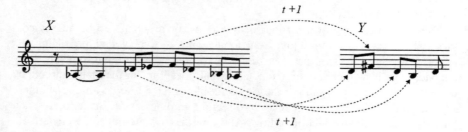

Figure 4.2

However, if we then *undo* this effect of transposition, shifting all of the points of this phrase back down a semitone, it is possible to experience an effect of *unveiling*, of a new visibility, as what was veiled, made invisible, comes into view. For each of the points of this un-transposed phrase can now be heard as either stating the centre – Db – or as being with respect to it, finding their meaning in relation to it, as points in its orbit, encircling it, constituting it as centre – as, in other words, *answering the very question at the heart of the experience of invisibility*, the question, that is, of the "tonal centre". This is shown in Figure 4.3, with Db, the "tonal centre", circled.

Figure 4.3

If, un-transposed, the second phrase offers an answer to the question of what had been made invisible, it is possible to discern that, insofar as what is veiled, made invisible, is the tonal centre, *it is transposition that performs the veiling function*, it is transposition that makes something that was "visible", "invisible". In the movement from one point to another, something else appears – something takes the place of another, a phrase is replaced by its transposition, and an effect of veiling, of concealment, is produced. So, if transposition is the cause of the effect of veiling, if in "Invisible", as we have suggested, transposition veils the tonal centre, making it "invisible", what is transposition such that it produces these effects? What are its properties, its mechanisms that would account for such a relation?

Transposition

The transference of a relation

In a prelude to the later work on geometrical space in which he developed the notion of a *vector*, William Rowan Hamilton proposed to constitute algebra as a "science of pure time", as geometry is a science of pure space, replacing the dimension of magnitude with relations of temporal order – *coincident, before, after*.[2] In the early sections of this text, Hamilton proposed a new notation to represent not only the ordinal relations between points but also the *relations between the relations* between these points. An "analogy", in which a difference between two distinct points in time (A, B) is equal to the temporal difference between another two points (C, D), was thus expressed,

$$B - A = D - C$$[3]

A "continued analogy", in which the points form an equidistant series, insofar as the "mean" values (the values situated on the inner side of the equation – B and C in the case of the analogy above, rather than, like A and D, at the "extremes") are coincident, in which they coincide temporally, was expressed thus:

$$B' - B = B - A$$[4]

48   Invisible

Hamilton called this repetition of a relation, of a difference, *transference* – "the repeated transference of one common ordinal relation, or the continued application of one common mental step".[5]

Hamilton's notation for the analysis of points in time was exactly the notation he would later use for the analysis of points in geometric space, where B − A means "the analysis of point B with respect to point A", so as to produce the "step", the movement, that would take you from point A to point B – what he would later call in his *Lectures on Quaternions* a *vector*. If we thus transfer this notion of "analogy" to pairs of points in space, and, in particular, to pairs of points in pitch space, B − A = D − C now means, "the analysis of pitch B with respect to pitch A produces a vector equal to – the same as – the vector produced by the analysis of pitch D with respect to pitch C". This analogy is "continued" where the mean points coincide, where, in other words, the endpoint of *a* and the initial point of *b* are the same point, B.

Transposition thus implies transference, in Hamilton's sense – the "repeated transference" of a relation; given two simple motifs, X and Y, where X is the pitches A and B, and Y is the pitches C and D, and where Y is the *transposition* of X, transposition implies that B − A = D − C. However, it is also possible to see that this is insufficient, as internal to almost any piece of music it would be possible to find many such purely arithmetic repetitions, many such relations between differences between pitches without this necessarily implying the experience of transposition, that this motif, Y, is motif X *heard elsewhere*. Rather, the experience of transposition implies not only repetition at the level of the differences internal to a sequence of pitches, internal to a motif, but, as a consequence of this repetition of internal difference, *a repetition at the level of the motif itself*. First, there is an experience of non-identity at the level of the points – motif X and Y are constituted by a different set of pitches; second, there is an experience of identity at the level of the "intervallic structure", the differences internal to the motif and its transposition; third, as a consequence of the identity experienced at the level of the differences internal to the motif and its transposition, there is an experience of identity at the level of the motifs themselves. An experience of identity at the level of the part is *transferred to the whole*, we could say, where the "part" is a vectoral *relation*. As such, transposition implies a relation of *equivalence*,[6] both at the level of the intervallic structure – "X and Y have the *same* intervallic structure, the same structure of differences" – and at the level of the motif itself – "X and Y are the same motif" – an equivalence which Ornette will link to *sound*, as we will see in Chapter 7.[7]

Equivalence quotients

So, if equivalence is not to be situated at the level of the points, but at the level of the relations these points manifest, this implies that the equivalence relation that pertains to transposition is a relation that relates not points, but relations – a relation that says, in effect, "this relation, *a*, is the same as this relation, *b*". And, in fact, Hamilton proposed exactly such a relation, a relation that relates not points but the relation between points, not positions in space but the directed distances – the *vectors* – that move "movable points" between positions in space.[8] This relation between relations he called a *quotient*, for, if "vectors" were produced by the analysis by *subtraction* of one point with respect to another point, a "quotient" would be produced by the analysis by *division* of one *vector* with respect to another *vector*:

$$d_y/d_x = q$$

If the analysis by division of a vector, d_y, with respect to another vector, d_x, produced a quotient, q, in synthesis by multiplication, the quotient *synthesised* with respect to the vector d_x would produce the vector d_y – would "move", we could say, transferring terms from Hamilton's description of synthesis by addition, a "movable point" from d_x "in the direction of" d_y.

So, if quotients relate relations, if quotients relate Hamiltonian vectors, or directed distances, is there an "equivalence quotient", a quotient that moves a "movable point" from one vector, *a*, "in the direction of" the *same* vector, *b* – "in the direction of" the vector with the same distance and direction? Yes – the equivalence quotient is obviously quotient *1*, insofar as *1* is produced by the division of some value with respect to itself – the value of some vector, *b*, with respect to *a*, another vector with the same value. *Q1* will thus, in synthesis by multiplication, "move a movable point" from the vector *a* "in the direction of" a vector, *b*, with "the same distance and direction".

It is also possible to see that transference in Hamilton's sense and transference in Stewart's sense come together in the notion of transposition; there is the experience of the transference of a relation, that a relation – a vector – is moved, *transferred*, elsewhere, to be realised by another set of points, and, as a consequence of the "something in common" at the level of the relation this Hamiltonian transference produces, there is the Stewartian "transference of a name" – we could imagine a little letter – "*a*" – transferred from one instance of a motif to the next, indicating that the two motifs are to be considered *the same motif*, with the "quality in common", which allows such a shift, the vectoral relation both manifest.

From points to relations

If an experience of transposition is contingent on an experience of identity, of equivalence, at the level of the transposed idea itself – that, in the case of melodic transposition, a melody and its transposition are the *same melody* – it is thus possible to perceive that what is entailed in an experience of transposition is *a shift from points to relations*, from the points A and B to the relation, the vector *d*, to the particular relation of coincidence or non-coincidence that separates one point from another. The consequences of this shift are crucial, for "the condition of identity" – what makes two motifs "the same motif" – is now to be situated at the level of the *relation* – at the level of the particular vectoral differences that separate one melodic point from another, and not at the level of the points themselves.

50   Invisible

So, if transposition is the cause of veiling, the cause of the invisibility to which the title refers, and if transposition implies a shift *from points to relations* – that identity is to be situated at the level of relations rather than any points that manifest those relations, such that two fragments that share an intervallic structure are to be considered the same fragment, the "same motif" – what is the relation between the two? What is the relation between an effect of invisibility and the shift from points to relations that transposition implies?

Invisibility

Relations and invisibility

If the identity of the motif is contingent on the identity at the level of its internal, constitutive relations, and not on the identity of any points that would manifest this relation, the identity of the motif, what makes it the same motif, regardless of the differences at the level of the points that would manifest it, is thus a strange, immaterial substance, a relation floating free, irreducible to any points constituting its particular visibility. As such, the shift from points to relations implies that the identity of the motif, what makes it what it is, is *constitutively invisible*; it is nothing but a relation emerging invisibly – or better, perhaps, *inaudibly* – at the intersection of any two of its "punctual" appearances – visible, audible points without which it could not appear, could not be heard, but to whose audibility, whose visibility, it can also never be reduced. However, is this really enough to account for what is at stake in this experience of invisibility? Is it really enough to locate invisibility on the side of the relation, rather than the "visible" points that manifest that relation? For it is not simply that the shift from points to relations, from identity at the level of melodic points to identity at the level of melodic relations, is experienced at the level of the tonic relation itself – a shift from tonic points to tonic relations – but that this shift to relations produces a point-effect, a kind of *phantom tonic*, a phantom "point" that persists as "hidden", "invisible", haunting the space as the spectral presence of a determinate endpoint to be discovered, to be unveiled.

A lost or hidden object

"The search for the agreement of a set of phenomena", says Mill in a section of his *Logic* on abstraction dealing with the formation of those general conceptions without which, he says, no induction could occur, "is in truth very similar to the search for a lost or hidden object". "At first", he says, "we place ourselves in a sufficiently commanding position, and cast our eyes around us, and if we see the object, it is well; if not, we ask ourselves mentally what are the places in which it may be hid, in order that we may there search for it: and so on, until we imagine the place where it really is".[9] The search for the general conception – the "general idea", or attribute, common to the whole class of things that share a general name – is marked by a certain loss, a privation, at the level of *sight* – the object, the point of agreement, we are looking for is lost to our gaze; in spite of our position

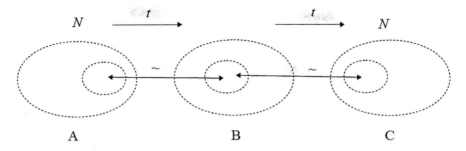

Figure 4.4

of supremacy, of assumed control, of *command*, we search *blind*, the object – the general "idea" – receding from sight. However, if this is the case, if the search for the point of agreement constituting a set of phenomena as a class, and which thus forms the "connotation"[10] of the general name which names that class, is the search for something lost, something hidden from sight, something with respect to which our sight fails, with respect to which we are, in some sense, *blind*, what is the cause of this privation, what is the cause of our loss of sight, which coincides, as Mill implies, with a loss of supremacy, of command, in our attempts to order the world?

Of course, Mill is referring to a process of "observation" *prior* to the process of naming – one determines the quality in common between two objects, constituting them as of the same class and thus as bearing the same general class name. However, there is, perhaps, another answer, one implied by Mill's distinction between two kinds of names, between one that is applied "univocally" and one that Mill, drawing directly on Dugald Stewart's theory of meaning shifts, calls "transitive" – a distinction directly correlative to the difference between the approach to meaning articulated by the Encyclopedists and the one articulated by Stewart's law.[11] In the case of a *univocal application* (Figure 4.4), an equivalence (~) relates a "quality" or "attribute" of an "object", A, to a quality or attribute of the object B; the property of A and the property of B, in other words, are the "same property" – in Stewart's terms, there is a "quality in common" that allows the transference (*t*) of the name (*N*) from A to B. When that name is transferred from B to another object, C, this application is "univocal" insofar as the equivalence that relates the property in A to the property in B now relates the *same property* in B to a property in C. Given the transitivity that pertains to equivalence, this means that the property in A and C must also be related by that equivalence, that they are, in other words, the "same quality"; the application is *univocal*.[12]

Univocal applications

In the case of a *transitive application* (Figure 4.5), however, an equivalence relates a property of A to a property of B, allowing the transference of the name from A to B, and an equivalence relates a property of B to a property of C, allowing the further transference of the name from B to C. But, in this instance, the quality in B

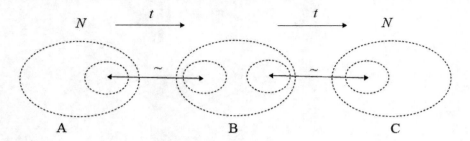

Figure 4.5 Transitive applications

to which A is related by means of an equivalence *is not the property in B to which the property in C is now related*.¹³ There is a "gap", a break, "internal to the space of the 'object'" – the two properties internal to B are not related, in other words, by means of an equivalence – they are not the "same quality".

The distinction between a *univocal* and *transitive* application is thus correlative to the distinction between two forms of *transference*, now in Hamilton's sense, two different forms of the "transference of a relation", the "repetition of a mental step", where the relation to be transferred, in this instance, is an *equivalence relation*. In both cases, the equivalence that relates A to B is transferred to relate B to C, but in the case of a univocal application, the "analogy" constituted by this transference is "continued", in Hamilton's terms – the "mean" points (properties) internal to B coincide – whereas in a transitive application, they do not.

At the heart of Stewart's law, which makes such transitive applications possible, is thus the shift from points to relations we have just seen in the case of transposition. In the work of the Encyclopedists, of which Stewart's work constitutes a critique, there is an assumption that an identity at the level of the name must reflect an identity at the level of the properties that make possible the transference of that name, but with Stewart, all that is needed to allow the "transference of a name" from object A to C is that the *relation* (the equivalence) relating some property of an object, A, to some property of an object, B, is *transferred* (in Hamilton's sense) so as to relate some property of B to some property of C – it is the repetition of the relation that matters, not the repetition of the point. There is a shift, in other words, from the identity of points – of properties – to the identity of relations – equivalences – that relate those points.

We could say, then, that *transference*, like transposition – the transference of a relation between properties – *performs a veiling function*. It is the shift from points to relations that transference implies that produces the effect of veiling, causing, in the case of the Encyclopedists, the search for an object that, in a sense, is nothing but a phantom produced by a misperception regarding the nature of names and naming, the misperception that an identity at the level of the signifier must imply an identity at the level of the property that constitutes the "connotation" of such a signifier – a property which, veiled by transference, is now experienced as "lost" or "hidden".

Free direction

So, what of the question of *direction*? "The melodic direction is pretty free", says Ornette in his discussion with Hentoff for the liner notes to *Something Else*, but what is "direction", melodic or otherwise, and what would it mean for it to be "free"? And if the "melodic direction" that pertains to this piece, in which there is an effect of invisibility, of veiling, is "pretty free", what is the relation, if any, between the two? What is the relation between "free direction" and "invisibility", including, perhaps, the relation between the movement of transposition we have situated as its cause?

Three directions

A melodic vector could be produced by means of Hamiltonian analysis by subtraction, so as to produce a "directed distance" between melodic points, without any necessary relation to the tonic vectors discussed earlier. Such vectors would then imply "direction", we might say, in three distinct senses;

1) First, there is direction as *endpoint* – "where one goes" – the point, B, "in the direction of which" the vector moves "a movable point". In this sense, at the level of the order that pertains to vectoral movement, "direction" is on the side of *consequence*, the point that follows at the level of the order this movement implies.
2) Second, there is "direction" at the level of "sense"[14] – at the level, that is, of whether the vector moves "a movable point" in the direction of a consequent point, B, *greater than* or *less than* the antecedent point, A, of that movement. This "sense direction" is the way in which Hamiltonian vectors are *directed* distances and is implied in vectors in pitch space by the signs for positive (+) and negative (−).
3) Third, there is "direction" at the level of "angle of inclination", which, in two dimensions, is the effect of the interrelation of distances on each axis.

Of course, interval-vectors in pitch space require only *one* dimension, and thus there is no "angle" that pertains to them in this sense. However, we can "artificially" produce such an angle for one-dimensional vectors by introducing a difference on the x axis that is unit (U) for all vectors on the y axis (or vice versa). Whilst the angles thus produced are nothing but the effect of the relation to the arbitrarily chosen difference on the x axis, these angles are comparable insofar as this difference is unit – that is, insofar as it is the same for every vector. Now two vectors with the same distance and direction will appear as parallel, as with the two vectors with the value +2 in Figure 4.6.

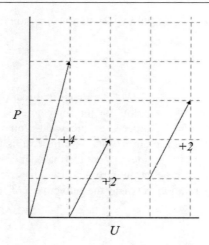

Figure 4.6

Given these different senses of "direction", and given the notion of melodic vectors, what would it mean for the direction that pertains to a melody to be "free" – what, in other words, is a "free direction"?

Free vectors

In physics, a vector is sometimes defined as the representation of an entity possessing both "magnitude" (or size) and direction, but there is within this field a further distinction, a further difference, between two kinds of vectors – or between two different ways of thinking about the *identity* of vectors – between vectors that are, on the one hand, *bound* – "anchored" – and those that are *free*.[15] If a bound vector is anchored to a particular location, to a particular position in space, to be considered only in relation to that position, the free vector is independent of any location, *its identity contingent not on its being any particular where but rather on its magnitude and direction* – any vector with the same magnitude and direction, in other words, can be considered *the same vector*. In this sense, we could say, a vector is "free" rather than "bound", *insofar as it is free of points*, insofar, that is, as *its identity is free of any points that would manifest it*, binding its identity to any specific position in space. This shift from points to relations, from the identity of the points to the identity at the level of the vectoral relations these points manifest, is thus exactly the shift we perceived at the heart of the phenomena of transposition – that not only that the vector, the "directed distance" between points is the same, that they are equivalent, but that, as a consequence of this experience of equivalence, of being the same, there is an experience of identity at the level of the motif itself. As such, transposition implies exactly the "freedom" of the *free vector*; it too is a "free identity", a *free relation*, its identity, its being the same, not contingent on its realisation by any specific set of points.

We can use Hamilton's $q1$ to represent the relation between two vectors with the same "magnitude" (distance, in Hamilton's instance) and "direction", for multiplying the distance and direction of any vector by 1 will obviously produce a vector with the same distance and direction. In a sense, we could say, "$q1$" *means* "the same distance and direction", insofar as, for instance, $+3$ multiplied by (quotient) 1 equals $+3$, where "+" indicates direction and "3" indicates distance. It is then possible to see that, at least in one sense, the "freedom" of the free vector does not pertain to direction as "sense" or "angle of inclination"; $q1$ means that direction in these senses is *not free* – that any vector produced by means of (multiplication by) $q1$ is bound to reproduce, in other words, whatever direction (as "sense" and "angle of inclination") pertains to the vector to which $q1$ relates them. The "freedom" of free vectors relates, rather, to direction as *point*, as *consequent*, to the level of "the point in the direction of which I move". *The vector as "free direction" is free of any determinate "consequent"*, for there is nothing at the level of $q1$, just as there is nothing in the conditions governing the identity of a free vector, that would determine "where" the vector, where this directed distance, is to "go", where it is "put" in space – it can "go" *anywhere*, as long as the points that constitute this "anywhere" manifest that specific directed distance, as long, we could say, as it is "parallel" (where "parallel" vectors, in this instance, also have the same "sense").

Free

In the liner notes to *Change of the Century*, his first album with the famous group of Charlie Haden, Billy Higgins and Don Cherry, Ornette wrote that the title to one of the tunes on the album, "Free", was "well explained by the title".

> Our *free* group improvising is well-documented here. Each member goes his own way and still adds tellingly to the group endeavour. There was no predetermined chordal or time pattern. I think we got a spontaneous free-wheeling thing going here.[16]

However, if we look closely at the composed melody for this piece, another interpretation, closer to the one we have been pursuing in relation to "Invisible", presents itself. For it would be possible to hear in this tune the movement we heard in "Invisible", to hear, in other words, in the ascending sequence of notes that starts with the Db, a fragment of the melody already heard but transposed, as in "Invisible", up a semitone. Figure 4.7 shows the melody to "Free", with durations given as units. The collection of notes, V, is represented as a transposition of U, with the transposition of W "deleted" from V, and with the order of U reversed (inverted on the temporal axis). (This rather complex explanation is clearer when the melody is heard.)

56 Invisible

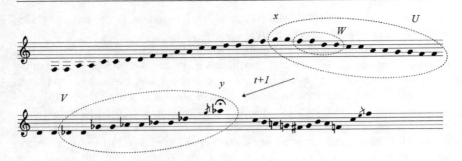

Figure 4.7

So, if "to follow" means to "go where I go", as we have now stated many times, what does it mean to follow in a transpositional space of "free relations", with their implied "free directions"?

What does it mean to follow?

If we can represent the relation between manifestations of a "free relation" by means of $q1$, it is possible to see that the consequent "where one goes", the end "point" in the direction of which $q1$ moves a movable point, *is itself a relation – $q1$* moves "a movable point" from a relation to the same vectoral *relation*. In terms of Hamiltonian analysis and synthesis, analysis by division implies the analysis of the vectoral relations that pertain to determinate motifs – of the vector "internal" to the motif Y, as manifest by two determinate pitches, C and D, with respect to the vector "internal" to the motif X, as manifest by two determinate pitches, A and B. In synthesis by multiplication, however, $q1$, produced by means of this analysis, "moves" "a movable point" "in the direction of" *another relation, without regard to which points realise this relation –* the vector that is the "endpoint" of this movement, in other words, can "go" anywhere, can be realised by *any* points, as long as the relation between the relations realised is $q1$; the vector is free precisely insofar as it is *free of points*.

The shift from points to relations that characterises both transposition and free vectors thus also affects the question of what it means to follow, to "go where I go", for, if in the previous chapter, to "go where I go" is to go to a common point – the point of tonic convergence – now to "go where I go" is to go to a common *relation* – now the relation constitutes the point of convergence, the "where" to which both "you" and "I" go, *regardless of the points that manifest that relation*. However, if this is the case, if there is no indication at the level of quotient synthesis as to "where" a relation is to "go", "where" – by which points – it is to be realised, any such indication, any law governing the "where" of realisation must be given in addition to quotient synthesis, must, in other words, be given by means of a separate law. Does such a law exist in Ornette's discourse?

Invisible   57

A law governing manifestations?

That's it, that's it!

The musician Ellis Marsalis recalls an experience he and Harold Battiste both had on separate occasions when playing with Ornette – an experience that bears on this question regarding free directions, on the question of where, given the freedom that pertains to a free direction, a transposition is to "go", by means of which specific pitches a transposition is to be realised. Both were playing piano, he says,

> and I started a cycle of 7th chords, just moving 'em up the scale, up the piano chromatically, and Ornette said, "That's it! That's it! Keep playing that!" … I didn't really understand what I was doing, it's just that whatever it was, Ornette related to it. Eventually it kind of disturbed Edward because I had forsaken the rhythmic responsibilities of the group in favour of trying to play harmonically what Ornette was hearing and trying to hear myself what was going on.[17]

"That's it! That's it!", says Ornette, but what is "that"? What is "that" such that "that" is "it", the "that" to which, whatever it was, Ornette related, that seemed, for Ornette, to satisfy some desire about what one is to keep playing? Is "that" the specific *chord*, the 7th, or the specific *movement*, $+1$, such that the space that was heard here is now "moved", as Marsalis suggests, elsewhere, manifest "up", chromatically from where it was? Or is it both, or neither, something else?

If each of the points of this "cycle" is a transposition, in the sense we have been discussing, where an experience of equivalence at the level of internal differences is then experienced as an equivalence at the level of the space itself – from "the differences internal to this space are the same" to "this is the same space, the same chord, heard – *moved*, as Marsalis suggests – elsewhere" – then $+1$ marks a difference between manifestations, between realisations of relations that are *free*. In this sense, $+1$ is an answer to the question of "where" free relations are to "go", which points will manifest them, which we could formulate thus: wherever the relations are first manifest, wherever the antecedent manifestation is, the consequent manifestation will be $+1$ "up" "chromatically", manifest a semitone away, "up" from the antecedent. When this is repeated for each new antecedent, where, that is, each new consequent itself becomes an antecedent, a "cycle" of manifestations appears. "That", in this sense, could thus be understood in the following way: whatever the movement relating an initial antecedent and consequent manifestation, X and Y, the subsequent movements will be equivalent. As in the situation Marsalis describes, if the initial movement was $+1$, so were the subsequent movements, thus forming what Marsalis calls an equivalence "cycle" of manifestations, each related by an equivalent movement. Such a law will produce a cycle of manifestations, as in the opening to "Invisible", shown in Figure 4.8, in which the same movement, $+1$, relates a to b, then b to c, and so on.

However, it is clear that this "law" is far too limited, for there are many moments in Ornette's music that might imply the manifestation of *free relations*

58 Invisible

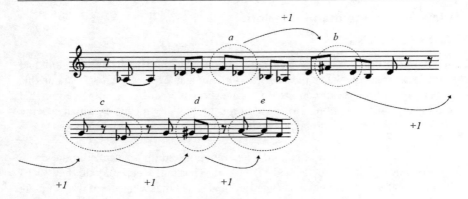

Figure 4.8

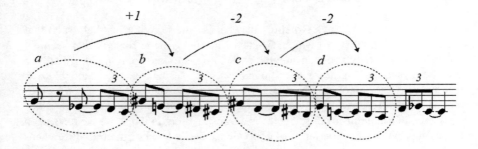

Figure 4.9

but where the appearance of such manifestation seems to be governed by nothing so straightforward as +1. For instance, what might be considered the "turnaround" section to Ornette's famous melody, "Turnaround", which appears on Ornette's 1959 album, *Tomorrow is the Question*, the relation between the manifestations of the set of intervallic vector-relations (−4, −1, −2) shifts from +1 to +2, as shown in Figure 4.9, where *a*, *b*, *c* and *d* now mark the initial points of the sequence of manifestations.

The opening of *W.R.U.*, from the 1960 album, "Ornette!", is a more complex instance, for, whilst a chromatic movement, +1, can be discerned in the sequence F, F#, G, G#, A, A# (marked in Figure 4.10 by curved, dashed arrows), insofar as this fragment manifests the ascending interval, +8, where the initial points of these manifestations are *a*, *b* and *c*, the relation between these points is not +1 – whilst *b* to *c* is +1, *a* to *b* is +2. This is shown in Figure 4.11, in which the transposition of the "free interval-vector", +8, no longer appears as a cycle, insofar as the transpositions "moving" this vector are different: +2 then −1.

Figure 4.10

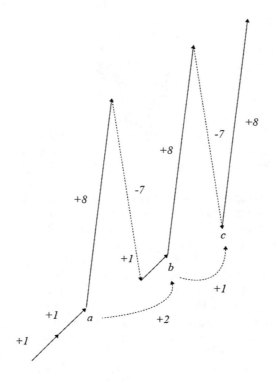

Figure 4.11

Only a half-step away

Let us then consider another possibility, one implied by something recounted by the guitarist Kenny Wessel, who appeared on Ornette's *Tone Dialling*, something Ornette had said to him about the relationship between chords. "All chords", he said, "are only a half-step away from any other chord" – a statement Wessel linked to the voice leading that would take you from the notes of a G minor triad – G, Bb, D – to the notes of an Eb triad – Eb, G, Bb – a shift entailing the movement of only one note – D – by a half-step (+*1*) to Eb.[18] It does not appear, however, that this is a satisfactory explanation, for the simple reason there exist many chords – say, a C major triad and an F# major triad – that cannot be related even by voice-leading that is simply stepwise, let alone by half-step (if by "stepwise" we mean "by one or two semitones"), as proven in Figure 4.12, which shows the possible relations between different inversions of C major and F# major triads. None can be linked by purely semitone movement (or less).

G $\xrightarrow{+6}$ C#	G $\xrightarrow{+3}$ A#	G $\xrightarrow{-1}$ F#
E $\xrightarrow{+6}$ A#	E $\xrightarrow{+2}$ F#	E $\xrightarrow{-3}$ C#
C $\xrightarrow{+6}$ F#	C $\xrightarrow{+1}$ C#	C $\xrightarrow{-2}$ A#

Figure 4.12

We instead propose the following, given in terms of "spherical" neighbourhoods[19] in a chromatic pitch space: with a "radius" of two semitones, at least one point of any triad is contained in a pitch space neighbourhood of a point of any other triad, where the radius is less than two semitones. This is illustrated in Figure 4.13, where the points of a C major triad are shown as solid points in chromatic pitch space, and the points of an F# major triad are shown as hollow points. With U_C, U_E and U_G as neighbourhoods of the points of a C major triad, at least one of the neighbourhoods of these points contains a point of the F# major triad. (In fact, both U_C and U_G contain points of an F# major triad.)

This is true for all major, minor and diminished triads, as no major, minor, diminished or augmented triads can be created from the complement of such neighbourhoods of the points of those chords. The exception is an augmented triad, where augmented triads can be thus created.[20]

With respect to the question of antecedent and consequent manifestation of free relations, Ornette's thesis could then be reformulated thus: the neighbourhood of any point of any manifestation of any chord contains a point of any manifestation of any other chord. However, by generalising both to spaces other than chords,

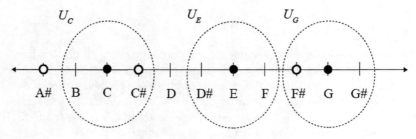

Figure 4.13

and to neighbourhoods of a point other than "spherical neighbourhoods" with a determinate "radius", we could further reformulate this thesis in terms of a general answer to the question of "where to go" with respect to free relations, of "where" they are to be manifest; a relation can manifest, we could say, *anywhere where any point of that manifestation is contained in the neighbourhood of any point of a prior manifestation.*

What does it mean to follow – revisited

In the previous chapter, we spoke of what it means to follow in terms of *tonics* and spaces with a tonic orientation. To "go where I go" in such a space was to go to the tonic, though, as we have discussed, the notion of "tonic", as "point of convergence", already implies that, insofar as we both play the same space, and that space is a space with a tonic orientation, "you" will go where "I" goes – the notion of tonic already implies, in other words, that no matter where "you" and "I" are in such a space, they are always going, converging to a common (tonic) point. If the tonic offered us something in common, a point that was shared and in the direction of which both "you" and "I" moved, the shift from points to relations represented by both transposition and free vectors disrupts this commonality, producing a correlative shift at the level of where I go. Now "where I go" – the point in the direction of which I move – is not a point but *a relation between points*, with no necessary implication of "where" – of which points, in other words, are to manifest that relation.

However, if this is the case, if the shift from points to relations entails a shift at the level of "where", of the endpoint of my movement, from "where I go" as point, to "where I go" as relation, without any implication of which points would manifest that relation, and if there is, correlative to the identity of relations, the experience of identity at the level of the points that manifest those relations – as with a motif and its transposition, considered as the "same motif" – this implies that "you" and "I" go to the same "where" – "you" goes where "I" goes – *even if, at the level of the points, there is a gap*, even if, at the level of the points, in other words, "you" is somewhere other than "I". From AB, "you" could go to CD and "I" could go to EF, even if $C \neq E$ and $D \neq F$. If we conceive these vectors as tonic vectors, as in the previous chapter, then it is possible to see that "you" goes from C to D and "I" goes from distinct pitches E to F, with D and F both mapped to tonic-as-origin coordinates, then "you" goes where "I" goes at the level of the coordinate, even though there is a gap, a non-coincidence, a *non-convergence*, at the level of the points coordinated to that coordinate – exactly the split we discerned at the end of the previous chapter.

In this sense, it would be possible to draw in our prior discussion of *knowledge*, of "knowing" with respect to "where to go", for if, in our previous chapter, there was a split at the level of the distinction between coordinate and coordinated, between knowing the coordinate and knowing the point coordinated to that coordinate, then here we have a correlative split between knowledge at the level of

62   Invisible

the *relation* and knowledge at the level of the points that are to manifest that relation. The shift from points to relations is thus, we could say, transposed into the dimension of knowledge; even if one "knows" the relation, this knowledge does not imply knowledge at the level of the points which are to manifest that relation.

Perhaps there is, we thought, to be discerned in Ornette's discourse the allusion to another law, another direction, regarding where such "free relations" are to go, which points are to manifest them. And in the words of one of Ornette's collaborators, we discerned the possibility of a law to be given in terms of neighbourhoods – a manifestation can go anywhere, we said, where any point of that manifestation is contained in the neighbourhood of any point of a prior manifestation. However, given the sheer inclusivity of this "law" in relation to chords specifically, *perhaps it is simply another way of saying "anywhere"*, with our account of neighbourhoods simply suggesting that no matter where one manifestation is, no matter what points manifest it, all other possible manifestations are close by – each, in fact, is (almost) as close as any other. The only solution, again, is to *leap*, contingently electing (unknown) points as known, so as to manifest the known relation.

And perhaps, in our search for such a "law", we had ourselves been drawn into the search for the phantom we had discovered haunting our transpositional structures, the effect of a point – a *point-effect* – "hidden", made invisible by the shift from points to relations characterising transposition and the *free relation*, the "free direction", it implies. In this sense, if "to follow" means "to go where I go", and if this "where" is the tonic, the relation to which will also situate me, tell me where I am, then the question of what it means to follow is itself haunted by this phantom; it is itself in danger of being drawn into the search for an impossible endpoint, a point whose hiddenness, whose invisibility, is, in one sense, nothing but a misperception regarding its relationality, its *freedom*, and for which reason its location will forever be impossible to uncover.

However, to this notion of "freedom" there is another, final detail to add, for with this subtle shift we have discerned at the heart of "free relations" in transpositional space, from points to relations, from the pitch to the vectoral relation relating points, an even stronger bind is induced, an even stronger necessity binding one point to another. For as soon as an antecedent point (C) is chosen to manifest a "free relation", as soon, that is, as one antecedent point (C) is experienced as "transposing" another antecedent point (A) (Figure 4.14) – *this necessarily induces the fixing, the binding of its consequent (D)*, it necessarily induces the fixing of *what follows* with respect to *what leads*, of *where "I" goes* with respect to *where "I" goes from* (Figure 4.15).

What emerges, then, in the movement from relations to manifestations, is a kind of *direction effect*, an *effect of direction*, of *what follows*, with the relation-as-vehicle propelling, "vectoring", "vehicling", the movable point by means of its inner necessities in the direction of another *determinate* point. Necessity emerges from contingency, imperative from freedom, "somewhere" from "anywhere". "Anywhere", that is, *as long as it's "parallel"*.

Invisible   63

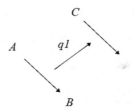

Figure 4.14

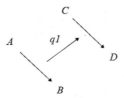

Figure 4.15

So, if in this chapter we have discerned a shift from points to relations, with effects at the level of veiling, of invisibility, as well as at the level of what follows, of where to go with respect to some antecedent, we turn now to what appears as a movement in the inverse direction. The movement from *points to relations* now appears as the inverse movement *from relations to points*, from the being of a point with respect to another point, to the being of the point itself, apparently without respect to any other point – a shift that has something to do, it seems, with a relation to women.

Notes

1 Hentoff, liner notes, *Something Else*.
2 Hamilton, "Theory of Conjugate Functions".
3 "Conjugate Functions", 10.
4 "Conjugate Functions", 13–14.
5 "Conjugate Functions", 17.
6 An *equivalence relation* is a relation that is reflexive (it relates a point to itself), symmetrical (if it relates x to y, it also relates y to x) and transitive (if it relates x to y, and y to z, then it also relates x to z).
7 In terms of the musical analysis that develops tools from set theory and elsewhere, transposition is most often conceived in a way correlative to geometrical translation; directed intervals – we could say Hamiltonian interval-vectors – move the points of a motif or phrase in the same direction by the same interval-distance. (See Schuijer, *Analyzing Atonal Music: Pitch-Class Set Theory and Its Contexts*, 52.) In order for such a "translational" shift to be a transposition, in order, in other words, for the points of the phrase to be moved elsewhere, however, the vector producing such a shift must

be anything *other* than an equivalence; it must be anything other than a relation, in other words, expressing "the same". For the only equivalence internal to the space of such translational movements is, of course, *0*, the vector, in other words, that leaves the points where they are – *un*-transposed. In this sense, the translational mode of transposition would seem ill-equipped when it comes to representing what is at stake in the experience of transposition, if what is at stake is the experience of equivalence: that, as a consequence of an experience of identity – of being the same – at the level of the interval-relation the motif or phrase manifests, there is an experience of identity, of equivalence, at the level of the motif or phrase themselves – that motif X and Y are "the same motif".

8 Hamilton, *Lectures on Quaternions*.
9 Mill, *System of Logic*, 433.
10 Mill is using "connotation" to refer to the common quality allowing a common denotation (a common name).
11 See Chapter 2 of this book for an explanation of Stewart's theory.
12 *Logic*, 28.
13 *Logic*, 442.
14 "Sense", in a mathematical sense, is defined as "the 'direction' of an inequality, i.e., whether it signifies 'greater than' or 'less than'". Penguin Dictionary of Mathematics, 291.
15 Fleisch, *Guide to Vectors and Tensors*, 2.
16 Coleman, liner notes to *Change of the Century*.
17 Litweiler, *A Harmolodic Life*, 51.
18 Wessel in private seminar.
19 For our limited purpose here, we could form simple "spherical" neighbourhoods of a point x in pitch space thus: a neighbourhood U_x of a pitch x is a neighbourhood containing all those pitches less than an arbitrarily chosen "radial" interval-distance from x. With this distance as two semitones, the neighbourhood U_C of the pitch C contains all those pitches whose interval-distance from C is less than two semitones. As this distance is "radial", this neighbourhood contains pitches on two semitones on "either side" of of the chosen pitch, C.
20 For instance, A#/Bb, D and F#/Gb augmented triads can be created from the complement of the neighbourhoods of the points of a C augmented triad.

Chapter 5

Lonely Woman (solitude)

Ornette met the French philosopher, Jacques Derrida, in Paris in 1997, a meeting that took place on Derrida's initiative and in the presence of the film and music critic, Thierry Jousse, working for the French music journal, *Inrockuptibles*. Ornette and Derrida spoke for many hours, Derrida's intellectual orientation introducing a conceptual clarity to both the questions Ornette was asked, as well as the answers Ornette was able to give in response. They spoke of many things, finding many points of common ground, particularly in relation to the question of language, a question that interested Ornette very much. However, in the course of this discussion, perhaps prompted by things Ornette had said in moments of their discussion not printed in *Inrockuptibles*, Derrida asked Ornette about women, and in particular about the relation between Ornette's music and his relation to women. "Pensez-vous que votre écriture musicale a fondamentalement quelque chose à voir avec votre rapport à la femme?", asked Derrida, to which Ornette offered the following response:

> Avant d'être connu en tant que musicien, quand je travaillais dans un grand magasin, un jour, pendant ma pause déjeuner, je suis arrivé dans une galerie où quelqu'un avait peint une femme blanche très riche qui avait absolument tout ce qu'on peut désirer dans la vie, et elle avait l'expression la plus solitaire du monde. Je n'avais jamais été confronté à une telle solitude, et quand je suis rentré chez moi, j'ai écrit un morceau que j'ai appelé *Lonely woman*.

Of course, this conversation was actually conducted in English and translated into French for publication in *Inrockuptibles*.[1] Let us nonetheless turn for a moment to the English *Genre* translation (of the French translation), made by Timothy S. Murphy, which reads as follows:

[Derrida]: Do you think that your musical writing has something fundamental to do with your relation to women?

[Ornette]: Before becoming known as a musician, when I worked in a big department store, one day, during my lunch break, I came across a gallery where someone had painted a very rich white woman who had absolutely everything

DOI: 10.4324/9781003412304-5

that you could desire in life, and she had the most solitary expression in the world. I had never been confronted with such solitude, and when I got back home, I wrote a piece that I called "Lonely Woman".

In an interview given in 2007, echoing comments he had made elsewhere regarding "sound medicine",[2] Ornette related the question of loneliness to cure, to "healing", by linking loneliness to *solitude*, as its correlative condition, as the condition from which one suffers when one is lonely. "My real concern for the things I would like to perfect in music", says Ornette, "is to heal the suffering and the pain and ...", hesitating, searching for the right words, "what [do] they call the ... when you are lonely?", he asked the interviewer. "Solitude", was the response. "Yeah", said Ornette, "*solitude*".[3]

A space of solitude

What Ornette describes to Derrida is thus an experience to which his piece "Lonely Woman" – one not at all insignificant in the history of music, described by him elsewhere as the first piece he recorded that was "harmolodic", the neologism he coined to name his approach – is a response.[4] This *confrontation* (confronté, says the French Ornette) with solitude, with an "expression" that is also an expression of solitude – a singular expression of the woman's being-sole – is the confrontation with a woman who had absolutely everything it would be possible to desire in life, with a woman in whom, it seems, nothing but a lack is lacking.

If we listen closely to this account Ornette gives of his experience, it is possible to discern in this "et" – *and* – and she had such an expression of solitude – where one might expect a "mais" – *but* – a woman who had absolutely everything, *but* she was lonely – something that links this having everything to solitude in something other than a relation of negation, as if there were another link between this solitude Ornette had encountered and the *everything* it would seem this woman possessed at the level of what it would be possible for her to desire. Let us draw in another English expression here, one that has now perhaps lost some of its resonance but of which it would be possible to hear in this "solitude" an echo – *feme sole* – an expression for which one dictionary simply offers the sense *unmarried woman,* but for which an earlier edition evokes the possibility of something else in this confrontation Ornette describes with solitude, with this woman who had everything one could desire in life, *and* who had such an expression of solitude – *feme sole* as not only a *spinster* or *widow*, but *feme sole* as a woman *entirely independent of her husband as regards property*.[5] Is there not something of the *feme sole* in this woman Ornette has confronted, who seems to lack nothing at the level of property, at the level of what of her desire it would be possible to own, and that it might be necessary to have from a husband? *Feme sole* thus enables us to link these two, apparently distinct, even conflicting, features together – the *solitude*, on the one hand, and the *having everything*, on the other – such that the "expression" Ornette confronts emerges not just as an expression of solitude, of being-solitary, but as an

Lonely Woman (solitude) 67

expression of *being feme sole*, of being a woman whose *having everything* undoes entirely – at least at the level of property – any dependence linking her to an other.

Isolated points

In terms of general topology, a point, x, is an *isolated point* of a set, A, if there exists a neighbourhood of x that contains no other point of A, the wider set in which x is contained, other than x.[6] x is, in other words, on its own, solitary, *isolated*. There is some "space" around x into which we can move, containing no other points, a surrounding "distance" empty of all other points, maintaining x in its solitude, its isolation. However, it is possible to see that, if the lonely woman Ornette describes is an isolated point, if there is, in other words, a neighbourhood that contains her *and no other points*, this isolation *is an effect of her "having everything"*. "Having everything" is what produces her as *feme sole*, as a woman entirely independent of an other with respect to property, with respect to what she *has* and which it might be necessary to have from this other.

An interval that will have everything in it

In February of 1960, just a few months after the release of Ornette's second album, *The Shape of Jazz to Come*, on which this piece, "Lonely Woman", would appear, the musician and composer Gunther Schuller, an early friend and champion of Ornette's work, interviewed him for "The Scope of Jazz", a weekly radio show he then hosted with the critic Nat Hentoff. In the course of this interview, something of the complexity of the space of Ornette's early thought opens up, as Schuller, who knew Ornette well, even having acted as a tutor to Ornette in matters of notation, questioned him at length on the sometimes unusual aspects of his music and ideas.[7] Early on in their discussion, the conversation turns to the question of *intervals*. "What do you mean by 'interval'?", Schuller asked Ornette directly – a question to which Ornette gave the following answer:

> Well, I mean a musical pitch that carries an idea that a person is playing, a change, or a person is playing a harmonic pitch to go with the change, or a person is playing a degree of a key, or a person is playing a degree of a chord. You still have to play a pitch of music to know you're doing that. And, to me, I try to conceive maybe one interval that will have harmony, changes, everything in it.[8]

A pitch that carries an idea – what to make of Ornette's response here, for isn't an interval, both in its musical and in its more general sense, precisely something that appears between *two* points – between two pitches – as the distance, the "gap", separating one from the other? As such, isn't it irreducible to a single point, rather requiring two points for its constitution? If in our discussion of invisibility we discerned, at the heart of the notion of transposition, a shift from points to relations, why now this apparent shift back, *from relations to points*, from the "interval" as

68 Lonely Woman (solitude)

distance, as difference, between points, to "interval" as the point itself, as the point, the pitch, that "carries an idea"?

In this reference to an interval – *a pitch that carries an idea* – that will have "harmony, changes, everything in it", it is also possible to hear an echo of the *having everything* of the lonely woman – the woman who "had everything you could desire in life" and who had such a solitary expression. So, what is the relation between the two, between the "having everything" of the lonely woman and the "having everything in it" of the solitary-pitch-as-interval? And if, in the case of the lonely woman, "having everything" is linked to *solitude*, what does this imply about Ornette's music as a space of solitude?

Interval

The transference of a name

In one passage from his essay on beauty, to which we have referred many times, Dugald Stewart wondered about the shifts to which the notion of an *interval* had been subjected since its origin in the *intervallum*, evidently borrowed from the phraseology of the camp: *inter vallo spatum* – the space between the stakes or palisades which strengthened the rampart. No one, says Stewart, had taken any notice of the insensible *transitions* by which this term was successively to be employed in a more enlarged sense, first to express a limited portion of longitudinal extension in general, and afterwards limited portions of time as well as of space. "How remote", Stewart exclaims in a footnote to this passage, "are some of the following applications of the word from its primitive meaning!"[9] Of course, the explanation Stewart gives for the existence of such "remote applications" is that the "transference of a name" – the transference of a signifier such as "interval" – is not, as the Encyclopedists had thought, that there is a quality common to *all* objects that share a name, the presence of which would constitute the condition for the transference of that name, but merely that there be a quality in common with at least *one* object already contained in the class of things that share that name: *one is enough*. This is what we have called Stewart's law.

So, if Ornette's "interval" implies a transference in Stewart's sense, a further transition or movement to a point even more remote than those to which Stewart refers, to what point of the existing class of meanings does Ornette's meaning relate by means of an immediate point of partial overlap, allowing the "transference of the name"? What is the relation between "interval" as "pitch that carries an idea" and the existing class of meanings connected to this name? And what is the "common quality", satisfying the condition established by Stewart's law, thus allowing such a shift? If we understand an "idea" as a *change* or *degree* of a chord or key, as Ornette suggests, the question then becomes, what does a pitch that carries a *change* or *degree* have in common with the "gap", the distance, that separates one pitch from another? What is it that the two have in common so as to allow the transfer of the signifier from the latter to the former?

In the terms we developed earlier, a musical interval can be conceived as the relation between pitches produced by the simple metric implied by Hamiltonian analysis: B – A. If we treat the product of this analysis as an absolute value, our interval is undirected – it is simply the distance between A and B, without regard to any directed movement from A to B or from B to A. If we do not treat the value as absolute, B – A produces a directed interval – a *vector*, or directed distance, in Hamilton's terms, which moves a "movable point" from A to B, but not (necessarily) from B to A. Using a broader sense of "vector" in relation to a space with a tonic orientation, we also spoke of the *degree* as an effect of coordination, of situation, as the *being somewhere* of a point with respect to a tonic point of origin, produced as the endpoint of the inverse, situating vector, when synthesised with respect to the tonic point of origin. So, our question is thus, what does interval as *relation* between points – expressed in terms of tonic and situating vectors – have in common with the *effect of situation*, of "being somewhere", produced by means of that relation? What do they have in common so as to satisfy "Stewart's law", the law governing the transference of a name from the interval as relation to the "interval" as point, as "pitch that carries an idea"?

There is, as we have discussed before, a kind of intimate relation between the situating vector and the endpoint, made visible when, in a simple coordinate space, the initial point of that vector is zero, the point of origin. Then the relation (the situating vector) and the endpoint share a name; "+5" is the coordinate five unit steps up – "+5" – from the point of origin, "–3" is the point three unit steps down – "–3" – from the point of origin, and so on. In this sense, the name – even when conceived in terms of musical intervals – 3rds, 5ths and so on – is already something the inverse situating form of the tonic vector has in common with the pitch that carries the effect of situation – what Ornette calls the degree or *idea* – something in common sufficient to satisfy Stewart's law and thus allow the transference of the name, "interval". However, when Ornette defines an interval as a "pitch that carries an idea", is this really all he has in mind? Is it really simply a question of a coincidence experienced at the level of technical nomenclature?

Transference of a relation

We propose instead the following: if the Ornettian Interval is redefined as *a pitch that carries an idea*, it is because, correlative to the merely "technical" coincidence at the level of the name the situating vector shares with its endpoint, *something of this relation itself has been transferred to the point*, something of the "gap", the "distance" *between* points has *itself* been transferred to one of the points this "gap", this distance, relates, and is now experienced as an immanent, audible property of the point itself, something, some "substance" or *Idea*, this point now "carries". This transfer to the point of something of the relation would then offer an answer to the question of what the interval as relation, as vector, distance, or "gap", has in common with an Ornettian Interval as *pitch that carries an Idea*. For what they have in common, allowing the transfer of the signifier, "interval", *is simply the*

70 Lonely Woman (solitude)

presence of something of the relation itself, albeit in a "disavowed", inverse form as the Idea the pitch-as-Interval now carries.

In this sense, perhaps, the Ornettian Idea could be nothing more than the effect of "up-ness" a point seems to carry as an effect of its relation to a point "down" with respect to it, or the effect of "before-ness" a point seems to carry as an effect of a relation to a point after with respect to it at the level of some order, or even the authority someone seems to bear within themselves as an effect of the order relation that constitutes the hierarchy that situates them as "above" or "greater". This is correlative, perhaps, to the effect of "sixth-ness" or "third-ness" a pitch seems to bear within it as a consequence of its being with respect to a coordinating tonic point of origin. And, in each of these instances too, the Idea-effect is correlative to the relation that situates the points that carry them. Thus "up-ness" is correlative to an upward relation situating the "up" point with respect to what is down, "before-ness" is correlative to an order relation situating the "before" point with respect to what is after, authority is correlative to both of these relations, insofar as it implies both order and "height" and so on.[10]

Everything in it

"Everything"

Let us now conceive the "everything" the point "has" "in it" as *everything that it would be possible to have from outside*, in the form of "harmony, changes, everything". In this sense, "everything" can be understood in terms of the "everything" taken to be absent from a music in which what Ornette has called a "set pattern" – the external, orienting, temporally ordered framework of chords and their tonal orientations – is missing.

In his interview with John Litweiler, Gunther Schuller reported something Ornette had said during the lessons Schuller had offered him on reading and notation, implying something further to the harmonic Ideas that pertain to "harmony" and "changes" and thus a possible generalisation of the Ornettian Idea to include in this "everything" the effects of relations other than those of harmony:

> Over a period of, when I think he was playing in blues bands in Texas, he had for some reason begun to associate certain pitches with certain characters. In other words, certain notes were always upbeats and they could only be upbeats.[11]

If "upbeat" and "downbeat" imply a temporal vector-relation – what moves "a movable point" one beat-unit step "forward" (in time) from the downbeat to the upbeat, an upbeat Idea can be conceived as the inverse (situating) form of this vector, now *transferred to the point*, such that the upbeat Idea is experienced as an immanent property of the pitch. The note ("always") has an upbeat "character" – it always carries "in it", in other words, an upbeat Idea.

"In"

Let us conceive "in" in terms of *the interiority of the point*. The Ornettian Interval is now a "space" with an interior and exterior, and what was taken to be exterior, in the form of "harmony, changes, everything", is now interior. The Ornettian Interval-point now has "harmony, changes, everything" "in" it.

"Having everything in it"

The "having everything in it" that pertains to the Ornettian Interval can now be formulated in the following way. *There is nothing that could be had from the exterior, in the form of "harmony, changes, everything", that is not already to be found on the interior. Everything* that can be had from the exterior, in the form of "harmony, changes, everything", is already to be found on the interior. The Interval *has everything in it.*

Pitch sole

In this sense, if the "lonely woman" is a *feme sole*, insofar as her "having everything" at the level of what it would be possible to desire frees her of dependence on others, the Ornettian Interval is a *pitch sole*, insofar as its "having everything in it" (at the level of Idea) frees it of dependence on exterior others. It is *solitary*, because there is nothing that could be had from the exterior that is not already to be found on the interior.

So, if an Interval is defined as *a pitch that carries an Idea*, and the *Idea* the pitch carries is defined as something of the relation *transferred to the point*, as something, some substance, this point now "carries", and if "everything" is to be given in terms of "harmony, changes, everything", how is it that an Interval can "have everything in it"? How is it that an Interval – a pitch that carries an Idea – can possess "everything" – "harmony, changes" – as some property interior to itself? We propose the following simple answer. An Ornettian Interval can have "everything" – harmony, changes, everything – "in it", insofar as the Idea the pitch now carries, somehow immanent, internal to itself, *is nothing but the inverse effect of the relation to those tonic points that constitute harmony, changes, everything* – insofar, that is, as the Idea is the effect of the pitch-as-Interval's relation to harmonic tonics, tonal tonics, to the points of changes and so on. The presence of the Idea *effect*, in other words, necessarily implies the ("disavowed") presence of its tonic *cause*.

"Behind all interpretation", say Ogden and Richards in their treatise on meaning, "we have the fact that when part of an external context recurs in experience, this part is, through its linkage with a member of some psychological context", "sometimes a sign of the rest of the external context"[12] – a sign sufficient to evoke, to "call up", the rest of the context in an act of "completion" we have linked to *transference*. There is, in effect, a *transference of the context*, contingent on a "quality in common" at the level of what Ogden and Richards call the "sign"; the sign is a "stimulus" "*similar*" to some part of the original stimulus and, thus, sufficient to

72 Lonely Woman (solitude)

evoke, to call up, the rest of its context. So, if there is an experience of an Ornettian Interval – if there is the experience of an Idea connected to a pitch as something that pitch carries – and if this Idea is nothing but the effect of the pitch-as-Interval's relation to tonic contexts "exterior" to it, then the experience of an Interval must imply the transference of this context, must imply the "disavowed" experience of the presence of this context, the relation to which produces the Idea as its effect.

Carries a complete idea

A little later in his interview with Schuller, and in the context of a discussion of connection and disconnection experienced in relation to Ornette's music, almost exactly Ornette's formulation for the Interval – the pitch that carries an idea – appears, but now to describe a *phrase*. If before, in their discussion of Ornette's Interval, it had been a pitch – a single point – that "carried an idea", here it is a phrase – a *collection* of points – that "carry an idea", and that idea, says Ornette, is "complete". "They say", says Schuller, referring to Ornette's sometimes hostile audience, that "none of the phrases make any sense. They don't connect up. It's just a bunch of notes". "Yeah that's right", responds Ornette, "but they don't realise that the phrases … carry a complete idea as it's played".[13]

What then, to make of this consonance at the level of expression, this appearance of the same fragment of speech, implying that both pitches and phrases can carry, can be the *vehicles* for, Ideas? To what extent does it imply a generalisation of the notion of "Interval" to refer not only to points singular but to points plural, to collections of points – correlative, perhaps, to the use of "signifier" to refer not only to single words but to words collected into phrases, and further? What also to make of this reference to completeness, to the notion that the Idea a phrase – and perhaps also a pitch – carries can be "complete"? What is this "completeness" that pertains to the Idea, and what does it have to do, perhaps, with the "having everything in it" that pertains to the Interval that Ornette has said that he tries to play? Does an Interval that "has *everything* in it" "carry a *complete* Idea"? And what, finally, of the relation between completeness, of a phrase that "carries a complete idea", and "disconnection" – the experience that Ornette's "don't connect up", that they're "just a bunch of notes"?

Phrase ideas

If we conceive of Ornettian Ideas in terms of *degrees* – the degree of a chord, the degree of a key, as suggested by Ornette – then there is a problem when we talk of Ideas in terms of the *multiple* points that pertain to phrases. For, if all of the points of a phrase are situated with respect to a common point, and if these points are different from one another, this will, of course, produce multiple "degrees" – multiple Ideas – insofar as the values that pertain to the situating vectors are also multiple. If Idea is understood in the sense we have been using with respect to "degrees", the only way for the different points of a phrase to carry the *same* Idea would be if each of the points of the phrase were related in *parallel* – situated, that is, with respect to different points so as to produce a consonance at the level of the Ideas these situating relations produce.[14] Now each point carries the "same Idea".

However, we could also conceive of the multiple Ideas produced with respect to a single tonic point in more general terms, as a single "tonic Idea" – each of the points of the phrase carries, for instance, an Eb tonic-Idea. Or, we could treat the phrase as a single point, much like a spoken phrase can be considered a single signifier; now the Idea a phrase carries pertains to the phrase as a whole, with the singularity of the Idea correlative to the singularity of the phrase and distinct from any Idea each of the individual points of that phrase may carry. In this sense, for instance, one could conceive of a *phrase Idea* in terms of the meaning or function a particular phrase has with respect to other phrases in a wider section or piece – something that tells us, perhaps, about the identity of the phrase, what it is for the other points in that section or piece – and which is experienced as an immanent property of the phrase itself.

Disconnection

So, what of this other dimension, identified by Schuller, that has to do with the *connectivity* that pertains to Ornette's music? "They say that none of the phrases make any sense. They don't connect up ..." What to make of this experience of *disconnection* to which Schuller refers, a reference to which Ornette responds with the notion of *completeness*, that those who experience disconnection fail to realise that "the phrase carries a *complete* Idea"? What is the relation, in other words, between disconnection and a completeness that we have linked to an *Interval* that "has harmony, changes, *everything* in it"?

In general topological terms, a set, *A*, is *disconnected* if it can be "decomposed" into disjoint summands – if, in other words, it can be conceived in terms of disjoint subsets (subsets without overlap), the union of which produces the set *A*.[15] Thus, a space composed of *isolated points* – points for which there exist neighbourhoods containing only those points and no others, as discussed earlier – is a *disconnected space* in this sense, for the simple reason that the isolating neighbourhoods constitute tesserae of disjoint subsets, the union of which produces the space. If Ornettian phrases carry a complete Idea insofar as they have everything in them and insofar as this "having everything" is linked to *solitude*, such that we can speak of the Ornettian Interval or "Interval-phrase" (a phrase that carries a complete Idea) as *pitch-sole* or *phrase-sole* – "Intervals" that, having everything in them, being *complete*, require nothing from outside, are entirely independent of exterior others – then this offers a relation between completeness and disconnection. An effect of disconnection is an effect of the isolation of the Interval, produced as it is by its internal completeness, its "having everything in it".

Movement

> After three years or so in Los Angeles, learning how to play bebop, I found I could use notes in a way that was equal to playing chords, but if I used notes as chords without them being chords, I was no longer restricted to doing sequences. At first I tried to understand how it would work in terms of writing music. That's how I started by improvising, and then took it to writing. I found that this idea doesn't allow you to compose in sequences, so I used "movement" as another word to describe each new melody.[16]

"I found I could use notes [...] as chords", says Ornette, "without them being chords", but notes used in this way, first in the context of improvisation, then composition, are somehow incompatible with "sequences" from which notes-as-chords nonetheless offer an escape, a way of playing and composing no longer subject to its limitations. Then, as a consequence of this incompatibility with the sequence, there is a transference of a signifier, "movement", to describe each new melody constituted in this way. But what would it mean for a note to be used "as" a chord? How could a single note appear in place of the multiple points that constitute a chord, taking their place, their function?

We propose the following: notes are "used as chords without them being chords" to the extent that these notes *carry a harmonic Idea*, the being of their relation to a harmonic context, the transference of which produces the Idea as its effect. In this sense, our discussion of an Ornettian Interval that "has harmony, changes, everything in it" already implies "notes as chords", already implies that the pitch-as-Ornettian-Interval is the bearer of harmonic Ideas that imply the transference of a wider harmonic context. This would enable us to conceive the space of a *Movement*, a *Movement space*, in Ornette's sense, as a space of Ornettian Intervals, the space of a "horizontal" melody, where the points of that space are caught up in "vertical" (harmonic) spaces – spaces that appear immanent to a point-as-chord in the form of the Ideas they carry. If we draw in the distinction between harmonic and tonal tonics we introduced in Chapter 3, this would produce a succession of Intervals (I), suspended from each of which are ("disavowed") branches linking these points to their harmonic (h) and tonal tonics (t), producing harmonic-tonic and tonal-tonic Ideas (i) as their effect, which are then experienced as immanent properties of the Ornettian Interval-notes-as-chords. This is an articulation of Ornettian *Intervals* producing what Ornette calls a *Movement* (Figure 5.1).

With Ornette's reference to "sequence" understood in terms of "changes" – a sequence of tonally oriented chords, as we suggested in Chapter 3, where this "sequence" is predetermined, decided in advance, then it is possible to see why composing Movements would cause a conflict at the level of "sequences", for the "harmonics" implied by a Movements already imply chords, already imply, in the form of notes-as-chords, harmonies, which are then in danger of coming into conflict with some underlying, predetermined sequence of chords. This is one way to make sense of something Ornette said to the reed player, Eric Dolphy, about an

Lonely Woman (solitude) 75

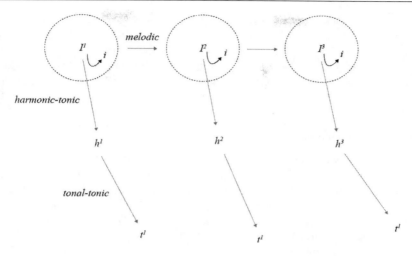

Figure 5.1

experience of coincidence at the level of harmony: "if someone played a chord, he heard another chord on that one".[17] If the chord someone is playing is part of a predetermined harmonic "sequence", and the note Ornette is playing is "used as a chord", this would produce the coincidence of harmonies Dolphy describes – another chord on that one, another set of chords overlaying the chord sequence someone else is playing.

Har-mo-lodic Movement

Ornette has told us that the word, "harmolodic", is a neologism, the combination of three distinct words, producing a new word naming his approach – *harmolodics* as the fusion of harmony – *harmonics* – and melody – *melodics* – with another signifier – *movement* – at their intersection (Figure 5.2).

h	a	r	m	o	n	i	c	s
			m	o	v	e	m	e	n	t
			m	e	l	o	d	i	c	s

Figure 5.2

And, in a sense, it is possible to see that the structure of this signifier – *harmolodic* – itself manifests the structure we have been discussing, of *melodic* "notes" that, "as chords" – *harmonics* – emerge as points of intersection between melody

76 Lonely Woman (solitude)

and harmony, thus constituting what Ornette calls a *Movement*. The Ornettian *Interval*-note-as-chord constitutes a point of meeting, of overlap, between *melodic* points that, as *Intervals*, "are" "chords" insofar as they carry harmonic Ideas "in" them – function *har-mo-lodic-ally* – as simultaneously melody and harmony. The structure of *har-mo-lodics* is, in this sense, itself transposed into the structure of the very signifier that names it.

A cure for solitude

So, let us turn finally to a question to which we alluded at the start of this chapter, that has to do with healing, with a cure, with Ornette's music as a cure for a condition Ornette has linked to loneliness, as what you are when you are lonely, the condition of *solitude*. A *cure for solitude*; what, given the account of solitude we have offered in this chapter, would such a cure entail? If solitude constitutes a malady, a condition to be healed, how could music – *Ornette's* music – constitute the cure for such a malady?

If solitude is to be conceived in terms of "having everything in it", and "having everything in it" is to be conceived in terms of the Idea – as "something of the relation transferred to the point" – then the solitude, the being *pitch-sole* of the Ornettian Interval, only emerges insofar as the pitch is *not solitary*, insofar as there is another – a tonic pitch – with respect to which that pitch is situated, an effect of situation then (mis)perceived as an immanent property of the point, independent of the relation to its tonic cause. The *being alone*, the being solitary, of the pitch in other words, is *nothing but the "disavowed" form of its being related*, of *not* being alone; what it "has in it" is nothing but the effect of what it has "outside" it, its being with respect to tonic others, the relation to which produces a property-effect, the effect that the pitch *has* something, independent of this being-for-others.

Richards conceived of the new rhetoric he proposed in his *Philosophy of Rhetoric* as a riposte to what he called the "proper meaning superstition" – the belief that a word has a meaning (one, ideally) independent of its context and use, and for the expression of which it should be uttered, with its supposition that words "just sheerly possess their sense", as men, he says, have their names, and "carry this meaning with them into sentences, regardless of the neighbour words",[18] building the meaning of a sentence "as a mosaic is put together of discrete independent tesserae".[19] Rather, says Richards, meanings are "resultants" which are arrived at only through the "interplay" of the interpretative possibilities of the whole utterance.[20] "A word, when isolated momentarily from its controlling neighbours", he says, "is free to develop irrelevant senses which may then beguile half the other words that follow it".[21] However, if meaning is, as Richards has said, a "resultant", the effect of the interplay of a word and its "controlling neighbours", the emergence of a sense, however relevant or irrelevant, already implies the presence of neighbours, already implies that the word, the point, in other words, is *not isolated* – just as an Idea a pitch carries as "Interval" can also only emerge insofar as that pitch is *not isolated*, insofar as it is experienced as related, as being with respect to, another point, the inverse form of the relation to which is then transferred to the point as the Idea it "carries".

So, if solitude is an effect of "having everything in it", and if this interiority of the *Idea* with respect to the *Interval* is a disavowed form of its exteriority in the form of the relation, then a *cure* for solitude would imply the avowal that what is experienced as inside, as interior to the point, is the contingent effect of its being with respect to the outside, its solitude the effect of its being for others. In this sense, a cure for solitude could be situated on the side of *change*, on the side of an experience that a change at the level of the "internal" Idea is correlative to a change at the level of the exterior relation. Change, in this sense, restages the constituting, prior moment of exteriority disavowed by an experience of interiority, it puts on show the relation, the being-out-for-others, disavowed by the shift to Idea, the being-in-oneself.

Loss of a relation, loss of an Idea

In Chapter 3, we saw that certain properties pertain to the tonic relation, where "tonic" is understood in the wider sense implied by the transference of this name from "tonal tonic" to "harmonic tonic". A point, we said, can change its tonic – more than one point can be a tonic for a point – but it cannot *at once* have more than one tonic, unless the points are linked together transitively. The relation is, in this sense, *exclusive*, it can be a relation to one point or another, but not both at once. Although the implied relation is different, the same exclusivity pertains to melodic direction; there can be, in other words, a change of direction, a shift to a new consequent at the level of the order that pertains to a melody, but this new direction is exclusive of the old. It is one or the other, never both; only one of these directions, in other words, can "be" the melody. In this sense, in both instances, a *loss* pertains to a change of direction. There is a *loss of direction* correlative to the exclusivity of the relation, for the exclusivity of the relation is such that, when I choose a relation to a determinate point, I lose my relation to the point to which I was previously related by means of that relation. A *gain* at the level of the relation, in these specific instances, *always necessarily entails a loss* at the level of my relation to any points to which I was previously related. If an *Idea* is a relation-effect, then such a loss at the level of a relation necessarily also implies a loss at the level of the Idea, for the exclusivity that pertains to the relation also pertains to the Idea; one can have more than one Idea, but not *at once* – it is one or the other, not both, unless these Ideas are linked together transitively.

However, this allusion to *loss* is perhaps sufficient to alert us to an insufficiency at the level of our cure for solitude, at the level of *change* – a change of relation producing a change of Ideas as its effect. For *loss* is not correlative to *lack*, the loss of a relation, of an Idea, is not correlative to the lack of a relation and its associated Idea. There may be, in other words, in the experience of loss, the experience of a *wrong*, of the loss of what is *proper to* the point, the loss of a relation and its

78   Lonely Woman (solitude)

correlative Idea that *rightfully belongs* to, that is the *rightful property of*, the point. *Change*, in this sense, may itself take on the quality of a search for *lost property*, for relations that will restore the Idea proper to the point, its proper being, what was rightfully its own, and of which it has wrongfully been dispossessed in this shift at the level of external relations.

Lack of a relation, lack of an Idea

In the liner notes to *Something Else!!!!*, Ornette's first album, on which "Invisible" would appear, Walter Norris, the pianist for this recording, described the process that characterised its creation, a process marked, he suggested, by a profound attention to change, to *difference*. "Each time we played the tunes", he said, "we'd change them around a different way. We did everything possible we could with them". This attention to change, to variety, to the dimension of *something else*, was echoed in Ornette's own words in these notes:

> I would prefer it if musicians would play my tunes with different changes as they take a new chorus so that there'd be all the more variety in the performance. On this recording, the changes finally decided on for the tunes are a combination of some I suggested and some the musicians suggested. If you feel the lines differently one day, you can change the harmony accordingly.[22]

In these words, another dimension emerges, another kind of "change", another sense of "something else" that is not the search for a lost, determinate point, realising a determinate relation, but the desire for change, for *difference*, for *otherness*, itself – *something else*, not as a search for a lost object but the desire for the relation that relates such objects, for what makes one to the other something else, something different. And it is possible to discern in this desire for something else, for *difference*, for *change* itself, the shift from points to relations we found in our discussion of *free relations*, of "free directions", the shift from "something else" as a *point* to "something else" as a *relation* that relates some point to a point other to it. There is, we could say, the repeated *transference of a relation* – the transference of a relation of *difference*, of otherness, from one set of points to another.

This shift from points to relations - from *something else* as point to *something else* as relation between points – is correlative to a shift to *lack*, the *lack of a relation*, for from the perspective of this desire – the desire for difference – the constitutive relation is "lateral" – it relates relation to relation, difference to difference – it merely says that difference will be *repeated*, that there will be an *equivalence of differences*, the "repeated transference of a relation (of difference)", *with no indication of which points will manifest that relation*. There is nothing, in other words, at the level of this desire that indicates "where" this difference will "go", where, by which points, it will be manifest – *only that it will be a difference*, only that this going will manifest this difference. Now, a point "lacks" a relation because there is nothing at the level of the shift to *free difference relations* that would imply a relation *proper* to that point, that would distinguish between a relation that is the rightful property of the point and thus, in danger of being wrongfully lost, and a relation that is improper, the *wrong relation*, and thus to be discarded in favour of *something else*. This lack at the level of a relation proper to a point is, again, correlative to a lack at the level of the Ideas the point is experienced as carrying as an effect of these relations. For if there is nothing at the level of the *free difference* that would determine "where" it would "go", by which points it would be manifest, then this is to say that there is nothing at the level of the *free difference* that would determine which Ideas are to be produced as the effect of these manifestations. The Idea produced can be any Idea, so long as it is the effect of the manifestation of a *free difference*.

"Ornette went on to say about his general goal", says Hentoff in his liner notes for *Something Else!!!!*, "that the direction of a tune in performance can vary from bar to bar", before quoting Ornette directly:

> If I don't set a pattern at a given moment, whoever had the dominant ear at the moment can take and do a thing that will release the direction from what it always was into something better. And I believe in going with him. The drummer can help determine direction too, because he can turn phrases around on a different beat, for example, thereby raising the freedom of my playing.[23]

If the note that is "always a downbeat", which Schuller refers to in his account of his lessons with Ornette, that always has a certain downbeat "character", carrying a certain downbeat Idea "in it", is related to solitude, then here, in these changes of direction, in this drumming that "turns phrases around on a different beat", we have a specific instance of the cure for solitude we have proposed, where *turning*, producing difference as its effect, is a *free turning*, the desire for turning, for a change of direction itself, regardless of the specific directions produced by means of this turning. If the Interval is solitary insofar as it carries a downbeat Idea in it, and thus requires nothing from the outside, now as a consequence of the intervention of the outside, in the form of a drumming that turns, this "having in it" is transformed into a lack, the lack of any "interior" beat-Idea proper to the point, correlative to a lack, produced by a shift to *free turning*, at the level of the beat relation it has exterior to it.

So, what are the consequences of these reflections regarding solitude – the *being-feme-sole* of the "Lonely Woman", the *being-pitch-sole* of the Ornettian Interval – as well as the *cure* for solitude we have discussed, for the question of what it means to follow? What are the consequences at the level of what it means to go, to move, where "I" goes?

What does it mean to follow?

In the first sense, the har-mo-lodic structure of an Ornettian Movement implies movement in two directions – first, the "horizontal" movement from isolated Interval

80 Lonely Woman (solitude)

to Interval, and, second, the "vertical" movement implied insofar as the Interval, as "note-as-chord", carries a harmonic Idea "in it", contingent on the ("disavowed") transference of a harmonic context exterior to it, the relation to which produces the harmonic Idea as its effect. With respect to the first of these, to "go where I go" thus means to go to an isolated point, a point experienced as contained in an isolating neighbourhood of a disconnected space. With respect to the second, there is a problem, however, insofar as the movement in the direction of an exterior orienting "where I go", which produces the Idea as its effect, is experienced as a property of the interior, without the need for a movement out that would make the "where to go" it implies manifest. For, when we recall the order that pertains to effects of situation,[24] it is possible to see that, with the Ornettian Interval, the initial movement *out* from a point to an orienting point of origin, which would then produce, on the return situating journey, the Idea as its inverse effect, *is already done.* If the point already carries an Idea "in it", this implies that one has *already moved* – there is no need to move *out* from the point, for the effects of such movement are already here, are already experienced as an immanent Idea-property the Interval has *in* it. In this sense, "to follow" is to go to a point to which the Interval has already gone in order to (re)produce the Idea the Interval carries "in it" as the effect of this movement. However, confronted with an Ornettian Interval, if the Idea it carries is nothing but the "disavowed" form of the relation experienced as transferred to the point, and if this relation relies for its constitution on *two* points, as the Hamilton vector relies for its constitution on the two points of subtractive analysis, how does one experience the relation/Idea when this other point is absent? How does one experience the relation/Idea if the pitch is solitary, if it is *pitch sole*, isolated from those neighbours with respect to which a vector could be produced? If there is no necessary relation between Idea-coordinate and coordinated, as we have said, then the only solution is to leap, with the possibility that "you" and "I", again, leap to different consequences, different points of harmonic orientation, producing different Idea coordinate-effects.

On the other hand, if we conceive of the space of Ornette's music not as a space of solitude, but as a space that constitutes a *cure for solitude*, and if this cure is conceived in terms of a shift to *free difference*, then the "endpoint" in the direction of which "I" moves is, again, itself a relation – a difference – with no indication of "where" this relation is to "go", by which points it is to be manifest. From the perspective of the desire for difference, the difference can go anywhere, so long as this going manifests this difference. In this sense, we could say that "to go where I go" in a space of free difference is *to go to difference*; you and I *converge to difference*, and, insofar as this difference relies on points to manifest itself, to *go to difference* means to go – to manifest – anywhere, by means of any points, such that this going manifests this difference. Anywhere, *so long as it's different.* Reformulating this desire for difference in terms of the curative shift from having to lacking, to go where "I" goes in a space of *free difference* means to go anywhere *such that this going manifests the lack of a relation*, such that this going manifests the lack of any determinate relation proper to the point and thus of any Idea that this point is experienced as carrying "in it". Going "anywhere", in this sense, *is the means of manifesting the lack of a determinate "somewhere"*.

So, if the "going anywhere" of a space of *free difference* implies a lack, the lack at the level of a relation proper to a point, and thus the lack of any Idea correlative to that relation, we now turn to a lack of a relation of a different, perhaps stronger kind, a lack that is not simply an "anywhere" expressing the lack of a determinate "somewhere" but a lack that is a *no relation*, the absence of a relation, a relation that is not one between two spaces that "haven't any relation" and which has something to do with conflicts in relations of love.

Notes

1 This was confirmed to me in a conversation with Thierry Jousse.
2 Coleman, "Jazz Conversations with Eric Jackson".
3 Coleman, "An Interview with Ornette Coleman", *Bonnaroo*.
4 Litweiler, *A Harmolodic Life*, 56–57.
5 *OED*, 416.
6 Hausdorff, *Set Theory*, 131–132.
7 Coleman, interview by Schuller, *The Scope of Jazz*.
8 Coleman, interview by Schuller.
9 Stewart, *Philosophical Essays*, 223.
10 This discussion bears, of course, on the question of what Rings calls "tonal qualia", the perceptual phenomenon of "scale-degree-ness", "the raw feel of experiencing a sounding pitch as, say, scale degree (3) or scale degree (5)". *Tonality and Transformation*, 43.
11 Litweiler, *A Harmolodic Life*, 94.
12 Ogden and Richards, *The Meaning of Meaning*, 57.
13 Coleman, interview by Schuller.
14 "Parallel", in this instance, has the sense we introduced in Chapter 4, where "angles" for one-dimensional vectors are produced by means of a unit difference on the axis opposing the pitch axis.
15 Hausdorff, *Set Theory*, 172.
16 Shipton, *A New History of Jazz*, 567.
17 Williams, *Jazz Panorama*, 283.
18 Richards, *The Philosophy of Rhetoric*, 54.
19 *Philosophy of Rhetoric*, 55.
20 *Philosophy of Rhetoric*, 55.
21 *Philosophy of Rhetoric*, 55.
22 Hentoff, liner notes to *Something Else!!!!*.
23 Hentoff, liner notes, *Something Else!!!!*.
24 See Chapter 3.

Chapter 6

Lonely Woman (no relation)

The tension in all love conflicts

When *The Wire* interviewed Ornette in 2005, it asked him about this piece, "Lonely Woman" and, in particular, about its temporal aspect. "How", asked the interviewer, "did you get the idea of the drums playing double against the saxophone?" "Playing fast?", Ornette asks. "That's the tension that I see in all love conflicts. It's like time is running out, but you're standing still".[1] Leaving aside for a moment the question of love, a question nonetheless intimately connected to the problems we have been discussing, of a woman who had everything but whose having everything introduced a problem at the level of her relations of love, what to make of Ornette's response here? What is this *tension* that characterises the relation between the saxophone and drums, a tension so striking in the history of music, described as both "double" and "fast"?

To introduce this question, let us turn to something Ornette said to Gunther Schuller, in his interview from 1960, about the question of notation and, in particular, of how to become a "precise reader", which, he says, he "never could".[2] At the origin of his early attempts to read, Ornette says, there was an experience of disorientation with respect to the aspect of time, and in particular to the level of tempo. Ornette refers specifically to "Cherokee" – another song about love – the first movement from Ray Noble's *Indian Suite*, written in 1938, a piece that would become the framework to which so much melodic improvisation would relate itself.

> I have never seen it notated, but it's always played, the melodies always played twice as slow as what they play it […] That's a good example, you know. And I said, well, they're playing as fast as they can play, and it sounds like a ballad […] That's one way I started reading. I started learning how to read like that, you know, that, whatever I read, it wasn't really the tempo that it was in. It was always either against it or above it. It was never that.[3]

"They're playing as fast as they can play", says Ornette, "and it sounds like a ballad". Could it be that this characterisation of Ornette's experience of "Cherokee", that echoes so closely the one we have just given of "Lonely Woman", of drums

DOI: 10.4324/9781003412304-6

"playing fast" against the saxophone, has something to tell us about the temporality of perhaps Ornette's most well-known piece and thus about the "tension" that Ornette perceives in all conflicts of love?

Cherokee

The first recording of "Cherokee" appeared in 1938, performed by the Roy Noble Orchestra under the composer's own direction. If we take the minims played by the bass in this performance (quarter note plus quarter note rest), the quarter note implied by the interplay of bass and intervening chords, and the whole note heard in the first bar of the melody as three distinct levels at which a beat could be experienced, this would then offer us three distinct tempos, to each of which a signifier of *medium, fast* or *ballad (slow)* could be transferred, with a half-note beat implying a *medium* tempo (c. 112 bpm), a quarter-note beat a *fast* tempo (c. 224 bpm), and a whole-note beat a *ballad* tempo *(slow)* (c. 56 bpm) (Figure 6.1).[4] In Charlie Parker's famous version of "Cherokee" recorded in 1942, the tempo is slightly faster, with a half-note beat offering a tempo of c. 152 bpm, a whole-note beat a tempo of c. 76 bpm, and a quarter-note beat a tempo of c. 304 bpm – tempos we could characterise with the same three signifiers – *medium, slow* and *fast*.[5]

Given these beats and the tempos they imply, we can determine for each a corresponding metre implying a *chain* lying within a simple duration space (see appendix). Such metrical chains contain the beat, the "feel" duration subdividing this beat (thus making it, for instance, a "simple" or "compound" metre), the metrical duration (the duration of a whole bar), as well as any intervening durations.[6] Thus, 4/4 implies the chain (♪, ♩, ♩, 𝅝) (represented here as an ordered set) containing the beat duration – ♩ – the "feel" duration – ♪ – the metrical duration – 𝅝 – as well as the intervening duration – ♩.[7] 6/8 implies the chain (♪, ♩., ♩.) containing the beat duration – ♩. – the "feel" subdivision – ♪ – as well as the metrical duration – ♩. and so on.[8]

When each of these durations internal to a metrical chain is realised as a "continued analogy", in Hamilton's sense (see Chapter 4) – the "transference of a relation" – such that the endpoint of a duration and the initial point of its repetition coincide, and such that the initial point of all realisations of those durations also coincide, it produces the space of a *measure*, or bar.[9] This is represented by the duration vectors in Figure 6.2, which realise the metrical chain (♪, ♩, ♩, 𝅝) to produce two bars of 4/4. The duration of each vector is given in terms of a quarter note unit on the

Figure 6.1

84 Lonely Woman (no relation)

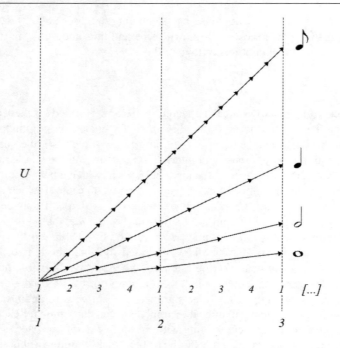

Figure 6.2

x axis, with the "angle" of each vector produced by means of a unit difference (*U*) on the *y* axis, as proposed in Figure 4.6. Vertical, dashed lines show the boundary points of each measure (i.e. the endpoint of one bar coincident with the initial point of the following bar).

With respect to our analysis of "Cherokee", with a quarter note beat producing a "fast" tempo, the implied metrical chain is (♪, ♩, 𝅗𝅥, 𝅝), where the metre is simple (the "feel" duration subdivides the beat in two) and where there is a metrical duration equal to four beats (coinciding with the metrical duration as written in Ray Noble's original score). This is the metrical chain given above as 4/4. With a whole-note beat producing a "slow", ballad tempo, the implied metrical chain is (♩, 𝅝, 𝅜, ▭) where the metre is simple (a half-note subdivides the whole-note beat "in two") and the metrical duration is equal to four whole-note beats, thus including an intervening "breve" twice as long as the beat and half as long as the metrical duration, as in the example of 4/4 given above.

We can represent the relation between these two, fast and slow metrical chains by *q*4. If we treat the "fast" chain as an ordered set, we can produce the "slow" chain by means of "scalar multiplication" – *q*4 (♪, ♩, 𝅗𝅥, 𝅝) = (𝅗𝅥, 𝅝, 𝅜, ▭). In other words, each duration in the "fast" chain produces the corresponding duration in the "slow" chain when multiplied by four. Inversely, the "slow" chain is "four times as slow" with respect to the fast chain. What we have discerned here, in the relation between the two times of "fast" and "slow", which we have characterised by means of "$q4$", is thus a first approach to the question of "tension". There is, between the fast and slow tempos, a simple relation, a simple "difference", given in terms of a difference between two metrical chains that lie within the duration space, and that difference is a "quotient difference", *4*.

Schuller's "Lonely Woman"

In 1961, the year after he interviewed Ornette for his WNBC radio show, Schuller published *A Collection of the Compositions of Ornette Coleman*, in which transcriptions of some of the compositions from Ornette's third album, *The Shape of Jazz to Come*, appeared, including a transcription of "Lonely Woman".[10] In this transcription, Schuller gave the metrical direction as *alla breve* – two half-note beats per bar – with a tempo direction of h = c. 88, around eighty-eight half-note beats per minute.

In the analysis implied by Schuller's transcription, with the beat as half-note (as given by ₵), the implied metrical chain is (♩, ♩, ○) – a half-note beat, a quarter-note feel (though the triplets in the melody might also imply a compound, triplet feel), and a whole-note metrical duration producing, Schuller's "fast" indication notwithstanding, a "slow" tempo – "it sounds like a ballad". With, however, the beat as eighth-note (as implied by the ride cymbal) and four beats in a bar, this implies the chain (♪, ♪, ♩, ♩), with the "feel" as sixteenth-note and the metrical duration as half-note, thus producing a "fast" tempo; "they're playing as fast as they can play", as Ornette says of "Cherokee". If we analyse (by means of Hamiltonian division) the beat duration of the slow chain (half-note) by the beat duration of the fast chain (eighth-note), it produces, again, as with "Cherokee", the quotient *4*. The "ballad" tempo is "four times as slow", or the "fast" tempo is "four times as fast".

Two "tensions"

At the level of the metrical chains that lie within the duration space proposed, we can thus identify at least two kinds of "tension".

1) On the one hand, there is the tension between two different chains lying within the space, where each of the durations of one chain is related by means of an integer quotient – as with *q4* above – to each of the durations of the other, and such that there exists a third chain lying within the space that contains them both. Given the existence of these relations between chains, this is the least "tense" form of tension.

2) On the other hand, there is the tension between two chains that lie within the duration space – say the chain for 4/4 and the chain for 6/8 – where not all of the durations of one chain are related to all durations from the other chain by

86 Lonely Woman (no relation)

means of the integer relation, correlative to the fact that 4/4 and 6/8 represent different approaches to metrical feel (simple and compound). This constitutes a more "tense" form of tension because of the absence of these relations.[11]

However, in spite of these two forms of tension, the first represented with respect to "Cherokee" and "Lonely Woman" by $q4$, it is possible to see that both these forms of tension emerge *internal to a wider space* – there is a difference between one chain and the other, with different degrees of intensity, but these differences, these disunities, nonetheless emerge *internal to a wider unity* – the unity represented by the duration space, which means that, even if two durations are not related directly, there will, at some point in the space, exist a third duration to which both are related by means of the integer relation that characterises the space. The question that faces us with respect to "Lonely Woman" is thus the following: is this really enough? Do such conceptions as implied by "Cherokee", on the one hand, and Schuller's transcription, on the other, really account for the "tension" to which Ornette refers, the tension at the heart of "Lonely Woman", between the time implied by the drums and the time implied by the melody instruments – a tension that Ornette sees in all love conflicts?

Analysis of "Lonely Woman"

Let us turn, for a moment, to our transcription of the performance of "Lonely Woman" that appears on *The Shape of Jazz to Come*. Figures 6.3.1–6.3.5 show a transcription of the performance of the melody to the "A" section of "Lonely Woman", as well as the first repeat. On the left is the A section played for the first time, and on the right is the A section played for the second time, juxtaposed for the sake of comparison. The layout is as follows:

- Timings shown on the horizontal timeline are the timings as they appear on the original recording, given with the unit as seconds.
- Pitches are transcribed as nodes on the staves, which are also the initial points of their real-time durations, with the tip of the arrowhead their real-time endpoints.
- Black, vertical, dashed lines show those cymbal hits taken to be "on the beat", where the beat is an eighth note, as shown in Schuller's score. (This is, of course, not the beat as given by cut common time, but the beat given where the tempo is interpreted as very fast, with the beat as an eighth-note, as in our analysis above.) Vertical lines that are not dashed show cymbal-hit beats where the nature of the recording – in particular, the number of coincident sounds – made it nearly impossible (for this transcriber) to determine aurally the position of the cymbal with respect to the timeline.
- The circled pitches show those pitches that coincide with the first beat of a bar in Schuller's score, with the numbers above indicating which bar that is.

- The numbers below the triangular, upwards-pointing arrowheads at the bottom of the score show the bar number as implied by the drums; if the vertical lines show eighth-notes, eight eighth-notes add up to the metrical duration, as Schuller proposes, and thus a new bar starts.
- The positions of the triangular arrowheads are adjusted to coincide with the initial note of the melody as heard on the recording. Smaller arrowheads show the second beat of the bar, as implied by the drums.
- The asterisks on the vertical cymbal lines show a Schullerian bar made up of eight cymbal eighth-notes if the adjustment just mentioned is not made. It thus shows the temporal "drift" with respect to the drummer's realisation of Schuller's metrical duration.

In effect, the relation between a large triangular arrowhead and a circle with the same value shows the extent to which the performance coincides with Schuller's analysis – at least with respect to the first beat of each bar. Vertical lines joining triangular arrowheads to circles show coincidence, whilst lines that are not vertical show non-coincidence with respect to Schuller's analysis. Where corresponding lines in the first and second performances of the melody appear as (roughly) parallel, this shows (close to) the same relative position with respect to Schullerian time – where parallel lines are not vertical, this shows that they are "out by (close to) the same amount".

"Lonely Woman" – phrase 1

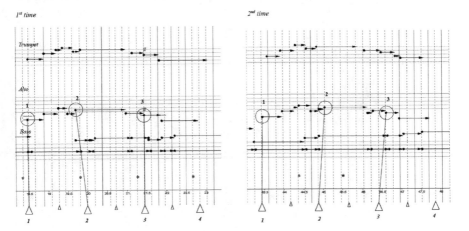

Figure 6.3.1

"Lonely Woman" – phrase 2

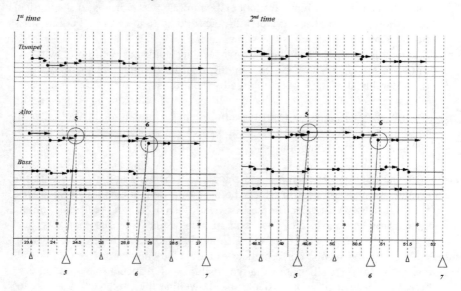

Figure 6.3.2

"Lonely Woman" – phrase 3a and 3b

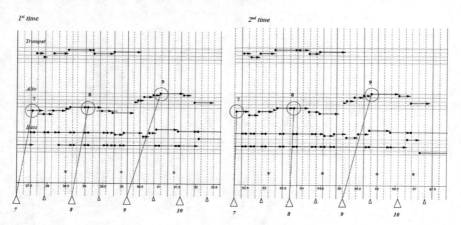

Figure 6.3.3

"Lonely Woman" – phrase 4

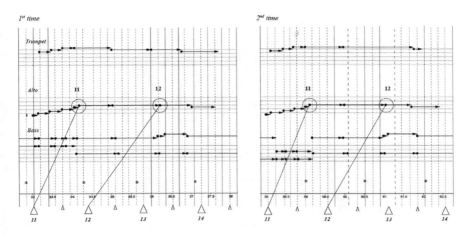

Figure 6.3.4

"Lonely Woman" – phrase 5

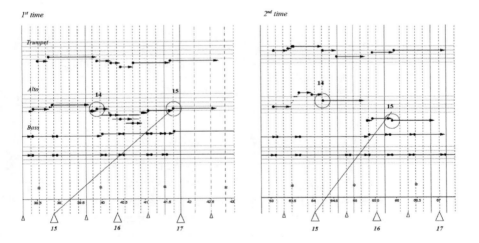

Figure 6.3.5

Analysis of transcription

Looking first at the relationship between the large triangular arrowheads and encircled pitches, it is possible to see that points of near-coincidence do occur; disregarding the coincidences at $1^{\triangle}$ (produced artificially by the author, as explained

90 Lonely Woman (no relation)

above), and using a somewhat generous notion of "proximity", there are near-coincidences at 3^Δ (1st time), as well as at 5^Δ and 6^Δ (both times) and 7^Δ and 8^Δ (2nd time). However, it is also possible to see that not only are the proximities at 7^Δ and 8^Δ (2nd time) not matched by corresponding proximities at 7^Δ and 8^Δ (1st time), but there are many other points of divergence at 9^Δ (both times), with progressively greater divergences through 11^Δ and 12^Δ to 15^Δ (both times), as reflected by the progressively slanted lines joining the first beat of the drum bar (marked by arrowheads) to the first beat of Schuller's bar (marked by circled pitches). By simply paying attention to these lines, it is thus already clear that there is something significantly amiss with Schuller's transcription, the direction to play "very freely" notwithstanding. But what is the precise nature of the problem? If Schuller's analysis entails a number of assumptions about the nature of the (temporal) space, the metre internal to that space, the specific durations chosen to represent note lengths, as well as the positions given to these durations in the measures that realise the metrical chains, at which level is the problem with Schuller's analysis to be situated? Where does he go wrong?

Let us, at least for a moment, persist with the assumption, as implied by Schuller's transcription, that the durations played by the melody instruments, on the one hand, and the durations played by the drums, on the other, belong to the same space – the duration space in the appendix. If we are to account for the dislocations we have discussed in terms of this assumption, a number of possibilities present themselves.

1) A first possibility, which we will disregard immediately, is that Schuller's temporal conception, as expressed in his transcription, is the right one, but that Ornette's group simply failed to realise it correctly. Whilst starting well, producing the near-coincidences mentioned above, after a while, the temporal relations became too difficult to maintain, and the different temporal strands began to dis-align.

2) A second possibility is that the metre Schuller has identified – *alla breve* – is correct, but the way Schuller has aligned the melody with the resulting bar space is not. Here, even the specific durations Schuller has chosen for the melody may broadly be correct, with adjustments to be made merely at the level of those notes heard on the first beat of the bar, and so on. This possibility would be given particular force if we were to discover a coincidence between the alignments of the first and second times – if, in other words, they were found to be "in or out by (close to) the same amount". Whilst such coincidences or near-coincidences can be found – a case for these could be made up until 6^Δ – at 7^Δ things begin to drift again, reaching a pronounced dis-alignment of (dis) alignments at 15^Δ. However, even if we were to discover a particular alignment of dis-alignments – if, in other words, the first and second times were found to be "out by the same amount" – this would not *necessarily* prove the thesis represented by our second possibility. For instance, the superimposition

of two temporal conceptions consistent *internal to themselves* with respect to tempo, duration and so on, regardless of how such features were constituted, would, quite contingently, produce a consistency of alignments *between* these temporalities, with no necessary implication that this consistency was the product of a shared space.[12]

3) A third possibility is that, whilst all of the durations heard are from the same duration space, the metre is incorrect, such that the grouping of durations produced by the bar realisations of this metrical chain results in the misalignments we have discussed. The single durations "go into" a single metrical duration, but not the one Schuller has identified. Again, such a possibility would be given force if we were to discover a consistency between the alignments of the first and second time, indicating that, whilst dis-alignments exist with respect to Schuller's score, there exists, nonetheless, another metrical concept of which this consistency is evidence.

4) A fourth possibility would be that, whilst we retain the unity of a shared duration space, everything else about Schuller's transcription is incorrect – the specific durations he has chosen, the metrical durations which contain them, the way these durations align with the bar coordinates, are all wrong, such that we are obliged to start again, rediscovering the specific elements that constitute the temporal relations characterising the temporal space of the piece. However, here there is a fear, which, in fact, haunts all of our possibilities, that the "search" for new metrical limits, for instance, *is in danger of producing its object*, that our attempts to simply "observe" some, for instance, metrical divisions in fact imposes these divisions on the music, such that they are then experienced as an immanent property of the music itself.

Given these reservations, produced not just by the dis-alignments between score and performance, but also the dis-alignment between alignments internal to the performance itself, it becomes very difficult to support the "quotient" interpretation related to our analysis of "Cherokee" that we have here been pursuing in relation to the temporality of "Lonely Woman". And, in fact, if we turn to Ornette's discourse about his music, we find many allusions to time and temporality, and many references to metre and rhythm that call such a relation into question, implying new ways to listen to the time of Ornette's music, and "Lonely Woman" in particular, as well as new ways with respect to the problem of "tension" we have been discussing, to be found, Ornette says, at the heart of conflicts in love.

A natural, freer time

In his interview with Gunther Schuller from 1960, to which we have now referred many times, the conversation turned to the question of time, and, in particular, to the question of the disposition of phrases with respect to beats and bars. "In other words", says Schuller, attempting to draw the different strands of Ornette's

92 Lonely Woman (no relation)

argument together, "the superimposition of a mathematical scheme over something [...], over music, is very foreign to you". "Yes, it is", Ornette replies, before calling into question the mathematical distinction between different forms of metre:

> In fact I can't really conceive how all times can be played in different accents when mathematically you could figure out all of them as being the same thing. If, you know, if you take 4/4 time and you break it up to 2/4 [...] you can make all of the times come out mathematically the same thing. So that really takes you back to – none of them are really different, if you're going to do it mathematically.[13]

Spread rhythm

Ornette developed these ideas in another interview with the critic, Nat Hentoff, calling into question the very notion that his music could be "timed", that the durations that constitute it can be subject to some kind of temporal *measure*. "My music doesn't have any real time", he says, "no metric time". "It has time, but not in the sense that you can time it".[14] If "metric time" implies the measure that pertains to a musical *metre*, the time that pertains to Ornette's music, he says, is "a natural, freer time", a time "more like breathing". "People have forgotten", he says, "how beautiful it is to be natural".[15] In this same interview, Ornette proposed a new temporal concept, which he calls "spread rhythm", and which, perhaps, better characterises his music. "I like spread rhythm", says Ornette, "rhythm that has a lot of freedom in it" – a rhythm he opposes to "the more conventional netted rhythm". "With spread rhythm", he says, "you might tap your feet a while, then stop. Then later start tapping again". "Otherwise", he says, "you tap your feet so much, you forget what you hear. You just hear the rhythm".[16]

Netted rhythm

Let us first conceive *netted rhythm* as the space of a rhythm caught in the net cast by a tapping foot. As with the realisation of a metrical chain, we can conceive of the net cast by a tapping foot as a continued analogy, in Hamilton's sense,[17] the repeated transference (t) of a relation-duration, a, such that the endpoint of a coincides with the initial point of its immediate repetition, b, and without any *necessary* implication of a longer metrical duration, and thus of metre (Figure 6.4).

In his interview with Schuller, Ornette linked this tapping foot – "patting your feet" – to *ideas*. "When you're patting your feet sometimes", he says, "the quarters [...] don't sound like quarters any more, and in fact they just sound like what you hear it as being [...] it takes on, like, an idea, more than just what it is".[18] Given this relation between a tapping foot and ideas, which we could conceive in the terms

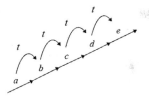

Figure 6.4

offered in Chapter 5, let us say that a rhythm is caught in the net cast by a tapping foot insofar as the durations that constitute the rhythms are experienced as being with respect to – situated by – the net duration. If the net duration is a duration from the duration space in the appendix, these situation effects can be given as the inverse form[19] of the quotient that relates each duration to the net duration – as, in other words, Ornettian *Ideas*. With the net duration as a quarter note, an eighth-note, half-note and whole-note are caught in the net cast by the foot tapping quarter notes insofar as each is experienced as situated with respect to that tapping, where ♪, 𝅗𝅥 and 𝅝 carry ½, 2 and 4 Ideas respectively, indicating that they are half, twice and four times the duration of the net duration (♩).

Figure 6.5 shows the melody to "The Sphinx"[20] caught (from point *x*) in the net cast by a tapping foot, with the net shown by the vertical, dashed lines, which mark the initial and end points of the net duration realised as a continued analogy. Vertical, dashed lines, in other words, represent "beats" (some of which are unmarked on this score, due to the absence of manifesting pitches). At *y*, the foot stops tapping. The durations represented in this transcription are "real" durations (durations calculated using clock time and represented as spatial extension), not quarter notes, eighth notes, and so on, though a tapping foot may imply a beat conceived in these terms. At *z*, the foot starts tapping again.

So, if *netted rhythm* allows us to account for the time of a tapping foot, and if the net cast by a tapping foot can be conceived in terms of a (repeated) duration from our duration space, with rhythms "caught in the net" insofar as they relate themselves to the net duration, thus carrying durational Ideas, in what space are rhythms caught when the tapping stops? What time orients them in the interval between the time of tapping, telling them *when* they are, in what kind of temporal space they are oriented, and to which point of that space?

Breathing in space

In his interview with Schuller, Ornette suggested the presence of another "measure", one, in fact, already alluded to in his interview with Hentoff, that allies durations to the coordinates of breath, in what appears to be the most straightforward of relations: if there is no more breath, there is no more passage, such that the endpoint of a passage is coordinated with, takes as its coordinate, the endpoint of

94 Lonely Woman (no relation)

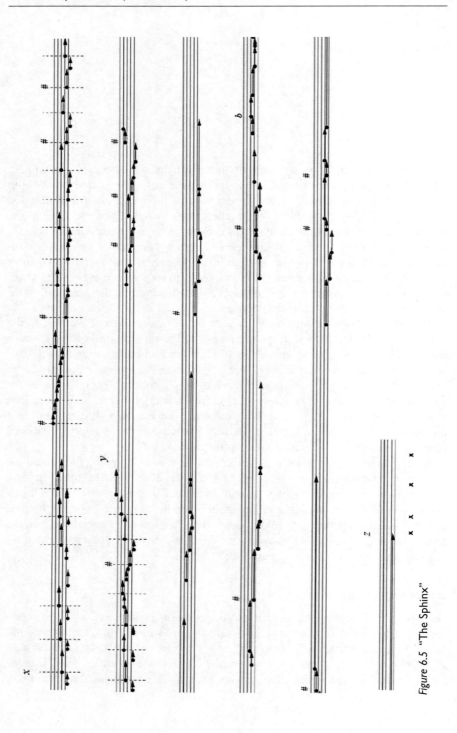

Figure 6.5 "The Sphinx"

an expiration, with indifference to the disposition of the phrase with respect to the coordinates of metre – of beats and bars and the boundaries they imply.

> I don't concentrate on mathematical things to express musical things. I just do it from the point of view of breathing in space [...] When I play a passage, when the breath leaves the passage, there's no more passage. But I don't think about in the sixth beat of the bar that I've got to start breathing here to do it, you know.[21]

So, if we take these two conceptions together – *netted rhythm* – the space of a rhythm caught in the net cast by a tapping foot – and *breathing in space* – phrases coordinated with respect to the boundaries, the endpoints, of breath, then we have a way to conceive of the alternating space of *spread rhythm* – first a space of the tapping foot, then the space of breath, then the space of a tapping foot again, the ordered movement from one to the other, each following the other in a temporal sequence.

However, if *spread rhythm* is conceived in terms of such an alternation, as the space of a tapping foot immediately followed by the space of a respiratory measure, and vice versa, it could also offer a new way to hear the temporal aspect of "Lonely Woman", not as an *alternation* of spaces, not the spaces each "next" with respect to the other, but as these two spaces *superimposed* – "next to" with respect to one another "vertically", rather than "horizontally", two different times, two different kinds of temporal space, in other words, *at the same time*. Now the "tension" between the time of the drums and the time of the melody is not a tension internal to the same space, not a tension that can be expressed by means of a relation (such as $q4$), relating two points internal to the same space, but as the tension, the disjunction, *between two entirely different spaces* – the space of a tapping foot (the drums), on the one hand, and the space of a respiratory measure (the melody instruments), on the other.

Hasn't any relation

During his interview with Ornette, Schuller turned the conversation to the question of what he called "continuity", of how to listen to the continuity of Ornette's music. If some listeners persisted with the attempt to relate the ideas in Ornette's improvisation to the composed theme – an attempt that at times produced a feeling of frustration, of failure – Schuller proposed a new way of listening, a new way of relating, in which the listener related each new idea not to the "expositional idea" (the composed theme), but to its immediate consequent, or rather, to its immediate antecedent. "I know that the way that I listen to your music, Ornette", he said, "is to take each incident, each note, each little idea, group of notes, by itself and relate it to what follows. Or rather, relate the new idea to the one just previous to it".[22] "I notice sometimes, for instance", he said,

96　Lonely Woman (no relation)

you'll do a phrase and you'll end on a certain note, and instinctively your next phrase, which may be an entirely different shape and may be louder or softer, it may be entirely different, but it may start with that same note. [...] There's always some kind of relationship. And it never is the same. Sometimes it's the note [...], sometimes it's the loudness or the tone maybe, but there's some kind of relationship.[23]

"There's always some kind of relationship. And it never is the same". This elegant theory, with its attention to local relations rather than the relation to an expositional theme, was, of course, a significant development of the ideas Schuller had proposed in relation to the "thematic improvisation" of Sonny Rollins, in which, unlike the harmonic orientation of "chorus improvisation", the thematic material constitutes a kind of constant "ideational thread",[24] a "fountainhead" "from which issues most of what is to follow".[25] However, in his attempt to find new ways to listen to Ornette's music, retrieving relations where it was assumed that there were none, implying a failure, a falling short, at the level of what constituted the unity of theme and improvisation, Schuller had, in fact, *himself* fallen prey to a failure of listening, had himself failed to listen, a failure that betrayed, perhaps, a desire *not* to hear, a desire not to have something Ornette had only just said to him – something about relations in his music – drawn to his attention. In these words of Ornette's, there is no failure to produce an expected relation, nor is there a relation to be discovered where it had been assumed there was none, but, rather, there is the attempt, the *deliberate effort*, to play *the absence of a relation*, to play a *no relation*, an idea that *"hasn't any relation"* to the next idea, though, musically, there is a drawing together:

I try to play an idea that hasn't any relation to the next idea but musically they come together.[26]

Of course, in Schuller's elegant theory of Ornettian relations, to "have a relation" means to have a "quality", a "property" *in common* – "relation" thus implies an "internal" point of intersection between one idea and the next. However, the notion of "relation" is, of course, much broader than this, going well beyond the idea of "something in common". In terms of the duration space in the appendix, two points "have a relation" (as represented by the presence of a quotient vector connecting them) if it is possible to multiply one of these durations by a positive integer (an integer quotient) in order to produce the other duration. Thus, ♩, a "quarter note", and 𝅗𝅥, a "half note", "have a relation", insofar as it is possible to multiply ♩ by a positive integer – 2 – to produce 𝅗𝅥, a "half note". ♩, a "quarter note", and ♩., a "three-eighths note", in this sense, "haven't any relation", insofar as ♩. is produced by multiplying ♩ by something other than a positive integer. In this precise sense, it would thus be possible to determine a distinction between a "hasn't any relation" *internal* to a space, and a "hasn't any relation" between a point internal to a space and one *external* to it – now "hasn't any relation" implies both an interior "no relation", as well as a "no relation" implied by the crossing of a boundary between inside and outside, between a point experienced as interior to a space, and one experienced as exterior, and even in another space altogether.

As such, it is possible to see that "hasn't any relation" is directly related to the question of "tension" we have been discussing. "Tension", as we have seen, implies first, a "difference", a *relation*, indicating that the durations *are* related but are not the same duration (as represented by an integer quotient other than 1); second, the absence of such a relation *internal* to the space (the absence of an integer quotient, but the implication of a non-integer quotient); and third, the absence of any such relation relating the points of that space to points *external* to that space, between points, in other words, of two entirely different spaces. The temporal ideas that constitute the "two times" of "Lonely Woman" which we have conceived in terms of *spread rhythm* – the time of the tapping foot "next to" the time of a respiratory measure – are in "tension", in this third sense, as two spaces constituted in entirely different ways and between the points of which there *isn't any relation*; the points of *netted time* haven't any relation to the points of a respiratory measure – the relations these spaces imply are entirely different, bearing no relation to one another. In this sense, "hasn't any relation" *is* the tension that Ornette sees in all love conflicts, where "hasn't any relation" implies the absence of a relation between the points of two distinct spaces, two distinct times, the time of rhythms caught in the net of a tapping foot, on the one hand, and the time of breath, on the other.

Of course, the signifier, "next", which describes the being of an idea with respect to another idea to which it apparently hasn't any relation, *already implies a relation* – a relation of *order*, in which what comes "next" with respect to some point, x, is the point, y, *immediately consequent* with respect to x at the level of that order. With the idea of "next", or "next to", to include not only points immediately consequent with respect to a point but also points *coincident* with respect to another point ("next to" in terms of a "vertical" "spatiality"), as in the case of "Lonely Woman", then two ideas which haven't any relation to one another already "come together" at this minimal level, are already related at the level of their being "next to", coincident with respect to one another in the temporal order that contains them both. In this sense, the two temporal ideas that constitute "Lonely Woman" – the space of a tapping foot, the space of a respiratory measure – although they *haven't any relation* to one another, although they are entirely distinct spaces constituted in entirely distinct ways, this temporal overlap, this "happening at the same time", produces a vast set of coincidences, a vast set of relations of temporal proximity, as the points of the two different spaces come together, touching one another at points of contingent temporal intersection. These purely *coincidental* relations invite other relations, of course, other points of contact; they constitute the pretext for the points of one space, for instance, to be drawn contingently into the space of the other, such that, for a moment, the melody finds itself caught in the net of the tapping foot, before disentangling itself, slipping through. Or, perhaps, the points of the space of the tapping foot find themselves, for a moment, drawn into the long

98 Lonely Woman (no relation)

durations of the space of a breath, its extended exhalations, which know nothing of the mathematics of the foot and its tapping.

So, if, in our discussion so far, the notion of *relation* has offered us the means to deal with *going*, with "going somewhere", insofar as the relation as "vector" constitutes the *vehicle*, the *means of movement*, of going, producing a "where to go" as its endpoint, what are the consequences for this movement if the relation, the means of movement, is missing? What will tell us "where to go" in the absence of a relation, in a space of *no relation*?

What does it mean to follow?

Of course, if *netted rhythm* is conceived in terms of a continued analogy, in Hamilton's sense, then all of the imperative effects, the "effects of direction", that pertain to the transference of free relations pertain here, for whenever the endpoint of the net duration falls, the next endpoint will simply be that point "plus" that duration, to recall a term from Hamilton's arithmetic. As with a *free vector*, when or where the relation "goes" *first* is not determined, but as soon as it is positioned, as soon as it is realised by some temporal point, the position of all future points follows as a necessary consequence of this initial choice; they are all, after this moment of initial contingency, "given in advance". With *breathing in space*, on the other hand, breath indicates the intervention of an entirely different temporal measure; now "where", or, rather, "when", a point is to "go" is an effect of the contingencies of breath, the durations of which are *transferred to the phrase*, such that the duration of the phrase now emerges as an effect of this transference, as the manifestation of this more "natural, freer time".

If the time that pertains to "Lonely Woman" is, however, the time of *spread rhythm*, in which there is an alternation between these two entirely different forms of time, constituted in entirely different ways and now superimposed, to "go where I go" is to go from a temporality, *X*, to a temporality, *Y*, *with which temporality X "hasn't any relation"*, with which it is in a kind of fundamental "tension" – to which it is "related", we could say, by a kind of *no relation*. Insofar as this alternation of non-related temporalities can be related to the tension we have been discussing – the tension that Ornette has said he sees in all love conflicts – to "go where I go" thus means to go somewhere – to some temporality – *such that this going, this movement, manifests this tension*, such that the non-relation of times from and to which I go manifests the "no relation" at the heart of the conflicts of love. In this sense, to follow – to go where I go – means to go *such that this "no relation" at the heart of love is "transposed"* – transferred – *from the field of love to the field of music*, such that music becomes the means by which the *no relation* of love manifests itself, by which it is expressed. There is a tension at the heart of conflicts in love that it is the work of music to express – a tension we can hear in the temporality of "Lonely Woman", but perhaps not only there. For *spread rhythm* would be a means to hear many of Ornette's pieces – the relation between the fragments that constitute "The Sphinx", as we have seen, but also the temporality of pieces such as "Congeniality" in which the alternating character of spread rhythm can be heard in the shift from one fragment to the next.

So, if thus far we have dealt with *tonic relations*, implying points of (external) convergence, *free relations*, implying points of (internal) convergence, where those points are *relations*, *solitude relations*, produced by means of a plenitude cured by lack, by the lack of a relation, and, just now, *non-relations*, the non-relation produced between points that "haven't any relation", we now turn to our final relation, so important in Ornette's universe, a relation that bears on the very question of unity, of what draws points together – *unison relations*.

Notes

1 Coleman, "A Question of Scale", 22.
2 Coleman, interview by Schuller: 23:53–23:59.
3 Coleman, interview by Schuller: 24:07–24:35.
4 Noble, "Cherokee", October 11, 1938: 0.09–0.18.
5 Parker, "Cherokee", track 12, *Bird in Time, Vol. 1*.
6 Where "q" stands for "quotient", as it is produced "analytically" (in Hamilton's terms) by dividing the consequent duration by the antecedent duration.
7 In the case of 4/4, this might account for why beat three is "stronger" than beats two and four.
8 It is important to note that metres in which, for instance, the beat was experienced as uneven (say long-short) would not appear as a chain in the duration space in the appendix – but one reason we are not proposing here a new theory of musical metre. For such theories of metre, see Hasty, *Metre as Rhythm* and, more recently, Just, *Organized Time*.
9 This is correlative to what Hasty calls "projection". See Hasty, *Metre as Rhythm* and Just, *Organized Time*.
10 Schuller, *A Collection of the Compositions of Ornette Coleman*, 17–19.
11 These two "tensions" might be seen as part of a wider distinction internal to the space between identity quotients ($q1$), non-identity integer quotients, non-integer quotients, and so on.
12 This is one reason to be sceptical about the sequence of mathematical relations uncovered in the analysis of "Lonely Woman" by Vickery and James – 14:5, 11:4, 41:15 and so on. See Vickery and James, *The Enduring Temporal Mystery*.
13 Coleman, interview by Schuller: 16.16–16.43.
14 Coleman, liner notes, *Croydon Concert*.
15 Liner notes, *Croydon Concert*.
16 Liner notes, *Croydon Concert*.
17 See Chapter 4.
18 Coleman, interview by Schuller: 23:25–23:29. In fact, there is some equivocation in Ornette's explanation, between the "sound" or "idea" a duration acquires when a performer pats their foot, on the one hand, and how a duration is *actually played*, on the other. Ornette begins with a reference to "sound": "when I tried patting my feet, I found out that it got a different sound, what I played". However, this immediately shifts, such that a patting foot will cause a performer to *actually play* notes longer or shorter: "if you're playing quarter notes for two bars [...] if you don't pat your feet you'll play those quarter notes like detached in some way that you know you're playing all quarters". However, there is then a reference to the sound of "ideas" distinct from the sound of what is actually played, from "what's there": "when you're patting your

feet sometimes the quarters, it don't sound like quarters any more, and in fact they just sound like what you hear it as being, you know, like it takes on like an idea, more than just what it is. Like it is this thing about music where that you can take anything that you've heard and if you know how to blend it with your own emotion and intelligence it can become an idea to you [...] more than just what's there". 22:36–23:45.

19 "Inverse" in terms of vectors (differences produced by Hamiltonian subtraction) means the opposing direction, as indicated by the signs for positive (+) and negative (−) when attached to a vectoral distance. "Inverse" in terms of *quotients* means the relation between *reciprocals* – i.e. the distinction between, for instance, 2/1 and ½.

20 Coleman, "The Sphinx", *Something Else!!!!*.

21 Coleman, interview by Schuller: 15:26–15:48.

22 Coleman, interview by Schuller: 32.32–33.26.

23 Coleman, interview by Schuller: 33:43–34.17.

24 Schuller, "Sonny Rollins and Thematic Improvising", 241.

25 Thematic Improvising", 243. Schuller's theory is a precursor to the approach Jost develops in *Free Jazz*, though Jost does not mention Schuller in his text.

26 Coleman, interview by Schuller: 33:37–33:43.

Chapter 7

Skies of America

The sensation of unison

"The Harmolodic Theory", the theoretical text Ornette promised in the liner notes to *Skies of America*, has never appeared, at least not yet, though in 1983 he would publish an article for *DownBeat*, entitled, "Prime Time for Harmolodics"[1] – a title that played on *Prime Time*, the name' he had given to his band of that time, as well as on, perhaps, "Prime Design", the title of the text published in 1960 by Buckminster Fuller, the man whom Ornette would once call his "main hero".[2] At the start of this difficult and, at times, enigmatic text, Ornette presents directly from Hermann Helmholtz's opus on tone and its sensations, first published in 1863 and translated into English as *On the Sensations of Tone*, the first sentence from the first chapter of the first part of Helmholtz's work, dealing with the composition of vibrations and their relation to tone and its qualities:

> Sensations result from the action of an external stimulus on the sensitive apparatus of our nerves.[3]

However, if Helmholtz's account had given priority to *sensation*, "in my musical concept", says Ornette, "not only the sensations of tone to the nerves is released, but the very reason for the use of tone", which is, he says, "the logic of ideas put into a single or collective unison".[4] This shift, from sensation to reason, from the sensation of tone to the reason for that sensation, which has to do with the "logic of ideas" put into some kind of relation, to which he gives the name "unison", then becomes the basis for a definition of "harmolodics", the signifier Ornette has used to name his approach. "Harmolodics", says Ornette, is:

> the use of the physical and mental of one's own logic made into an expression of sound to bring about the musical sensation of unison.[5]

And the word "unison", refers, he says, to "the sound of one's own voice".[6]

What to make of these enigmatic statements? What is the "sensation" to which Ornette refers – the "sensation of unison" – and what does it have to do with the

DOI: 10.4324/9781003412304-7

102 Skies of America

Helmholtzian "sensation of tone" on which it seems to depend? And, if the "sensation of unison" is brought about by a logic that is "one's own" when the physical and mental of which are made into an expression of sound, what is this "logic", and, insofar as it is related to a "logic of ideas", what does it have to do with the Ornettian Idea we have already encountered? And what does unison have to do with the voice, with a voice that is one's own? In what sense, in other words, is the "sensation of unison" the sensation of *the sound of one's own voice*?

In April 1972, together with the conductor, David Measham, and the London Symphony Orchestra, Ornette recorded *Skies of America*, a piece originally written for orchestra and the members of his own group. However, due to union restrictions regarding the employment of foreign musicians, only Ornette and the London Symphony Orchestra would appear on this recording, together with an unknown drummer, a situation Ornette would later describe in terms of a law regarding the mixing of classical music and jazz.

> when I was in London, I couldn't use Prime Time because it was against the law to mix classical music and jazz. They wouldn't let me do it. That's how I wrote it. So all I did was record the unison themes.[7]

"All I did", says Ornette of his difficult time with the London Symphony Orchestra, "is record the unison themes", themes characterised by the particular form of relation to which Ornette refers in his essay on harmolodic theory, and which he calls "unison" – a relation of *one-sound*, of a sound that is "one", "the same".

Hamiltonian unison

In terms of Hamiltonian analysis, a musical unison is, of course, a zero vector – the difference produced when some pitch is analysed (by means of subtraction) with respect to itself (and sometimes also when this difference is *12*, or some multiple of *12*, so as to produce, as a consequence of octave equivalence, "octave unisons", "double-octave unisons", and so on). Insofar as musical unisons also imply temporal coincidence – temporal "unison" – two points are "in unison" when the analysis of the temporal position of one point with respect to another point also produces a zero relation. In terms of a relation more broadly, such a "unison" implies a simple form of equivalence relation – a relation that is reflexive, symmetric and transitive.[8] However, if we look at our transcription of the opening of *Skies of America* (Figure 7.1) whilst the melodies appear in *temporal* unison – in a form of "homophonic" coincidence – they precisely do *not* appear in unison in terms of pitch, rather constituting a searing harmonic *disunison*, as distinct pitches form rich, dissonant chords. Not counting octave repetitions, the first harmonic simultaneity contains five distinct pitch classes – G, F, Db, C, Ab, Bb (marked x in Figure 7.1).

So, if the identity, the being one, the same, at the level of the "sound" that pertains to this theme is not to be situated at the level of the pitches that constitute them, such that the relation between them would be a difference of *0*, at what level

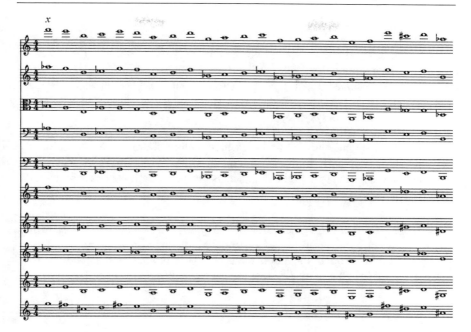

Figure 7.1 Skies of America – opening theme

is it to be situated? In what sense is there a "sound" that pertains to this theme that can be characterised as "one", as the same, equivalent, as an identity? In what sense, in other words, is this theme a "unison theme"? In an attempt to address these questions regarding "unison", questions that also have to do with sensation, with logic and with voice, we will turn to some of the contexts in which this signifier has appeared, moments in Ornette's discourse that may help us to shed light on this enigmatic term, so important in the Ornettian universe, and its relation, perhaps, to other, more conventional uses of the term. We will begin, however, with something Ornette has said regarding tuning, something that bears directly on the relation to Helmholtz and the notion of "unison" his work implies.

Sharp or flat in tune

In his famous text, Helmholtz had sought to connect the boundaries of two sciences that, although drawn together, he said, by many natural affinities, had hitherto remained distinct – the boundaries of physical and physiological acoustics, on the one hand, and of musical science and aesthetics, on the other.[9] For it was, he thought, precisely to the theory of the sensation of hearing, with its source in the phenomena of acoustics – the vibratory motions of elastic bodies and their laws, whether the motion of external objects or of the ear – that music was to look for the foundation of its structure.[10] The regular motions that produce musical tones had been exactly investigated by physicists, said Helmholtz. They are oscillations, vibrations or swings – up or down, or to and fro motions – of the sonorous body, and it is necessary that they should be regularly *periodic* – that, in other words, they should be a motion that "constantly returns to the same condition *after exactly equal intervals of time*".[11] The length of these equal intervals between one state of motion and its next exact repetition is to be called the length of the oscillation, vibration or swing, or the *period* of the motion.[12]

However, Ornette has described a realisation that bears directly on this relation between frequency and musical tone to which Helmholtz refers, a realisation, he says, that came very early in his development on the saxophone, and which calls into question the notion that a relation, such as the one Helmholtz describes, would need to be "exact".

> I realised you could play sharp or flat in tune. That came very early in my saxophone interest. I used to play one note all day and see how many different sounds I could get out of the mouthpiece. (I'm still looking for the magic mouthpiece) ... I'd hear so many different tones and sounds.[13]

Tuning neighbourhoods

Let us characterise this realisation – the realisation that you can "play sharp or flat in tune" – in terms of what might be called a "tuning neighbourhood". If, in a wider set of frequencies, F, there is a neighbourhood of frequencies, U_x, experienced as realising a given pitch, p, with a and b as its boundary points, there is a subset of frequencies of $U_x - U_{xi}$ – experienced as "in tune"; all frequencies contained in U_{xi}, in other words, are experienced as "in tune" realisations of a chosen pitch, p. The complement of U_{xi} in U_x is thus all those frequencies experienced as successful realisations of the chosen pitch, albeit "out of tune", and the complement of U_x in the wider frequency space, F, is all those frequencies *not* experienced as realisations of the chosen pitch, p.[14] These neighbourhoods are shown in Figure 7.2.

We can thus play "sharp and flat in tune", as Ornette suggests, insofar as the in-tune neighbourhood, U_{xi}, contains more than one point; we play "sharp in tune" by moving to the upper frequencies contained in that neighbourhood, and "flat in tune" by moving towards the lower frequencies of that neighbourhood (as shown

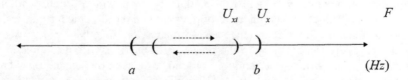

Figure 7.2

by the discontinuous arrows moving to the right and left in U_{xi}), with no implication of a central point constituting the "proper" tuning for that particular pitch.

If it is possible to play "sharp and flat in tune", as Ornette realised early in his interest in the saxophone, if it is possible to play "*one note* all day" with sharp and flat tunings, this implies that the identity of the musical tone, of a musical pitch, is *not* contingent on an identity at the level of the oscillations of a sonorous body, not contingent on the rate of those oscillations being "exactly the same", as Helmholtz suggests; rather, in other words, more than one frequency can be experienced as the "same note". Correlative to this, if unison implies identity at the level of pitch – that two pitches are the *same pitch* – to be expressed, perhaps, as a zero vector, Ornette's experiments with tuning reveal that this does not necessarily imply identity at the level of those frequencies experienced as realising those pitches. "Sharp and flat in tune", in other words, implies precisely that an effect of unison at the level of pitch does *not* rely on a "unison" at the level of frequencies that manifest those pitches; identity can appear in the midst of difference, unison in the midst of disunison, and vice versa.

Transference of a pitch name

So, if an effect of "one note" can be produced by frequencies that are other than one, if different frequencies can, in other words, produce an effect of unison, of a "one" at the level of the note these frequencies manifest, what do such frequencies have in common such that they share a unison, name, what do they have in common, in other words, such that they "are" both, for instance, "C"? The answer implied by our notion of "tuning neighbourhood" is that what two frequencies have in common so as to share a name, such as "C", *is their relation to that same tuning neighbourhood*; both f^1 and f^2 can share the name, "C", insofar as they are experienced as being *contained in*, as *interior points*[15] of, the tuning neighbourhood experienced as manifesting that pitch. The "common quality" apparently absent from their immanent properties is to be found instead on the side of their *relations*, on their being, that is, with respect to the boundary points, a and b, such that f^1 and f^2 are both greater than a and less than b.

The notation of unison

Let us now turn to an instance in which Ornette refers directly to the notion of "unison", an instance that has to do not with frequency and pitch but with what Ornette has elsewhere called an Idea. "If C and E is a major third", asks Ornette in his interview with Andy Hamilton for *The Wire* magazine, "and D and F is a minor third, which one is highest?" "C and E is the biggest interval", Hamilton answers tentatively, "but F is the highest note". "So you think the D is higher than the C and the E?", Ornette asks, before describing a notion of "sound" situated at the level of Idea, something that has to do with what he calls the "notation of unison":

So you think the D is higher than the C and the E? Only by name, not by sound. The reason why you say D and F [are higher] is that you're looking at F as being the 4th of C, but it's the minor 3rd of D. It's a minor 3rd, it's not a 4th. It has nothing to do with theory, it just has something to do with the notation of unison. There are lots of things in music like that.[16]

Higher by name

If the letter names C, E, D and F form part of the alphabetically ordered set of musical letter names (A, B, C, D, E, F, G), then D and F are "higher", insofar as C < D and E < F at the level of the order that pertains to the set. We could represent this by means of vectors in a space of letter names ordered alphabetically, as shown in Figure 7.3, in which the vector relating F to D appears "higher" in the space than the vector relating E to C; the D and F are higher than the C and E, as Ornette says, "by name".

Higher by sound

However, there is another order that pertains to the Ornettian Ideas these pitches "carry" – ma 3rd, mi 3rd and so on – that is not the order that pertains to the letter names. Ideas form their own order, which is the order that pertains to the numerical values used to represent them. In this order, ma 3rd follows mi 3rd and so on,

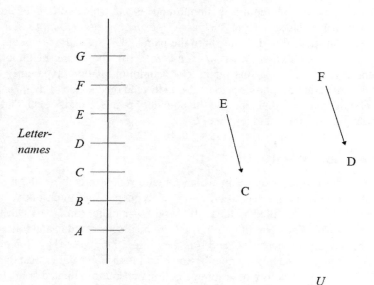

Figure 7.3

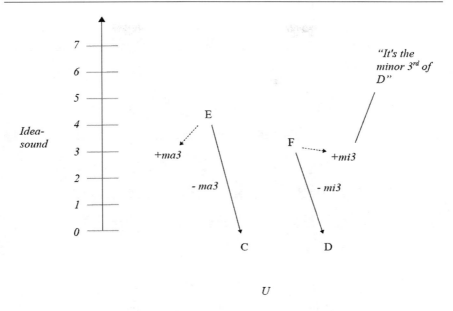

Figure 7.4

which can be represented as vectors in a space of numerically ordered Ornettian Ideas (expressed in Figure 7.4 as semitones). Now (E, C) is "higher than" (F, D) "by sound" – by Ornettian Idea-sound.

Conceiving the top line of the score to *Skies of America* as the manifestation of a tonic-oriented space, with C as tonic, for instance, this produces "4", "3", "7" and "1" as the Idea-sounds produced by the tonic relation this space implies, carried by the notes F, E, B, C. If, correlative to the parallel transference of the intervallic relations internal to the melody, we then transfer the tonic relation in parallel to the second line of the score, this, of course, produces the same four Idea-sounds, as carried by Ab, G, D, Eb and so on. Now the melodies are in "unison", insofar as the "son" that pertains to uni*son*, is the "son" of Idea-sound (Figure 7.5).

Transference of an Idea name

If "unison" here implies the unison of Ideas – that two distinct pitches carry the same Idea – and if the Idea is conceived in terms of something of the relation transferred to the point, as we proposed in Chapter 5, then a unison at the level of the Idea necessarily implies a unison at the level of the relation, that two points, A and B, are related to two other points, C and D respectively, by means of the same relation. As with the frequencies "sharp and flat in tune", what two pitches, p' and p'', have in common such that they share an Idea-name – for instance, "6th"– is thus, again, a relation – here their relation to a point of tonic orientation, their being "a

108 Skies of America

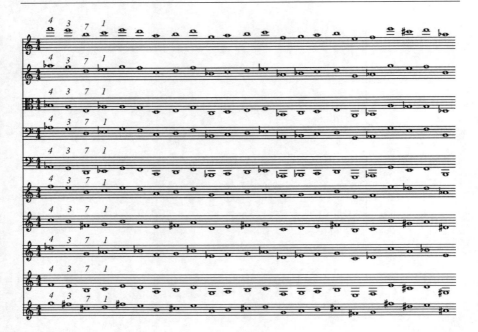

Figure 7.5

sixth up" from the pitch coordinated to the origin coordinate – a relation which is then transferred to the point as an Idea the point carries "in it".

A different unison for the same notes

The same four notes

In an interview with Bill Shoemaker for *Jazz Times* magazine, and echoing earlier statements he had made in the original sleeve notes to *Skies of* America, Ornette has also suggested that the harmolodic notion of unison has something to do with the system of clefs and, in particular, with the transferences produced by shifts at the level of clef relations. In this interview, he starts by referring to the notational marks that appear on the second space, the third line, the fourth line and the fourth space of a stave, read as the letter names, A, B, D and E, in the treble clef. (At points in the foregoing discussion, we will refer to the stave lines and spaces as numbered in ascending order, with the bottom line as 0, the first space as 1, the second line as 2, and so on, such that A, B, D and E in the treble clef appear as 3, 4, 6 and 7.)

In the treble clef, when you play A, B, D, and E, that A is C, the B is a C for alto, the D a C for the tenor, and the E is the C for the soprano. So, it's not really four

Figure 7.6

different notes, it's the same four notes. So, therefore it's deceiving to believe that the piano is the transposed clef for all voices. What it really does is uses those four words to make harmonies, keys, and chords. The treble clef does not have a pure voice.[17]

If A, B, D and E are not really four different notes but "the same four notes", this implies that the four notational marks to which the signifier-letters – "A", "B", "D" and "E" – are to be transferred as a consequence of a treble clef relation (Figure 7.6) – – are in fact to be related to four distinct clefs – bass, alto, tenor and soprano – so as to transfer the letter-signifier "C" to each of them. In Ornette's terms, "it's not really four different notes; it's the same four notes".

A different unison for the same notes

However, if we are to read apparent difference as identity – four different notes as "the same four notes" – this is because such an apparent difference is already the effect, the outcome, of an inverse, "transpositional" movement that goes not from difference to identity, but identity to difference, from the same note to (the appearance of) four different notes. "In harmolodics", says Ornette, "those four voices are transposed into one voice", producing "a different unison for the same notes".

> If I asked you to play soprano G natural on the piano, that's C natural for the treble clef. C natural for the soprano would be E. You can't hear those as voices, so you call them chords and keys. In harmolodics, those four voices are transposed into one voice. For instance, the A, B, D and E would be B, C, E and F on the alto clef, and G, A, C and D on the tenor clef. The same notes. So you have a different unison for the same notes.[18]

The "same four notes" (the same notational marks on lines/spaces 3, 4, 6, 7) "transposed" into the treble clef would appear as A, B, D and E; the "same four notes" transposed into the alto clef would appear as B, C, E and F; the "same four notes" transposed into the tenor clef would appear as G, A, C and D, and so on, yielding "a different unison for the same notes". In this sense, what appears as A, B, D and E is not really four notes but "the same four notes", "C", for bass, alto, tenor and soprano clefs, when the four notational marks, 3, 4, 6 and 7, representing "C" for each of these clefs, are "transposed into one voice", when they are read as marks internal to a single clef – the treble clef. Now "the same notes" (for four different clefs) appear as "four different notes" (for the same clef).

Although Ornette does not refer to *Skies of America* in his interview with Shoemaker, looking at the top line of our transcription of the opening theme to *Skies of America*, we see that the "different unisons" Ornette describes, produced as they are by these shifting clef relations, appear in a reduced form at the beginning of the melody. The "unison" produced by an alto clef relation – "B", "C", "E", "F" – appears first, in a reordered form, as "F", "E", "B", "C", marked as U in Figure 7.7. U is followed by V, the treble clef "unison" – "A", "B", "D", "E" – appearing reordered as "E", "D", "A", "B", which is then followed by W, the "D", "A" and "G" of the tenor "unison".

With these "unisons" not as "four different notes" but "the same four notes", the first four notes of the *Skies of America* theme are now "the same four notes", "D"; the second four notes, as Ornette describes, are "the same four notes", "C"; pitches 9–12, if we introduce a treble and soprano clef relation together, are now "the same four notes", "B", for the soprano, bass, alto and tenor clefs; and pitches 13–16 are all "the same four notes", "A", for these same clefs (Figure 7.8).

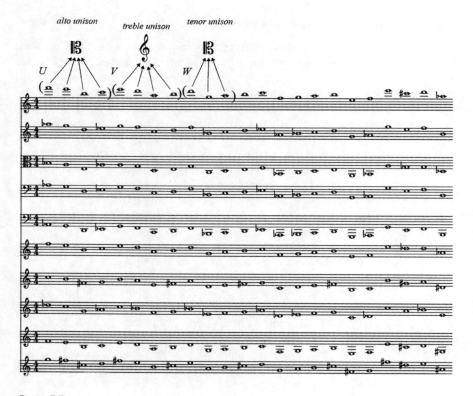

Figure 7.7

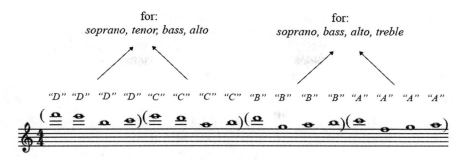

Figure 7.8

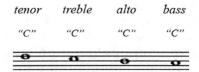

Figure 7.9

Writing these notes – "D", "C", "B", "A" – on a treble stave, they then appear as "the same four notes", "C", for the tenor, treble, alto and bass clefs (Figure 7.9).

However, if these notes are "not really four different notes" but "the same four notes", sharing the letter name, "C", what, if anything, do they have in common, such as to allow the "transference of a name", "C", from one to the other? What is the "quality in common" linking one to the other, so as to produce identity in the midst of apparent difference, the "same note" appearing as "four different notes"?

Transference of a letter name

The relation between the letter names of the musical alphabet is, in the sense we elaborated in Chapter 4, "free"; the letter name can, in a sense, "go" anywhere, but as soon as a single letter name is transferred from the orienting point of the clef to the line of the stave, the other letter names must be transferred in "parallel", so as to retain, that is, the relative proximities that pertain to the "musical alphabet". Thus, for instance, with the vectoral relation between the second space on the stave (3) and the third space on the stave (5) as +2, the vectoral relation between the two letter names to which 3 and 5 are mapped will also be +2. If 3 is mapped to "C", for instance, then 5 will be mapped to "E", the letter +2 – two steps up in letter space – from "C", and so on. In this sense, what all stave points have in common such that they share the name, C, *is this relation to all other points of the space*. All "Cs"

112 *Skies of America*

have in common, in other words, their being one step up (or some octave equivalent) with respect to the stave point mapped to "B", their being three steps down (or some octave equivalent) with respect to all points mapped to "F" and so on.

The harmolodic clef – 8

Harmolodic reading

At a lecture-demonstration given at Harvard in 1980 together with three other renowned Ornette collaborators, Charlie Haden, Dewey Redman and Billy Higgins, Don Cherry described something in which some of the ideas we have been discussing come together, something he called the "harmolodic clef", a clef of Ornette's own devising, written as a figure 8 – a sign with echoes, perhaps, of infinity.[19] "When Ornette writes a clef", says Cherry,

> he writes the treble clef, and then he writes the harmolodic clef, which is a figure 8, and then you have the bass clef. So that means that you could play ... look at the lines and spaces of the music and no matter what transposed instrument you play the melody [...] it will still come out the melody, and it will still be in harmony with the instrument you're transposing from.[20]

To read from the harmolodic clef thus means a number of different things. First, the musician, looking at the lines and spaces, introduces these lines and spaces into a relation with a clef, such that the alphabetical octave-letter names are transferred to these lines and spaces. Second, these octave-letter names are introduced into a relation to sounding pitch, insofar as the keys or strings or valves on a particular instrument are themselves mapped to the set of letter names. These two aspects of harmolodic reading produce a number of possible permutations, depending on whether different musicians are reading from the same clef, on the one hand, and whether they play an instrument with the same "transposition", on the other. Two instruments reading from the same clef may, of course, produce different sounding pitches as a consequence of this reading if they play instruments with a different transposition. And, inversely, two instruments reading from different clefs may produce the same sounding pitch as a consequence of a different transposition.

It doesn't change the sound you're making

Harmolodic reading thus produces (1) "parallel" relations in alphabetical letter space, as a consequence of the clef relation, and (2) "parallel" relations in a space of sounding pitch, as a consequence of the specific ways that these alphabetical letter names are mapped to sounding pitches for instruments with different "transpositions". It was beyond the skills of this transcriber to identify all of the different instruments in the orchestral texture playing the "unison theme" for the opening to *Skies of America*, but it is possible to see that transposing instruments reading from the same score without compensatory transposition will produce (at least some) of the parallel movement heard (see Figure 7.5). Where instruments with different transpositions read from the same clef, these parallelisms will be exact – the intervallic relations between pitches that constitute the melody will be exactly the same – but where instruments read from a different clef, they may not be. This is simply a consequence of the "unevenness" that pertains to the sounding pitches that correspond to the "musical alphabet"; a "step" in alphabetical letter space, in other words, may be either a half or whole step in pitch space (or even larger where accidentals are concerned). For instance, notational marks on the second space and third line will form an ascending tone in the treble clef and an ascending semitone in the alto clef. However, in an interview for the Guardian, Ornette suggested that such "unevenness" at the level of intervallic differences does not necessarily produce difference at the level of what he calls "sound". Two such intervals, in other words, can have the *same sound* – he gives the example of the notational marks, B and C, in the treble clef, as written on the third line and third space:

> B and C is a half-step right? But in the bass clef it's a whole step. That's crazy […] and it doesn't change the sound you're making.[21]

"B and C is a half step [+*1*]" (in the treble clef):

"But in the bass clef it's a whole step [+*2*]":

"and it doesn't change the sound you're making".

However, if the shift from the half-step between B and C in the treble clef to the whole step between D and E in the bass clef "doesn't change the sound you're making", if the points, B and C, have the same, unchanging "sound" as the entirely distinct points, D and E, to what does this signifier, "sound", refer? What is this one, unchanging "sound" if not the sound of the points, the pitches, that are changing, not one, not the same?

Transference of a sound name

Let us call this "sound" that both (B, C) and (D, E) share, "sound X"; what (B, C) and (D, E) share, such that the signifier, "sound X", can be transferred from one to the other, is the "step" they manifest. "Sound X" is the name of an intervallic step-sound, the sound of a step in pitch space, which does not change, even when the points that manifest this step change, and even when the step manifest in pitch space is +1 rather than +2, or +2 rather than +1. And, in fact, such a notion of "sound" was already implied by Ornette's allusion to the sound of Ideas, distinct from the pitches that carry those Ideas. If C – E is "higher" than D – E "by sound", it is because sound is to be conceived at the level of the Ideas these pitches carry, which make both C and D tonics – pitches that carry tonic Ideas and that are in Unison at the level of their Idea-sound.

Unison

What, then, do these coordinates we have discussed – "sharp or flat in tune", "the notation of unison", "a different unison for the same notes", the "harmolodic clef" – imply about the Ornettian notion of Unison? If "unison" is the mark of a relation between *sounds*, a mark of their being *one*, the same, an identity, as implied by the Hamiltonian equivalence, 0, which relates two pitches "in unison" one with respect to the other, what notion of Unison is implied here, to what relation relating what "sounds", such that they are experienced as being "one", as an identity, as the same, does Unison refer? What is Unison in Ornette's sense?

One-sound

The first thing to note is that the fragments from Ornette's discourse we have discussed imply a distinction between three different forms of *sound*, to which we could give the names *point-sound*, *relation-sound* and *Idea-sound*, to denote an experience of sound at the level of the *point*, as with the sound of a frequency, or of a pitch; an experience of sound at the level of the *relation*, as implied by the shift from C – B to E – D that "doesn't change the sound you're making"; and an experience of sound at the level of the Ornettian *Idea*, as implied by the E that is "higher than" F "by sound", insofar as this "sound" is the sound of the Ideas E and F, as Ornettian Intervals, "carry". Each of these notions of "sound" implies a distinct form of *unison*, of *one-sound*: (1) *one-point-sound* – as with the frequencies that are the same frequencies, or two pitches that are the same pitch; (2) *one-relation-sound* – as with the relation that doesn't change in the shift from B – C to D – E, or the relation that stays the same in spite of their different notational manifestation as 3 or 4 in stave space; and (3) *one-Idea-sound* – as with the "notation of unison", where unison implies that two pitches both carry the same idea.

From one-point-sound to one-relation-sound

In each of these fragments from Ornette's discourse, it is also possible to discern the shift, which we uncovered in the chapter on transposition and effect of invisibility, from points to relations, from an experience of identity, of equivalence, of being "one", the same, at the level of points, to an equivalence, an identity, being "one", at the level of the relations these points manifest, albeit, at times, in its "disavowed" form as the Ornettian Idea. In the case of "sharp or flat in tune", there is a shift from an experience of identity at the level of the frequencies – the assumption that an experience of identity at the level of the pitch must imply an identity at the level of the frequencies that manifest those pitches – to an identity at the level of the relations those frequencies manifest. What each frequency has in common such that they are experienced as being the same pitch is their *relation* – their being "in" – with respect to the same "tuning neighbourhood". In the case of the "notation of unison", there is a shift from an experience of identity at the level of pitch to an identity at the level of the Ideas these pitches "carry" – which is to say, a shift to an identity at the level of a *relation* to an external, orienting point, which is then transferred to the point as an Idea it is experienced as carrying "in" it, as we discussed in Chapter 5. And in the case of "a different unison for the same notes", there is a shift from an experience of identity at the level of the notational marks to an experience of identity at the level of the relations these marks manifest. Two marks, 3 and 4, in other words, can both "be" "C", insofar as they have in common their relation to all other points of the space – their being, for instance, one step down from the mark mapped to "D", or one step up from the mark mapped to "B", and so on.

If this is the case, if in each of these instances we have discovered a shift from an experience of identity, of being "one", the same, at the level of points, to an identity, a being "one", the same, at the level of the relations, and if both the points and the relations imply a different notion of *sound – point-sound, relation-sound* – then this would imply a shift at the level of the notion of *unison* itself – from a unison, an identity, an equivalence, a being "one sound", of points, to a Unison, a being "one sound", of relations. Now Unison replaces the mark for equivalence as the "one" relating the sound that pertains to a relation, that says of this relation, as manifest by points A and B, and this relation manifest by the points C and D, that they have the same sound – that they are "one", the same, an identity at the level of relation-sound, a relational *Unison*. In this sense, the opening theme of *Skies of America* is a "Unison theme" in a har-mo-lodic sense: first, insofar as a Unison relation relates the interval-relations manifest "horizontally" by each melodic line, and, second, insofar as, internal to each melodic line, Unison relations relate the "vertical" relations manifest by each point of that melody, and, on account of which, each note of the melody is the "same note", "C". Thus, whilst the first, "horizontal" or "melodic" sense is correlative to transposition, internal to each manifestation of these interval relations, what appears as difference – "four different notes" – is, in fact, identity – "the same four notes" – insofar as identity is contingent not on the

116 *Skies of America*

identity of points (which appear as the differences, the different notes that make up the melody) but on the identity at the level of the "vertical" relations they manifest.

One's own logic

So, if Ornettian Unison is to be situated on the side of the relation, as an equivalence, an identity of relations, what of the "logic" to which Ornette refers in "Prime Time for Harmolodics"? What of the "logic" that is "one's own" and that, when made into an "expression of sound", produces, brings about, as Ornette says, Unison as a "sensation"? What, in other words, is this logic that brings about a Unison that is not a unison of points but a Unison of relations?

Its own law

In fact, the notion of "logic" does appear elsewhere in Ornette's discourse, in the context of a discussion of exactly the shifting relation between names and sounds at the heart of harmolodic reading but produced instead by a misunderstanding regarding the naming of notes on the alto saxophone. In possession of his first instrument – a gold-plated Conn alto saxophone – but without a teacher, which he could not afford, and with only the aid of a book, Ornette set about teaching himself to play:

> I remember thinking, as the book said, the first seven letters of the alphabet were the first seven letters of music, ABCDEFG. But the standard concert scale is CDEFGAB. So I thought my C that I was playing on the saxophone was A, like that, right? Later on I found that it did exist thataway only because the E-flat alto, when you play C natural, it is [concert] A [transposed]. So I was right in one way and wrong in another – I mean, sound, I was right. Then I started analysing why it exists thataway, and to this very day I realize more and more that all things that are designed with a strict logic only apply against something: It is not the only way it's done. In other words, if you take an instrument and you happen to feel it a way you can express yourself, it becomes its own law.[22]

We could call the (mis)perception that the "C that I was playing on the saxophone was A" a first Ornettian "law", a first instance of a singularly Ornettian "logic", according to which the reader effects a harmolodic substitution, replacing "C" with "A", transferring the letter name, "A", to something to which the letter name, "C", has already been transferred. If such a transference implies the parallel transference of the rest of the space of letter names, it is possible to see that, in spite of the differences produced by means of Ornette's misunderstanding – the difference between "A" and "C" – such a misunderstanding will produce a Unison at the level of the intervallic relations, correlative to the Unisons produced by means of harmolodic reading. For instance, a melody written "A", "B", "D" and "E" will sound as (Eb alto) "C", "D", "F" and "G", as an effect of the logic of Ornette's misunderstanding, a misreading which nonetheless manifests an equivalent intervallic structure – $+1$, $+2$, $+1$ – when expressed as vectors in the letter space introduced earlier.

The sound of one's own voice

However, there is, of course, something else we have so far failed to address, something that surprised us on the pages of Ornette's defining text on "harmolodics", which has to do with the voice and its relation to Unison. Unison as "the sound of one's own voice", as a sound irreducible to Helmholtzian "sensation of tone", on the frequencies and combinations of frequencies on which it nonetheless seems to depend. What then does what we have discussed thus far have to do with the Ornettian "sensation of unison", with the sensation of the sound of one's own voice? In what sense is Ornettian Unison *voice*, and what does this voice have to do with the sensation that pertains to tone, in Helmholtz's sense?

I would know it was you

During his interview with Ornette for his radio show on WBAI, Gunther Schuller turned the conversation to the question of tone, and, in particular, of Ornette's tone, related as it was to the difficulties many had in listening to Ornette's music. "One hears specific comments about your tone", says Schuller, which a lot of people, he imagined, "associated with something other than what they're expecting to hear".[23] In fact, Ornette had his own association to relay: "I was talking to a neurologist and a psychologist the other night", he said, "and he was telling me that the tone I have with the music that I play was very associated with …"[24] – at which point Ornette's association is cut short. "Oh, your tone", interrupts Schuller, "your music is unthinkable without that tone, absolutely one thing".[25] "When I think of hearing the notes you play, played with a different tone, I may say, I can't even imagine it".[26] Ornette then relates this tone, this "one thing" without which his music would be unthinkable, to the voice:

"Just like the words that one speaks, regardless of if I was in – wherever I was, and I heard your voice, I would know it was you, you know. I would know that was you".[27]

The voice, like the tone, as a mark of identity, of a voice that is *one's own*, regardless of changes in space or time, the voice of one, of what stands for the one that I am.

The magic mouthpiece

In fact, the question of tone, connected as it is, as Ornette suggests, to the voice, has already emerged in the context of our discussion of tuning, in the context of the possibility of playing "sharp or flat in tune", "I realised you could play sharp or flat in tune", Ornette says, immediately shifting to the question of tone:

118   Skies of America

I used to play one note all day and see how many different sounds I could get out of the mouthpiece. (I'm still looking for the magic mouthpiece). I'd hear so many different tones and sounds.[28]

If there is a mouthpiece for which Ornette is still searching, however, its "magic" is not to produce a fixed tone, an identity at the level of the specific constellation of frequencies constituting a "tone" but to produce *difference*, a difference without assumed limit – "I used to play one note all day", says Ornette, and "see *how many different sounds* I could get out of the mouthpiece". Thus, in this conversation of tone, which Ornette links to the voice as a guarantor of knowledge regarding identity – as what would make it possible to *know it was you* – there emerges the desire for difference we encountered in our discussion of (a cure for) solitude, a desire for a difference that is *free*, not the desire for a specific difference, a difference as point, but difference as relation, for difference itself, regardless of which points manifest that difference. But how could it be that an effect of identity – the fact of being you and no other – can be produced by difference, by a tone – a voice – constituted by means of a *free difference*, by a relation indifferent to the identity of points, supposing instead an identity at the level of the relation, of difference itself, of what relates two points as "different"?

Phantom centre sound

In an interview with Richard Williams, Ornette spoke of the accusation his music had suffered from Bob Brookmeyer and others,[29] one closely related to complaints regarding his tone, that he was playing "out of tune". In this interview, Ornette relates the question to tuning temperament, introducing the notion of a "non-tempered psyche".[30] However, in the midst of this allusion to the history of tuning systems, something else emerges, a kind of constant, a still point in the storm of intonational difference, something to which the complaints about his music had turned a deaf ear. What had been heard as dis-alignment, as being "out" with respect to some expected alignment, was, in fact, "my emotions raising my tone to another level". In the midst of shifts at the level of frequency and tone, "I could still hear", Ornette says, "the centre of what I was reading".[31] But if one can play "sharp or flat in tune", implying a tuning neighbourhood, as we have described, containing multiple frequencies all of which are experienced as "in tune" manifestations of the same pitch, where is this centre Ornette is hearing to be found? For "sharp or flat in tune", as articulated by our "tuning neighbourhood", implies that *there is no centre*, there is no frequency that "is" the pitch; each frequency in that neighbourhood is, precisely, *equivalent* at the level of their *relations*, their being contained within the in-tune neighbourhood introduced earlier, and thus as manifestations of that pitch.

In Chapter 4, we discussed an effect of invisibility that conceals another "centre", a "tonal centre" that is "difficult to discover", which, like the "lost or hidden object", a hidden quality common to all objects that share a name, emerges as an effect of the shift from points to relations implied by both transposition and

Stewart's law – the shift, that is, from an experience of identity at the level of points to an experience of identity at the level of the relations these points manifest. This shift, from points to relations, we said, was correlative to a shift from a "bound" to a *free* space, from a space the identity of which is conceived in terms of its points to a space conceived in terms of the identity of its free relations. Such a space is *free*, in other words, insofar as its identity is *free of points*, with the experience of a concealed, "invisible" tonic end*point*, or of a lost or hidden object-quality, emerging as a kind of phantom in the space of freedom, the consequence of a misperception regarding the condition of an experience of identity such a space implies. In this sense, the shift from points to relations, from the identity conceived in terms of points to identity conceived in terms of relations, is always in danger of producing an effect of loss or hiddenness, the effect that the shift from points to relations hides, veils, the point in terms of which the identity of the space is properly to be conceived – the pitch that *is* the tonic, the frequency that *is* the pitch. If freedom implies *anywhere*, in other words, that the relation can "go" anywhere, be manifest by any points, so long as those points manifest that relation, the phantom centre implies a determinate *somewhere*, a determinate singular *one-where*, a singular, determinate point lost, made "invisible" by the shift from points to relations, binding to freedom, somewhere to anywhere.

The sound of one's own voice

In this sense, to our two notions of unison – the unison, the equivalence, the being one, of points, and the Unison, the equivalence, the being one, of relations – we could add a third form of unison, irreducible to either of them – the unison, the *one-sound* not of determinate points nor of the relations they manifest but the "sound" of a phantom "one" that emerges in the shift from one to the other, the sound, the *voice*, of a singular "one" that would *be* the identity that, with the shifts from points to relations, any determinate point, any determinate voice, can only manifest. What Ornette "still hears", the "centre" that persists in the midst of the space of *free relations* his experiments with tuning and tone imply, is thus a *phantom*, an "invisible", inaudible point-effect, that is neither the sound of the specific frequency-differences played nor the sound of the relation to the same "tuning neighbourhood" that makes of these differences an equivalence but the sound of the invisible, of the inaudible, of a phantom object "lost" in this shift from one to the other; the sound of a phantom one, *the sound of one's own voice*. And, if the different strands of the musical texture of *Skies of America* constitute the different manifestations of the same, free relations, then the phantom sound such differences produce, the *one-sound* that haunts this space of freedom, of relations free of points, is a collective "one", a collective "unison", "the sound of one's own voice", insofar as the voice of one emerges as a sound irreducible to any one voice, irreducible to anything that is heard – the voice of an absent one that is the effect of a misperception regarding the nature of identity such a space of freedom implies.

120 *Skies of America*

However, as in our discussion of "something else" in relation to a cure for solitude, it is perhaps possible to draw an important distinction between a difference that emerges as an *effect* of the search for a "lost or hidden object", for a determinate difference that would "be" the centre, would "be" the one veiled by transference, and a desire for difference that is the *cause* of that centre, that is the proliferation of differences that produce the centre as their effect. The search for a lost or hidden object and the desire for free difference thus imply two distinct approaches to the question of difference and the effect of "one" it produces. On the one hand, difference emerges "destructively", as the ear discards differences in its search for the lost or hidden "one" – the one, for instance, frequency that would "be" the pitch, or the one pitch that would "be" the tonic. On the other hand, difference is a mode of creation; one seeks difference itself, from which the centre-one emerges as a "by-product" – a distinction that is, in effect, the distinction between a desire for one that produces difference as its effect and a desire for difference that produces an effect of one.

So, if to follow implies convergent movement, that "you" goes where "I" goes, as Ornette says to Charlie Haden sometime in the late 1950s, what does Ornettian Unison, with its distinction between points, relation-Ideas, and the phantoms produced in the shift from one to the other, imply about what it means to follow? What does it mean to "go where I go", when "I" goes in a space of Unison relations?

What does it mean to follow?

With Unison as an equivalence between relations, regardless of the points that manifest this relation, to "go where I go" is, as in Chapter 4 on free relations, to go anywhere such that this going manifests this relation; one can play any frequency, so long as it manifests the relation of being "in" with respect to the tuning neighbourhood mapped to a single, unison pitch; one can play any pitch, so long as it manifests the same Idea (implying a unison of "disavowed" relations); one can read a set of notational marks in any clef and on any transposing instrument, so long as the letter names transferred to those points manifest the same relations. This shift from the unison of *points* to the Unison of *relations* implies that an effect of relational Unison can be produced by means of "punctual" *disunison* (disunion in terms of points) – that, in other words, a *following*, a "going where the other goes", can be produced by means of a *not-following*, by going – manifesting – somewhere other than where the other is going. Inversely, punctual "following", a punctual *unison*, a "going where the other goes" at the level of the point, does not necessarily imply a Unison at the level of the relations that point manifests. Punctual disunison can manifest a Unison, and relational disUnison can be manifest by means of punctual *unison*. However, in this space of freedom, this shift from a space of points to a space of free relations, from a unison of points to a Unison of relations, another "unison" emerges, the sound of an "invisible", inaudible "one", that is neither the sound of any determinate point, nor of any relations those points manifest, but a phantom "sound" produced by the shift from one to the

Skies of America 121

other. In this sense, Unison in disunison – the effect of relational Unison produced by punctual disunison – correlative to a following in not-following, a convergence in divergence, produces a point of phantom following, a point of phantom unison, of convergence, irreducible to the not-following of our punctual divergence, or to the following of our relational convergence – the sound, the voice, of a lost following, a lost convergence, a lost unison, the voice of a lost one.

To this distinction between points, relations and the phantoms produced by the shift from one to the other, there is one final thing to add, however, one final point of complication, that has to do with something stated by Julian Adderley in the article he wrote on Ornette's music and ideas for *DownBeat* in 1960, something that bears, in particular, on the question of clef relations and the Unisons they imply. Ornette, says Adderley in this article,

> has the unique idea that the alto voice should be thought of in the alto clef. Consequently, his E-flat alto C natural concert is really B-flat in the alto clef.[32]

It is not clear how Adderley produces Bb in the alto clef in the manner described, for, in order to produce a concert C-natural on the Eb alto saxophone, one must of course play the note, "A", for that instrument. "A" written in the treble clef (on, for instance, the second space up) then appears as "B" for the alto clef, not as "Bb". In any case, what is significant for our discussion is the first half of this statement, that Ornette has the idea that "the alto voice should be thought of in the alto clef". For although Ornettian Unison implies a shift from points to free relations, that the relations that pertain to the identity of the point given the name, for instance, "C", can go *anywhere*, so long as this going manifests these relations, this implies that, for the alto voice, these relations *cannot* go anywhere, that they must in fact be manifest by particular, determinate points – the points, that is, that pertain to the alto clef. This is, we admit, a perplexing reversal. For if everything we have discussed regarding Ornettian Unison implies *free relations* – a relation free of points, implying identities unbound from the identity of any particular points – why this sudden moment of unnecessary binding, why the sudden insistence that relations for a particular voice "go" a particular somewhere, that they are to be realised by these determinate points?

To conclude, we propose a simple, provisional hypothesis. If an experience of binding, with, perhaps, echoes of bondage, calls for freedom, for a shift that will free relations from their bondage to specific points, as we saw in our discussion of a cure for solitude, perhaps such a sensitivity to freedom, to music in its unbound, unfettered aspect, calls at times for some minimal moments of binding, for points at which a space of relations, floating free, finds a means of manifestation, finds a "punctual" mooring in what is heard.

Notes

1 Coleman, "Prime Time for Harmolodics".

122 Skies of America

2 Fuller, *Prime Design*.
3 Helmholtz, *On the Sensations of Tone*, 7.
4 "Prime Time", 54.
5 "Prime Time", 54.
6 "Prime Time", 54.
7 Coleman, interview by Katz.
8 *Reflexivity* means that for every x in A, $x\,R\,x$; *symmetry* means that for all x, y in a set A, if $x\,R\,y$ then $y\,R\,x$; and *transitivity* means that for all x, y, z in A, if $x\,R\,y$ and $y\,R\,z$ then $x\,R\,z$.
9 Helmholtz, *On the Sensations of Tone*, 1.
10 *Sensations of Tone*, 4.
11 *Sensations of Tone*, 8.
12 *Sensations of Tone*, 8.
13 Litweiler, *Harmolodic Life*, 25
14 This neighbourhood is the ordered-set neighbourhood proposed by Hausdorff, which we discussed in Chapter 1.
15 A point, x, is an *interior point* of a space, S, if there exists a neighbourhood of x contained within S.
16 Coleman, "A Question of Scale", 24.
17 Coleman, interview by Shoemaker.
18 Coleman, interview by Shoemaker.
19 Or, again, the bow-tie Ornette's "main hero", Buckminster Fuller, used to represent "teleology".
20 Cherry, "Old and New Dreams Harvard Lecture-demonstration", part 4, 1:26–1:48.
21 Coleman, interview by Purcell, "Free Radical".
22 Litweiler, *A Harmolodic Life* , 25.
23 Coleman, interview by Schuller: 10:33–10:49.
24 Interview by Schuller: 11:03–11:16.
25 Interview by Schuller: 11:16–11:21.
26 Interview by Schuller: 12:12–12:19.
27 Interview by Schuller: 12:21–12:29.
28 Litweiler, *A Harmolodic Life*, 25.
29 Litweiler, *Harmolodic Life*, 70.
30 Coleman, "Pipes of Joujouka", 23.
31 Coleman, "Pipes of Joujouka", 23.
32 "Cannonball Looks at Ornette", 21.

Chapter 8

Conclusion

You go where I go

"You follow me", said Ornette Coleman to Charlie Haden at one of their earliest meetings, sometime in the late 1950s, "and you go where I go". But what, given our attention to Ornette's discourse, to all of its enigmas and complexities, does it mean to follow? What does it mean to go where Ornette goes?

We began by identifying the need for an approach that would give attention to Ornette's discourse as a means to approach these questions without the assumption of idealised figures or the authority of authorial intention, and in Chapters 1 and 2, we offered such an approach, drawing in elements of an analysis of discourse informed by psychoanalysis, including the notion of discourse as other, quilting and transference, as well as tools from topology, including the notion of relation, neighbourhood and space. With these tools in hand, we turned to an analysis of Ornette's work, with each chapter oriented with respect to a fragment, or fragments, from Ornette's discourse bearing directly and indirectly on his music.

Those signifiers that performed a quilting function in relation to Ornette's discourse were signifiers, we suggested, that implied a particular form of relation, on the one hand, but in a way that had been subject to a significant shift at the level of meaning for which the notion of transference allowed us to account, on the other. We suggested that the relations these quilting signifiers imply may imply space, as well as constitute the *vehicle*, the means of movement, characterising the way "you" and "I" traverse that space, and thus how "you" *follows* "I", how "you" "goes" "where" "I" "goes".

In Chapter 3, we introduced the notion of a *tonic relation* in the context of the problem of knowledge, of "knowing where to go". We drew in the work of William Rowan Hamilton and, in particular, his notion of a vector as a *vehicle* that moves "movable points" from A to B, from analyser to analysand, from known to unknown. We developed two forms of vector – *tonic* and *situating* – to account for the solution Ornette proposed to the problem of knowledge, which he gave in terms of "tonics" and "thirds". And we discovered that "tonic" already implies a structure of convergence, of following; it already implies that all of the points internal to the same tonic-oriented space "go where the others go".

DOI: 10.4324/9781003412304-8

124 Conclusion

In Chapter 4, we turned to the notion of a *free relation* and the effect of invisibility it produces in the form of a phantom tonic haunting the space of freedom. We linked Ornette's reference to the "free direction" of "Invisible" to transposition, to Hamiltonian *analogy* – the "transference of a relation" – as well as to the notion of a *free vector* – a vector the identity of which is contingent not on the identity of its spatial position but of its magnitude and direction. The shift from points to relations implied by these three related notions – transposition, analogy, the free vector – then had consequences at the level of what it means to follow, of what it means to go where another goes, implying that the point to which "you" and "I" converge is now a *relation*, with no necessity that such a convergence would imply a convergence at the level of the points that manifest those relations.

In Chapter 5, we dealt with the question of *solitude* and the relation it implies, finding in Ornette's idiosyncratic definition of an "Interval" that "has everything in it" a musical correlative to the solitude of the "Lonely Woman", a woman "who had absolutely everything you could desire in life" and who had "the most solitary expression". Linking this solitude to the topological notion of an "isolated point", as well as to the har-mo-lodic structure of "notes-as-chords", we conceived of the space of an Ornettian Movement as a disconnected space – disconnected, that is, only insofar as its connections are "disavowed". And we conceived the *cure* for solitude as both the avowal of such connections and of their lack.

In Chapter 6, the second of our chapters on "Lonely Woman", we gave attention to the temporal aspect of Ornette's famous piece, with its distinctive drawing together of melody and accompaniment, finding in Ornette's reference to "tension" – to the tension that he sees in all love conflicts – a kind of *no relation*, the absence of a relation correlative to the drawing together of two entirely distinct spaces, two entirely distinct forms of time, as implied by Ornette's notion of *spread rhythm*.

And, finally, in Chapter 7, we turned to "Prime Time For Harmolodics",[1] the text that most closely approximates a manifesto for Ornette's approach, with particular attention to its reference to "unison", which we conceived in terms of *unison relations*. *Unison*, in Ornette's sense, we said, implies the shift we had already discerned in Chapter 4, from points to relations, from a "unison", a being *one*, the "same", *equivalent* – an identity – at the level of the sound that pertains to points, to a *Unison* at the level of the "sound" that pertains to the relation. This shift, from the being-one of *point-sound* to the being-one of *relation-sound*, disavowed in the being-one of *Idea-sound*, invokes, however, another "one-sound", another "unison", which is the sound of the *voice* that pertains to a phantom "one" – *the sound of one's own voice* – which emerges as the sound of a point that would *be* the identity, *be* the "one", lost, made "invisible", by the shift from points to relations Ornettian Unison implies.

Convergent movements

Each of the relations these chapters investigate thus implies ordered movements through spaces in the direction of particular points of consequence, of "what

Conclusion 125

follows", the convergence to which implies a particular sense of what it means to follow, of what it means to "go where I go". In the chapter on *tonic relations*, "to follow" means to *converge to tonic*. In the chapter on *free relations*, the shift from points to relations implies *convergence to a (free) relation*. In the chapter on *solitude relations*, convergence is "*har-mo-lodic*", moving in two directions, implying convergence to a "disavowed" point of harmonic orientation, as well as to another solitude, another interval-point of melodic consequence, with a *cure* for solitude implying *convergence to free difference*, to a relation of difference, regardless of the points that manifest that difference. In the chapter on *no relations*, to follow means to *converge to "tension"*, to *no relation*, to a "no relation" manifesting the tension Ornette sees in all love conflicts. And, in the chapter on *unison relations*, to follow means, again, to *converge to relations*, with Ornettian Unison implying, as with a *free relation*, both a Unison at the level of the relation, regardless of the points that manifest that relation, as well as a "unison" at the level of a phantom "one" emerging in the shift from points to relations such a space of relational Unison implies. In this sense, Ornette's discourse implies a distinction between four different forms of convergence: (1) convergence at the level of *points*, (2) convergence at the level of *relations*, with no necessary implication of convergence at the level of the points that manifest these relations, (3) convergence at the level of the *Idea*, which is to say, convergence at the level of a relation in its "disavowed" form, and (4) convergence at the level of the phantom point-effect, of a "one" that is "lost or hidden", made "invisible" by the shift from (1) to (2).

A transpositional logic

In the first instance, we could say, then, that Ornette's discourse is marked by the logic of *transposition*, in its broadest, most general sense, where transposition implies *the transference of a relation* from one set of points to another, implying a relational identity sufficient to produce an experience of identity at the level of the spaces these points manifest. If such transferred relations *sound*, if they are, in the sense implied by Ornette's discourse, *relation-sound*, transposition thus implies the *transference of a sound*, such that two distinct sets of points, each with their own *point-sound*, where the relation of one with respect to the other is one of "dis-unison", will nonetheless have the "same sound", will be "in Unison", insofar as they manifest the same relations – the same *relation-sound* – as implied by one of Ornette's definitions of harmolodics:

> Harmolodics means transposing any sound whatsoever into your own playing, without having to give up your own identity in the process.[2]

However, this shift to a transpositional logic, as we have seen, is complicated by two features. First, the shift from points to relations transposition implies produces *phantoms* – the experience, in other words, that such a shift hides, makes "invisible", determinate points to which the identity of the space is properly to be bound

126 Conclusion

– the point that "is" the tonic, the frequency that "is" the pitch, and so on – correlative to the effect of loss or hiddenness produced by (the shift from points to relations implied by) Stewart's law. Second, at moments in Ornette's discourse, the shift from points to relations his work implies is "disavowed" by a shift (back) from relations to points, as in the case of the Ornettian Interval, defined not as a *relation* – a "distance" between points – but as *the point itself*, with the disavowed interval-relation now an Idea it "carries" "in it", as its internal "sound substance". In Chapter 5, we linked this shift back from relations to points to *solitude*, to the experience that a point has something – an Idea – "in it" correlative to its independence, its isolation, from other points, with the *cure for solitude* thus implying an avowal that the Idea is, in fact, an effect of the point's relation to what is *outside* it, a relation to which, in a space of *free difference*, it *lacks*. If such a cure for solitude would seem to imply that Ornette's discourse is to be situated once again on the side of the relation, however, in the final chapter we encountered yet another shift to determinate points, in the insistence that there is a clef proper to each instrument – that an alto instrument must play in the alto clef, a tenor instrument in the tenor clef, and so on.

But perhaps this uncertainty in Ornette's discourse, this shift from points to relations and back again, reflects an uncertainty at the heart of "freedom" itself. For if freedom implies a space conceived in terms of the identity of the relation, regardless of the points that manifest that relation, such a space, in order to "appear", become "visible", audible, at all, *must nonetheless rely on points to manifest itself*; it must rely, in other words, on a shift (back) from relations to those points from which, as "free", it has freed itself. In order for a free space to appear, to become "visible", as *free*, in other words, it must risk *appearing*, it must risk, that is, appearing as "bound", as *not free*, as a space the identity of which is to be conceived in terms of determinate, punctual manifestations rather than the relations these particular manifestations manifest. And if such a misperception calls again for the inverse movement from points to relations, which would free relations from their punctual binds, this misperception regarding points is nonetheless in danger of persisting in a "phantom" form, as the promise of a return to points in terms of which the identity of the space would *properly* to be conceived, but which is now hidden, made "invisible", by the shift from binding to freedom. Harmolodic thought would thus seem to vacillate in this split, this non-coincidence, of points and relations, points and Ideas, here to be situated on the side of the relation, here on the side of the point, insofar as the relation is "bound" to it in its disavowed form as the Idea it carries "in it", and here to be found on the side of neither point nor relation but on the side of a phantom that is reducible to neither – produced, instead, in the shift from one to the other.

I don't want them to follow me

"You follow me", says Ornette to Charlie Haden, "and you go where I go", but in his interview with Will Kineally for *Cadence* magazine in October 1995, Ornette

Conclusion 127

made a statement that not only calls into question the notion that to play with Ornette is to follow, to "go where Ornette goes", but that seems, instead, to *directly contradict* this earlier statement to Charlie Haden, the one about following, made at one of their first meetings sometime in the late 1950s:

> human existence exists on multiple levels, not just on a two-dimensional level, not just having to be identified with what you do and what you say. Those things are the result of what people see and hear that you do. But the human beings themselves are living on a multiple level. That's how I have always wanted musicians to play with me: on a multiple level. I don't want them to follow me. I want them to be themselves, but to be with me.[3]

"I don't want them to follow me", says Ornette, "I want them to be themselves, but to be with me". What to make of this surprising denial of something that, to Charlie Haden in the late 1950s, was clearly affirmed: the wanting at the level of following, this demand that Haden follow him, that he go where Ornette goes. Why this apparent reversal from wanting to not wanting, from following to not following? How could something that was so clearly affirmed now be so emphatically denied?

If "to follow" means "to go where I go", as we have now said many times, if "to follow" has, in other words, the structure of convergence, of movements – goings – that converge to common "wheres", common endpoints, it is possible to see that Ornette's discourse implies followings, convergences, that are, at once, *not-followings*, and not-followings that are, at once, *followings* – a space, that is, in which convergence at one level coincides with divergence at another, and vice versa. The shift from points to free relations implies that the identity of the space is to be situated at the level of the relation and not at the level of the points that manifest those relations, and thus that following, convergent movement, "going where the other goes", at the level of the relation does not necessarily imply a following – a going where the other goes – at the level of the points that manifest those relations. One can, in other words, "play the same space" even if the points that manifest that space are entirely different. Even if the relation is experienced in its "disavowed" form as Idea, there can be an effect of convergence, of following, of *Unison*, at the level of Idea, without this necessarily implying a unison at the level of the points that "carry" that Idea, as implied by Ornette's assertion that C and E are "higher" than D and F "by [Idea] sound".

And if the shift from points to relations produces phantoms, a lost or hidden "one"-point in terms of which the identity of the space is properly to be conceived, this "one", this "unison" that is the *sound* of a voice that is *one's own*, only emerges insofar as the shift from points to relations implies the possibility of manifestations that are *not one*, that are not "the same" – insofar, that is, as it implies the possibility that there is a difference, a disunison, at the level of the points manifesting the same Unison relations. Phantom punctual followings – the phantom points to which both "you" and "I" (would) go – only emerge, in other words, insofar as, in the manifestations of a Unison relation, "you" does *not* necessarily go where

128 Conclusion

"I" goes, does *not* necessarily follow, insofar as there is a possibility of Unison in disunison and relational identity in the midst of punctual difference.

Notes

1 Coleman, "Prime Time for Harmolodics".
2 Wilson, *Ornette Coleman: His Life and Music*, 87.
3 Coleman, interviewed by Jarrett.

Appendix

Figure 9.1 shows a simple duration space, which is a necessary basis for the analysis offered in Chapter 6. The "points" in this space are common, written durations – quarter notes, eighth notes, and so on. The relations between points (durations) are *quotients*,[1] simply because they are the product of division. Thus, a half note divided by a quarter note produces a quotient of *2*, simply because ½ divided by ¼ = 2. In this duration space, quotients only relate durations to their multiples; in other words, there exists a quotient relating two durations only if the smaller duration divides the larger duration equally. Thus, there is no quotient relating a dotted eighth note and a quarter note, because ¼ is not a multiple of a dotted-eighth note – i.e., ¼ divided by 3/16 does not equal a whole number. Quotients thus represent pathways in a duration space linking durations that "go into" other durations without remainder. The existence of such a pathway reflects the fact that, given, say, a quarter note, it is possible to easily produce, to "get to", a whole note, simply by "adding" four quarter notes "end to end". "*Q4*", in a sense, means, at least in part, "how many times a smaller duration must be repeated 'continuously' (end to end) in order to produce the larger duration". Faint grey lines indicate positive prime integers other than 2 and 3. We have not included these for the sake of clarity.

Whilst this space as a whole is a non-total partial order,[2] *chains* lie within the space, where a chain is defined as a totally ordered set; each point of the chain, in other words, is related to every other point of the chain by means of the relation. For instance, the eighth-note triplet, quarter-note triplet and half-note form a chain, for the relation relates eighth-note triplets to quarter-note triplets, quarter-note triplets to half-notes, and eighth-note triplets to half-notes. These chains feature in our discussion of metre in Chapter 6. We notate these chains as ordered sets, however, to distinguish, for instance, the chain (eighth-note triplet, quarter-note triplet, half-note) from the chain (eighth-note triplet, quarter-note, half-note). This is necessary because both are distinct chains of the partial order, but their interval notation is the same (eighth-note triplet, half-note).

Appendix

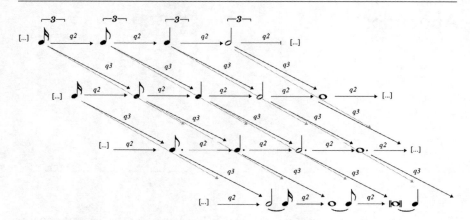

Figure 9.1

Notes

1 See Chapter 4 for Hamilton's quotient.
2 Where "<" means "is a divisor of" and $x < y$ thus means "x is a divisor of y" or "y is a multiple of x", this space is a partial order because it is reflexive (x is a multiple of itself), not symmetric (it does not follow necessarily that x is a multiple of y where y is a multiple of x) and transitive (if y is a multiple of x and z is a multiple of y, then z is a multiple of x). It is a non-total *partial* order in the sense that this relation does not necessarily relate all the points of the space to one another – it is not necessarily the case, for instance, that y will always be a multiple of some other point of the space, x, or, inversely, that x will be the divisor of some other points of the space, y.

Bibliography

Aarden, Brett. *Dynamic Melodic Expectancy*. PhD book, Ohio State University, 2003.

Adderley, Julian Cannonball. "Cannonball looks at Ornette Coleman". *Downbeat* 27, no. 11 (May 26, 1960): 20–21.

Agawu, Kofi. *Music as Discourse*. Oxford: Oxford University Press, 2009.

Agawu, Kofi. *Playing with Signs*. Princeton: Princeton University Press, 1990.

Angermuller, Johannes. *Poststructuralist Discourse Analysis: Subjectivity in Enunciative Pragmatics*. London: Palgrave Macmillan, 2014.

Arnheim, Rudolf. "Perceptual Dynamics in Musical Expression". In *New Essays on the Psychology of Art*. Berkeley, Los Angeles, and London: University of California Press, 1986.

Arthur, Claire. "Taking Harmony into Account". *Music Perception: An Interdisciplinary Journal* 34, no. 4 (April 2017): 405–423.

Austin, John L. *How To Do Things With Words*. 2nd ed. Cambridge MA: Harvard University Press, 2005 (orig. 1962).

Ayrey, Craig. "Debussy's Significant Connections: Metaphor and Metonymy in Analytical Method". In *Theory, Analysis and Meaning in Music*, edited by Anthony Pople, 127–151. Cambridge: Cambridge University Press, 2006.

Babbitt, Milton. "Set Structure as a Compositional Determinant". *Journal of Music Theory* 5, no. 1 (1961): 72–94.

Benjamin, William E. Review of *The Structure of Atonal Music* by Allen Forte. *Perspectives of New Music* 13, no. 1 (1974): 170–190.

Ben–Tal, Oded. "Characterising Musical Gestures". *Musicae Scientiae* 16, no. 3 (October 2012): 247–261.

Benveniste, Emile. *Problems in General Linguistics*. Florida: University of Miami Press, 1971.

Biancorosso, Giorgio. "Whose Phenomenology of Music? David Huron's Theory of Expectation". *Music & Letters* 89, no.2 (August 2008): 396–404.

Block, Steven. "Organised Sound: Pitch-class Relations in the Music of Ornette Coleman". *Annual Review of Jazz Studies*, no. 6 (1993): 229–252.

Borisovich, Yu., N. Bliznyakov, Ya. Izrailevich and T. Fomenko. *Introduction to Topology*. Translated by Oleg Efimov. Moscow: MIR Publishers, 1985 (orig. 1980).

Bregman, Albert. *Auditory Scene Analysis*. Cambridge, MA: MIT Press, 1990.

132 Bibliography

Brodsky, Seth. *From 1989, or European Music and the Modernist Unconscious.* Oakland: University of California Press, 2017.

Brown, Gillian, and George Yule. *Discourse Analysis.* Cambridge: Cambridge University Press, 1983.

Buchler, Michael. "Are There Any Bad (or Good) Transformational Analyses?" *Integral* 30 (2016): 41–45.

Burgoyne, Bernard. "Autism and Topology". In *Drawing the Soul: Schemas and Models in Psychoanalysis*, edited by Bernard Burgoyne, 190–217. London: Karnac Books, 2003 (orig. 2000).

Burgoyne, Bernard. "Topology: Secrets of Space". Seminar presented at Topology: Spaces of Transformation conference, Tate Modern, London, November 2011, January and March 2012. Available at https://www.tate.org.uk/search?q=secrets+of+space (Accessed 4th July, 2018).

Burgoyne, Bernard. "What Causes Structure to Find a Place in Love?" In *Lacan and Science*, edited by Jason Glyos and Yannis Stavrakakis, 231–262. London: Routledge, 2018 (orig. 2002).

Burgoyne, Bernard. "What is a Psychoanalyst?" Talk presented at The Future of Psychoanalysis conference, UKCP, 5 May 2000. Available at https://jcfar.org.uk/wp-content/uploads/2016/03/What-is-a-psychoanalyst-Bernard-Burgoyne.pdf (Accessed 3rd September, 2021).

Carlsen, James C., Pierre I. Divenyi, and Jack A. Taylor. "A Preliminary Study of Perceptual Expectancy in Melodic Configurations". *Bulletin of the Council for Research in Music Education* no. 22 (Fall 1970): 4–12.

Cenkerová, Zuzana, and Richard Parncutt. "Style-Dependency of Melodic Expectation: Changing the Rules in Real Time". *Music Perception: An Interdisciplinary Journal* 33, no.1 (September 2015): 110–128.

Cherry, Don. "Old and New Dreams Harvard Lecture-demonstration". Lecture-demonstration presented at Harvard University, 29 February, 1980. Available at https://www.youtube.com/watch?v=JCaLtlL-s6I (Accessed 3rd July, 2017).

Chew, Elaine. "Towards a Mathematical Model of Tonality". Thesis (Ph.D.) Massachusetts Institute of Technology, Sloan School of Management, 2000. Available at https://dspace.mit.edu/handle/1721.1/9139?show=full#:~:text=http%3A//dspace.mit.edu/handle/1721.1/7582.

Chion, Michel. *The Voice in Cinema.* Translated by Claudia Gorbman. New York: Columbia University Press, 1999 (Orig. 1982).

Clarke, Shirley, director. *Made in America.* Caravan of Dreams Production, 1986. 1hr, 25m.

de Clercq, Trevor, and David Temperley. "A Corpus Analysis of Rock Harmony". *Popular Music* 30 (2011): 47–70.

Cogswell, Michael. "Melodic Organisation in Two Solos by Ornette Coleman". *Annual Review of Jazz Studies* 7, no. 7 (1994): 101–144.

Cohen, Morris R. *A Preface to Logic.* New York: Henry Holt and Co., 1944.

Cohn, Richard. *Audacious Euphony: Chromaticism and the Triad's Second Nature* (Oxford Studies in Music Theory). Oxford: Oxford University Press, 2012.

Cohn, Richard. "An Introduction to Neo-Riemannian Theory: A Survey and Historical Perspective". *Journal of Music Theory* 42, no. 2 (Autumn 1998): 167–180.

Cohn, Richard. "Maximally Smooth Cycles, Hexatonic Systems, and the Analysis of Late-Romantic Triadic Progressions". *Music Analysis* 15, no. 1 (March 1996): 9–40.

Cohn, Richard. "Neo-Riemannian Operations, Parsimonious Trichords, and their 'Tonnetz' Representations". *Journal of Music Theory* 41, no. 1 (Spring 1997): 1–66.

Coleman, Ornette. "A Conversation With Frank J. Oteri". Interview by Frank J. Oteri, September 10, 2007. Available at https://www.youtube.com/watch?v=ojl2dTA79ec&t =47s (Accessed 3rd September, 2021).

Coleman, Ornette. "Dialling Up Ornette". Interview by Bill Shoemaker. *Jazz Times* 25, no. 10 (December 1995): 42–45. Available at https://www.pointofdeparture.org/archives/ PoD-6/PoD6TheTurnaround.html (Accessed 3rd[rd] September, 2021).

Coleman, Ornette. "Driven to Abstraction". Interview by Howard Mandel. *The Wire* 140 (October 1995): 37–40.

Coleman, Ornette. "Free Radical". Interview by Andrew Purcell. *Guardian*, June 29, 2007. Available at https://www.theguardian.com/music/2007/jun/29/jazz.urban (Accessed 3rd June 2019).

Coleman, Ornette. "Interview with Ornette Coleman". Interview by Gunther Schuller. *The Scope of Jazz*, WBAI, February 7, 1960. Available at https://ethaniverson.com/rhythm -and-blues/ornette-1-forms-and-sounds/ (Accessed 2nd September 2021).

Coleman, Ornette. "Interview with Ornette Coleman". Interview by Eric Jackson. *Jazz Conversations with Eric Jackson*, WGBH, December 3, 1981.

Coleman, Ornette. "Interview with Ornette Coleman". Interview by Michael Jarrett. *Cadence* (October 1995). Available at http://www2.york.psu.edu/~jmj3/p_ornett.htm (Accessed 2nd January, 2021).

Coleman, Ornette. "Interview with Ornette Coleman". Interview by Clara Gibson Maxwell. *Cadence* (November 1999). Available at http://www.kaloskaisophos.org.pagesperso -orange.fr/ac/acocint.html.

Coleman, Ornette. "Interview with Ornette Coleman". Interviewer unknown. *Bonnaroo Music and Arts Festival 2007*. Available at https://www.youtube.com/watch?v =8CoPGDfMWFc and https://www.youtube.com/watch?v=WdqRfHdbnXE. (Accessed 21st September 2021).

Coleman, Ornette. Liner Notes to *Change of the Century*. CD, Atlantic Masters 81227 3608-2 (orig. 1959).

Coleman, Ornette. Liner Notes to *The Empty Foxhole*. CD, Blue Note Records 28982, 1994 (orig. 1966).

Coleman, Ornette. Liner Notes to *The Music of Ornette Coleman*. CD, BGO Records BG0CD1049, 2012 (orig. 1968).

Coleman, Ornette. Liner Notes to *This Is Our Music*. CD, Atlantic Masters 81227 3137-2 (orig. 1960).

Coleman, Ornette. Liner Notes to *Skies of America*. CD, BGO Records BG0CD1049, 2012 (orig. 1972).

Coleman, Ornette. "Memories of Ornette". Interview by Richard Williams. *Melody Maker* (17 July 1971): 28.

Coleman, Ornette. "My Dinner With Ornette". Interview by Larry Katz. *The Katz Tapes* (blog), July 2015. Available at http://thekatztapes.com/my-dinner-with-ornette/ (Accessed 3rd September, 2021).

Coleman, Ornette. "Ornette: In His Own Language". Interview by Nate Chinen. *Jazz Times* (November 2006). Available at https://jazztimes.com/features/profiles/ornette-coleman -in-his-own-language/ (Accessed 21st September 2021).

134 Bibliography

Coleman, Ornette. "Ornette and the Pipes of Joujouka". Interview by Richard Williams. *Melody Maker* (17 March 1973): 22–23.

Coleman, Ornette. "The Other's Language: Jacques Derrida interviews Ornette Coleman, 23 June 1997". Interview by Jacques Derrida. Translated by Timothy S. Murphy. In *Genre: Forms of Discourse and Culture* 37, no. 2 (2004), 319–329.

Coleman, Ornette. "Prime Time for Harmolodics". *Down Beat* 50 (July 1983): 54–55.

Coleman, Ornette. "Quand Ornette Coleman improvisait avec Jacques Derrida". Interview by Jacques Derrida. *Les Inrockuptibles* (August, 1997). Available at https://www .lesinrocks.com/actu/ornette-coleman-et-jacques-derrida-la-langue-de-lautre-94053-20 -08-1997/ (Accessed 22nd September 2021).

Coleman, Ornette. "A Question of Scale". Interview by Andy Hamilton. *The Wire* 257 (July 2005): 22–26.

Coleman, Ornette. "Something to Think About". In *Free Spirits: Annals of the Insurgent Imagination*, edited by Paul Buhle, Jayne Cortez, Philip Lamantia, Nancy Joyce Peters, Franklin Rosemont, Penelope Rosemont, 117–120. San Francisco: City Light Books, 1982.

Coleman, Ornette. "To Whom It May Concern". *Down Beat* 34 (January 1967): 19.

Cook, Nicholas. *Analysing Musical Multimedia.* Oxford: Oxford University Press, 1998.

Cooke, Deryck. *The Language of Music.* Oxford: Oxford University Press, 1959.

Crystal, David. *Linguistics.* Harmondsworth: Penguin Books, 1971.

Dahl, Sofia, and Anders Friberg. "Visual Perception of Expressiveness in Musicians' Body Movements". *Music Perception* 24 (2007): 433–54.

Daintith, John, and R. D. Nelson. *The Penguin Dictionary of Mathematics.* London: Penguin, 1989.

David, Catherine. *The Beauty of Gesture: The Invisible Keyboard of Piano and T'ai Chi.* Berkeley: North Atlantic Books, 1996.

Davis, Allison, Burleigh B. Gardner, and Mary R. Gardner. *Deep South: A Social Anthropology Study of Caste and Class.* Chicago: University of Chicago Press, 1941.

Davis, Francis. *In the Moment: Jazz in the 1980s.* Oxford: Oxford University Press, 1986.

Dolar, Mladen. *A Voice and Nothing More.* Cambridge: MIT Press, 2006.

Dollard, John. *Caste and Class in a Southern Town.* 3rd ed. New York: Doubleday Anchor Books, 1957 (orig. 1937).

Dorsey, James. "Theme and Improvisation in a Composition by Ornette Coleman". *Jazz Research Papers* 12 (1996): 48–54.

Dowling, W. J., K. M.-T. Lung, and S. Herold. "Aiming Attention in Pitch and Time in the Perception of Interleaved Melodies". *Perception and Psychophysics* 41 (1987): 642–656.

Dunsby, Jonathan, and John Stopford. "The Case for a Schenkerian Semiotic". *Music Theory Spectrum* 3 (Spring, 1981): 49–53.

Euclid. *The Thirteen Books of the Elements: Vol. 1* (Books I and II). Translated by Thomas L. Heath. New York: Dover, 1956.

Euler, Leonhard. "Elementa Doctrinae Solidorum". *Novi Commentarii Academiae Scientiarum Petropolitanae* 4 (1758): 109–40.

Euler, Leonhard. "Solutio problematis ad geometriam situs pertinentis". *Commentarii academiae scientiarum Petropolitanae* 8 (1741): 128–40.

Fairclough, Norman. "Introduction". In *Critical Language Awareness*, edited by Norman Fairclough. London: Longman, 1992.

Feather, Leonard. *The Encyclopedia of Jazz in the Sixties.* New York: Horizon Press, 1966.

Bibliography 135

Feld, Steven. "Flow Like a Waterfall: The Metaphors of Kaluli Musical Theory". *Yearbook for Traditional Music* 13 (1981): 22–47.

Fink, Bruce. *Lacan to the Letter: Reading Écrits Closely.* Minneapolis: University of Minnesota Press, 2004.

Fink, Bruce. *The Lacanian Subject: Between Language and Jouissance.* Princeton: Princeton University Press, 1997.

Fink, Robert. *Repeating Ourselves: American Minimal Music as Cultural Practice.* Berkeley: University of California Press, 2005.

Fleisch, Daniel. *A Students' Guide to Vectors and Tensors.* Cambridge: Cambridge University Press, 2012.

Fowler, H. W., and H. G. Le Mesurier. *The Concise Oxford Dictionary of Current English.* 3rd ed. Oxford: Oxford University Press, 1938.

Forte, Allen. *The Structure of Atonal Music.* New Haven and London: Yale University Press, 1973.

Forte, Allen. "A Theory of Set-Complexes for Music". *Journal of Music Theory* 8, no. 2 (Winter 1964): 136–183.

Fréchet, Maurice. "Sur quelques points du Calcul fonctionnel". *Rendiconti del Circolo Matematico di Palermo* 22 (1906): 1–74.

Freud, Sigmund. "A Case of Hysteria". In *The Standard Edition of the Complete Psychological Works of Sigmund Freud, Volume VII (1901–1905).* Translated by James Strachey. London: Vintage, 2001 (orig. 1953).

Freud, Sigmund. "Group Psychology". In *The Standard Edition of the Complete Psychological Works of Sigmund Freud, Volume XVIII (1920–1922).* Translated by James Strachey. London: Vintage, 2001 (orig. 1955).

Freud, Sigmund. *On Aphasia.* Translated by E. Stengel. Madison CT: International Universities Press, 1953.

Freud, Sigmund. "On Narcissism: An Introduction". In *The Standard Edition of the Complete Psychological Works of Sigmund Freud, Volume XIV (1914–1916).* Translated by James Strachey. London: Vintage, 2001 (orig. 1955).

Frink, Nathan, A. *An Analysis of the Compositional Practices of Ornette Coleman as Demonstrated in His Small Group Recordings During the 1970s.* MA dissertation, University of Pittsburgh, 2012.

Frymoyer, Johanna. "The Musical Topic in the Twentieth Century". *Music Theory Spectrum* 39, no. 1 (Spring 2017): 83–108.

Fuller, R. Buckminster. *Critical Path.* New York: St Martin's Press, 1981.

Fuller, R. Buckminster. *Nine Chains to the Moon.* Carringdale, Illinois: Southern Illinois University Press, 1963 (orig. 1938).

Garfinkel, Harold. *Studies in Ethnomethodology.* Englewood Cliffs, NJ: Prentice Hall, 1967.

Gibbs, Raymond. *Metaphor Wars: Conceptual Metaphors in Human Life.* Cambridge: Cambridge University Press, 2017.

Giddins, Gary. *Rhythm-a-ning: Jazz Tradition and Innovation in the '80s.* Oxford: Oxford University Press, 1985.

Gioia, Ted. *West Coast Jazz: Modern Jazz in California, 1945–60.* New York: Oxford University Press, 1992.

Godøy, Rolf Inge, and Harald Jørgensen, eds. *Musical Imagery.* Lisse: Swets & Zeitlinger, 2001.

136 Bibliography

Godzich, Wlad. Review of *Fondements d'une sémiologie de la musique*, by Jean Jacques Nattiez. *Journal of Music Theory* 22, no.1 (Spring 1978): 117–33.

Goldberg, Joe. *Jazz Masters of the Fifties*. London: Collier-Macmillan, 1966.

Golia, Maria. *Ornette Coleman: The Territory and the Adventure*. London: Reaktion Books, 2020.

Goodman, Nelson. *Languages of Art: An Approach to a Theory of Symbols*. Indianapolis: Hackett Publishing, 1976.

Greimas, Algirdas. *Structural Semantics: An Attempt at a Method*. Translated by D. McDowell, R. Schleifer and A.Velie. Lincoln: University of Nebraska Press, 1983.

Grice, H. P. "Logic and Conversation". In *Syntax and Semantics 3: Speech Acts*, edited by Peter Cole and Jerry L. Morgan, 41–58. New York: Academic Press, 1975.

Gridley, Mark. *Jazz Styles: History and Analysis*. London: Prentice-Hall International, 1997.

Gritten, Elaine, and Anthony King, eds. *Music and Gesture*. Aldershot: Ashgate, 2006.

Gritten, Elaine, and Anthony King, eds. *New Perspectives on Music and Gesture*. Oxford: Routledge, 2016 (orig. 2011).

Haden, Charlie. "Charlie Haden on the Creation of Free Jazz". Interviewed by Tavis Smiley, *The Tavis Smiley Show*, 11 November 2004. Available at https://www.npr.org/templates /story/story.php?storyId=4164843&t=1633526069532 (Accessed 24th August 2014).

Haden, Charlie. "Interview with Charlie Haden". Interviewed by Ethan Iverson. *Do The Math* (blog), March 2008. Available at https://ethaniverson.com/interviews/interview -with-charlie-haden/ (Accessed 24th August 2014).

Haden, Charlie. "Jazz Legend Charlie Haden on His Life, His Music and His Politics". Interviewed by Amy Goodman, *Democracy Now*, 1 September 2006. Available at: http:// www.democracynow.org/2006/9/1/jazz_legend_charlie_haden_on_his (Accessed 24th August 2014).

Hamilton, William Rowan. *Lectures on Quaternions: Containing a Systematic Statement of a New Mathematical Method; ... With Numerous Illustrative Diagrams, and ... Geometrical and Physical Applications*. Dublin: Hodges and Smith, 1853.

Hamilton, William Rowan. "Theory of Conjugate Functions, or Algebraic Couples; with a Preliminary and Elementary Essay on Algebra as the Science of Pure Time". *Transactions of the Royal Irish Academy* 17 (1837): 293–422.

Harper-Scott, J. P. E. *The Quilting Points of Musical Modernism: Revolution, Reaction and William Walton*. Cambridge: Cambridge University Press, 2012.

Harris, Zellig S. *Discourse Analysis Reprints*. The Hague: Mouton & Co., 1963.

Haser, Verena. *Metaphor, Metonymy and Experientialist Philosophy: Challenging Cognitive Semantics*. Mouton: Berlin, 2005.

Hasty, Christopher. *Metre as Rhythm*. Oxford: Oxford University Press, 1997.

Hatten, Robert S. *Interpreting Musical Gestures, Topics and Tropes: Mozart, Beethoven, Schubert*. Bloomington, IN: Indiana University Press, 2004.

Hatten, Robert S. "Metaphor in music". In *Musical Signification: Essays in the Semiotic Theory and Analysis of Music: Vol. 12 No. 1*, edited by Eero Tarasti, 373–391. Berlin: Mouton de Gruyter, 1995.

Hatten, Robert S. *Musical Meaning in Beethoven: Markedness, Correlation, and Interpretation*. Bloomington, IN: Indiana University Press, 1994.

Hatten, Robert S. "A Theory of Musical Gesture and its Application to Beethoven and Schubert". In *Music and Gesture*, edited by Anthony Gritten and Elaine King, 1–23. Aldershot: Ashgate, 2006.

Bibliography   137

Hausdorff, Felix. *Grundzüge der Mengenlehre.* Leipzig: Verlag von Veit & Comp., 1914.

Hausdorff, Felix. *Set Theory,* 3rd ed. Translated by John R. Aumann, et al. New York: Chelsea Publishing Company, 1957.

Helmholtz, Hermann L. F. *On the Sensations of Tone as a Physiological Basis for the Theory of Music.* Translated by Alexander J. Ellis. New York: Dover Publications, 1954.

Hentoff, Nat. *The Jazz Life.* New York: Da Capo Press, 1978.

Hentoff, Nat. Liner Notes to *Something Else!!!! The Music of Ornette Coleman.* CD, Original Jazz Classics Remasters 0888072328457, 2011 (orig. 1958).

Hentoff, Nat. Liner Notes to *Tomorrow Is The Question!* CD, Original Jazz Classics Remasters OJC20 342-2, 2003 (orig. 1959).

Howe, James. "Argument Is Argument: An Essay on Conceptual Metaphor and Verbal Dispute". *Metaphor and Symbol* 23 (2007): 1–23.

Huovinen, Erkki, and Anna-Kaisa Kaila. "The Semantics of Musical Topoi: An Empirical Approach". *Music Perception: An Interdisciplinary Journal* 33, no. 2 (December 2015): 217–243.

Huron, David. *Sweet Anticipation: Music and the Psychology of Expectation.* Cambridge MA: MIT Press, 2006.

Isaacs, James. Liner Notes to *The Complete Science Fiction Sessions.* CD, Columbia/Legacy C2K 63569, 2000 (orig. 1982).

Jakobson, Roman. "Two Aspects of Language and Two Types of Disturbances". In *On Language,* edited by Linda Waugh and Monique Monville-Burston. Cambridge, MA: Harvard University Press, 2002.

James, Alex. "Review of Free Jazz, Harmolodics and Ornette Coleman, by Stephen Rush". *Popular Music* 37, no. 2 (May 2018): 316–18.

Johnson, Mark. *The Body in the Mind: The Bodily Basis of Meaning, Imagination, and Reason.* Chicago: The University of Chicago Press, 1987.

Jost, Ekkehard. *Free Jazz.* New York: Da Capo Press, 1994 (orig. Graz [Austria]: Universal Edition, 1974).

Juslin, Patrick, and Petri Laukka. "Improving Emotional Communication in Music Performance through Cognitive Feedback". *Musicae Scientiae* 4 (2000): 151–83.

Kerman, Joseph. *Contemplating Music: Challenges to Musicology.* Cambridge, MA: Harvard University Press, 1985.

Kerman, Joseph. "How We Got into Analysis, and How to Get Out". *Critical Inquiry* 7, no. 2 (Winter 1980): 311–31.

Klein, Michael L. *Music and the Crisis of the Modern Subject.* Bloomington, IN: Indiana University Press, 2015.

Klein, Michael L., Nicholas Reyland, and Byron Almen, eds. *Music and Narrative Since 1900 (Musical Meaning and Interpretation).* Bloomington, IN: Indiana University Press, 2013.

Kramer, Lawrence. *After the Lovedeath: Sexual Violence and the Making of Culture.* Berkeley: University of California Press, 1997.

Kramer, Lawrence. *Classical Music and Postmodern Knowledge.* Berkeley: University of California Press, 1995.

Kramer, Lawrence. *Franz Schubert: Sexuality, Subjectivity, Song.* Cambridge: Cambridge University Press, 2003.

Kramer, Lawrence. "Musicology and Meaning". *The Musical Times* 144, no. 1883 (Summer 2003): 6–12.

138 Bibliography

Kristeva, Julia. *Revolution in Poetic Language*. Translated by Margaret Waller. New York: Columbia University Press, 1984.

Krumhansl, Carol. *Cognitive Foundations of Musical Pitch*. Oxford: Oxford University Press, 1990.

Krumhansl, Carol."Perceived Triad Distance: Evidence Supporting the Psychological Reality of Neo-Riemannian Transformations". *Journal of Music Theory* 42, no. 2 (Autumn, 1998): 265–81.

Krumhansl, Carol, and E. J. Kessler. "Tracing the Dynamic Changes in Perceived Tonal Organization in a Spatial Representation of Musical Keys". *Psychological Review* 89 (1982): 334–68.

Kuhl, Ole. "The Semiotic Gesture". In *New Perspectives on Music and Gesture*, edited by Elaine Gritten and Anthony King. Aldershot: Ashgate, 2006.

Lacan, Jacques. "The Agency of the Letter". In *Écrits: A Selection*. Translated by Alan Sheridan. London: Routledge, 2006 (orig. 1977).

Lacan, Jacques. *The Ethics of Psychoanalysis: The Seminar of Jacques Lacan, Book VII, 1959–1960*. Edited by Jacques-Alain Miller, Translated by Dennis Porter. New York: W.W. Norton and Company, 1992.

Lacan, Jacques. *The Other Side of Psychoanalysis: The Seminar of Jacques Lacan, Book XVII*. Edited by Jacques-Alain Miller, Translated by Russell Grigg. New York: W.W. Norton and Company, 1991.

Lacan, Jacques. *The Psychoses: The Seminar of Jacques Lacan, Book III, 1955–1956*. Edited by Jacques-Alain Miller, Translated by Russell Grigg. New York: W.W. Norton and Company, 1993.

Laclau, Ernesto, and Chantal Mouffe. *Hegemony and Socialist Strategy: Towards a Radical Democratic Politics*. 2nd ed. London: Verso, 2001 (orig. 1985).

Lake, Steve. "Prime Time and Motion". *The Wire* 19 (September 1985): 30–5.

Lakoff, George. *Women, Fire, and Dangerous Things: What Categories Reveal About the Mind*. Chicago: University of Chicago Press, 1987.

Lakoff, George, and Mark Johnson. *Metaphors We Live By*. Chicago: University of Chicago Press, 1980.

Larson, Steve. "Musical Forces, Melodic Expectation, and Jazz Melody". *Music Perception: An Interdisciplinary Journal* 19, no. 3 (Spring 2002): 351–85.

Larson, Steve. "Musical Forces and Melodic Patterns". *Theory and Practice* 22/23 (1997–98): 55–71.

Larson, Steve. *Musical Forces: Motion, Metaphor, and Meaning in Music*. Bloomington, IN: Indiana University Press, 2012.

Larson, Steve, and Leigh Vanhande. "Measuring Musical Forces". *Music Perception: An Interdisciplinary Journal* 23, no. 2 (December 2005): 119–36.

Lee, David Neil. *The Battle of the Five Spot: Ornette Coleman and the New Jazz Field*. Toronto: Mercury Press, 2006.

Le Guin, Elisabeth. *Boccherini's Body: An Essay in Carnal Musicology*. Berkeley: University of California Press, 2005.

Lerdahl, Fred. "Atonal Prolongational Structure". *Contemporary Music Review* 4 (1989): 65–87.

Lerdahl, Fred. *Tonal Pitch Space*. Oxford: Oxford University Press, 2005.

Lewin, David. "Cohn Function". *Journal of Music Theory* 40, no. 2 (Autumn, 1996): 181–216.

Bibliography 139

Lewin, David. "A Formal Theory of Generalized Tonal Functions". *Journal of Music Theory* 26, no. 1 (Spring, 1982): 23–60.

Lewin, David. *Generalized Musical Intervals and Transformations*. New Haven: Yale University Press, 1987.

Lidov, David. *Is Language a Music? Writings on Musical Form and Signification. (Musical Meaning and Interpretation)*. Bloomington, IN: Indiana University Press, 2005.

Lidov, David. "Mind and Body in Music". *Semiotica* 66 (1987): 69–97.

Litweiler, John. *The Freedom Principle: Jazz After 1958*. New York: William Morrow and Co, 1984.

Litweiler, John. *Ornette Coleman: A Harmolodic Life*. New York: William Morrow and Co, 1992.

Mandel, Howard. *Miles, Ornette, Cecil: Jazz Beyond Jazz*. London: Routledge, 2008.

Martin, T. E. "The Plastic Muse, Part 1". *Jazz Monthly* (May 1964).

Mazzola, Guerin. *Flow, Gesture and Spaces in Free Jazz: Toward a Theory of Collaboration*. Berlin: Springer-Verlag, 2009.

Mazzola, Guerin. *The Topos of Music: Geometric Logic of Concepts, Theory and Performance*. Basel: Birkhäuser Verlag, 2002.

McAdams, Stephen. "Musical Forces and Melodic Expectations: Comparing Computer Models and Experimental Results". *Music Perception: An Interdisciplinary Journal* 21, no. 4 (June 2004): 457–98.

McClary, Susan. *Feminine Endings: Music, Gender, and Sexuality*. Minneapolis: University of Minnesota Press, 1991.

McGlone, Matthew. "What Is the Explanatory Value of a Conceptual Metaphor?" *Language and Communication* 27 (2007): 109–26.

McKerrell, Simon, and Lyndon C. S. Way, eds. *Music as Multimodal Discourse: Semiotics, Power and Protest*. London: Bloomsbury Academic, 2017.

McRae, Barry. *Ornette Coleman*. London: Apollo, 1988.

Meyer, Leonard B. *Emotion and Meaning in Music*. Chicago: University of Chicago Press, 1956.

Meyer, Leonard B. *Explaining Music: Essays and Explorations*. Berkeley: University of California Press, 1973.

Meyer, Leonard B. *Music, the Arts, and Ideas: Patterns and Predictions in Twentieth-Century Culture*. Chicago: University of Chicago, 1967.

Miles, Stephen. "Critics of Disenchantment". *Notes* 52, no. 1 (September 1995): 11–38.

Miles, Stephen. "The Limits of Metaphorical Interpretation". *College Music Symposium* 39 (1999): 9–26.

Mill, John Stuart. *System of Logic: Ratiocinative and Inductive*. 8th ed. London: Longman Green and Co., 1891 (orig. 1843).

Molino, Jean. "Fait Musical et Sémiologie de la Musique". *Musique en Jeu* 17 (1975): 37–62.

Monelle, Raymond. "The Absent Meaning of Music". In *A Sounding of Signs: Modalities and Moments in Music, Culture and Philosophy: Essays in Honor of Eero Tarasti on his 60th Anniversary*, edited by Robert S. Hatten et al., 67–89. Imatra: International Semiotics Institute, 2008.

Monelle, Raymond. "Structural Semantics and Instrumental Music". *Music Analysis* 10, no. 1 (1991): 73–88.

140 Bibliography

Monson, Ingrid. *Saying Something: Jazz Improvisation and Interaction*. Chicago: University of Chicago Press, 1996.

Moore, Gregory H. "The Emergence of Open Sets, Closed Sets, and Limit Points in Analysis and Topology". *Historia Mathematica* 35 (2008): 220–41.

Morris, Robert D. *Composition with Pitch Classes: A Theory of Compositional Design*. New Haven, CT: Yale University Press, 1987.

Narmour, Eugene. *The Analysis and Cognition of Basic Melodic Structures: The Implication-Realization Model*. Chicago: University of Chicago Press, 1990.

Narmour, Eugene. *Beyond Schenkerism: The Need for Alternatives in Music Analysis*. Chicago: University of Chicago Press, 1977.

Nattiez, Jean-Jacques. *Fondements d'une sémiologie de la musique*. Paris: Union générale d'éditions, 1975.

Nattiez, Jean-Jacques. *Music and Discourse: Towards a Semiology of Music*. Translated by Carolyn Abbate. Princeton: Princeton University Press, 1990 (orig. 1987).

Ogden, C. K., and I. A. Richards. *The Meaning of Meaning: A Study of the Influence of Language Upon Thought and of the Science of Symbolism*. 2nd ed. (revised). Conneticut: Martino Publishing, 2013 (orig. 1927).

Osborne, Peter. "Contemporary Art is Post-Conceptual Art". Public Lecture, Fondazione Antonio Ratti, Villa Sucota, Como, 9 July 2010. Available at https://api.fondazioneratti .org/assets/PDFs/XVI-CSAV_Lectures/Leggi-il-testo-della-conferenza-di-Peter -Osborne-in-PDF1.pdf (Accessed 3rd September, 2021).

Palmer, Bob. Liner Notes to *The Complete Science Fiction Sessions*. CD, Columbia/Legacy C2K 63569, 2000 (orig. 1972).

Parker, Ian. "Lacanian Discourse Analysis in Psychology". *Theory and Psychology* 15, no. 2 (April 2005): 163–82.

Parker, Ian. "Lacanian Discourse Analysis: Seven Elements". In *Lacan, Discourse, Event: New Psychoanalytic Approaches to Textual Indeterminacy*, edited by Ian Parker and David Pavón-Cuéllar. London: Routledge, 2014.

Parker, Ian. *Psychology after Discourse Analysis: Concepts, Methods, Critique*. Routledge: London, 2015.

Parncutt, Richard, and Gary McPherson, eds. *The Science and Psychology of Music Performance: Creative Strategies for Teaching and Learning*. Oxford: Oxford University Press, 2002.

Pêcheux, Michel. *Analyse automatique du discours*. Paris: Dunod, 1969.

Pêcheux, Michel. *Automatic Discourse Analysis*. Translated by David Macey. Atlanta: GA Rodopi, 1995.

Poizat, Michel. *The Angel's Cry: Beyond the Pleasure Principal in Opera*. Translated by Arthur Denner. Ithaca: Cornell University Press, 1992.

Popoff, Alexandre, and Jason Yust. "Meter Networks: A Categorical Framework for Metrical Analysis". *Journal of Mathematics and Music* (2020). Available at: https://www .tandfonline.com/doi/full/10.1080/17459737.2020.1836687 (Accessed 3rd September, 2021).

Porter, Lewis. "The 'Blues Connotation' in Ornette Coleman's Music and Some General Thoughts on the Relation of Blues to Jazz". *Annual Review of Jazz Studies* 7 (1994): 75–95.

Porter, Lewis, Michael Ullman, and Ed Hazell. *Jazz: From its Origins to the Present*. London: Prentice-Hall International UK, 1992.

Bibliography 141

Pow, Zubillaga. "Symbolic Listening: The Resistance of Enjoyment and the Enjoyment of Resistance". In *Music-Psychoanalysis-Musicology*, edited by Samuel Wilson, 151–63. London: Routledge, 2018.

Priestly, Brian. *Mingus, A Critical Biography*. London: Palladin, 1985.

Quignard, Pascal. *La haine de la musique*. Paris: Gallimard, 1996.

Rahn, John. *Basic Atonal Theory*. New York: Longman, 1980.

Rasmusson, Ludvig. Liner Notes to *At the "Golden Circle", Stockholm, Volume One*. CD, Blue Note Records 72435 35518 2 7, 2002 (orig. 1965).

Ratliff, Ben. *The Jazz Ear: Conversations Over Music*. New York: Times Books, 2008.

Régnault, François. "Psychoanalysis and Music". Translated by Asunción Alvarez. *The Symptom* 11 (2010). Available at http://www.lacan.com/symptom11/?p=51 (Accessed 24th August 2014).

Renwick, William. "Structural Patterns in Fugue Subjects and Fugal Expositions". *Music Theory Spectrum* 13, no. 2 (Autumn 1991): 197–218.

Richards, I. A. *The Philosophy of Rhetoric*. Oxford: Oxford University Press, 1936.

Riemann, Bernhard. *Grundlagen für eine allgemeine Theorie der Functionen einer veränderlichen complexen Grösse*. Göttingen: Inauguraldissertation, 1851.

Rings, Steven. *Tonality and Transformation*. Oxford: Oxford University Press, 2011.

Rings, Steven. "Tonic". In *The Oxford Handbook of Critical Concepts in Music Theory*, edited by Steven Rings and Alexander Rehding, 106–35. Oxford: Oxford University Press, 2020.

Rink, John. Review of *Music and Gesture*, edited by Elaine Gritten and Anthony King. *The British Journal of Aesthetics* 47, no. 2 (April 2007): 224–26.

Rockwell, John. *All American Music: Composition in the Late Twentieth Century*. London: Kahn & Averill, 1985.

Rosen, Charles. "Music a la Mode". *New York Review of Books* 41 (June 1994): 55–62.

Rush, Stephen. *Free Jazz, Harmolodics and Ornette Coleman*. New York: Routledge, 2017.

Russ, Michael. Review of *The Analysis and Cognition of Basic Melodic Structures: The Implication-Realization Model*, by Eugene Narmour. *Music & Letters* 73, no. 3 (August 1992): 450–54.

Sacks, Harvey. *Lectures on Conversation*. Oxford: Blackwell, 1992.

Sarath, Ed. "A New Look at Improvisation". *Journal of Music Theory* 40, no. 1 (Spring 1996): 1–38.

Sasaki, Masashi. "Two Types of Modulation in Ornette Coleman's Music: 'From the Direction Inside the Musician' and 'From Listening To Each Other'". *Kyoto Seika University Bulletin* 39, English edition (2011): 3–19.

Saslaw, Janna. "Far Out: Intentionality and Image Schema in the Reception of Early Works by Ornette Coleman." *Current* Musicology 69 (Spring 2000): 97–117.

Saslaw, Janna. "Forces, Containers, and Paths: The Role of Body-Derived Image Schemas in the Conceptualization of Music". *Journal of Music Theory* 40, no. 2 (Autumn 1996): 217–43.

Saussure, Ferdinand de. *Course in General Linguistics*. Edited by Charles Bally and Albert Sechehaye, Translated by Wade Baskin. New York: McGraw-Hill Paperbacks, 1966.

Schenker, Heinrich. *Harmonielehre*. Vienna: Universal Edition, 1906.

Schenker, Heinrich. *Harmony*. Edited by Oswald Jonas, Translated by Elisabeth M. Borgese. Chicago: University of Chicago Press, 1954.

142 Bibliography

Schoenberg, Arnold. *Fundamentals of Musical Composition*. Edited by Gerald Strang and Leonard Stein. London: Faber and Faber, 1967.

Schoenberg, Arnold. *Theory of Harmony*. Translated by Roy E. Carter. Berkeley: University of California Press, 2011 (orig. 1922).

Schuijer, Michiel. *Analysing Atonal Music: Pitch-Class Set Theory and its Contexts*. Rochester NY: University of Rochester Press, 2008.

Schuller, Gunther. *A Collection of the Compositions of Ornette Coleman*. New York: MJQ, 1961.

Schuller, Gunther. Liner Notes to *Free Jazz*. CD, Atlantic Masters 81227 3609-2, 2002 (orig. 1997).

Schuller, Gunther. Liner Notes to *Ornette!* CD, Atlantic, 8122 73714-2, 2003 (orig. 1962).

Schuller, Gunther. "Ornette Coleman". In *The New Grove Dictionary of American Music*, edited by Wiley Hitchcock and Stanley Sadie, 467–69. London: Macmillan, 1986.

Schuller, Gunther. "Sonny Rollins and Thematic Improvising". In *Jazz Panorama*, edited by Martin Williams, 239–52. London: The Jazz Book Club, 1965 (orig. 1958).

Schwarz, David. *An Introduction to Electronic Art through the Teachings of Jacques Lacan: Strangest Thing*. London: Routledge, 2014.

Schwarz, David. *Listening Subjects: Music, Psychoanalysis, Culture*. Durham, NC: Duke University Press, 1997.

Scruton, Roger. "Understanding Music". *Ratio* 25, no. 2 (1983): 97–120.

Searle, John. *Speech Acts*. Cambridge: Cambridge University Press, 1969.

Shipton, Alyn. *A New History of Jazz*. London: Bloomsbury Academic, 2001.

Shoemaker, Bill. "Dialing Up Ornette". *JazzTimes* 25, no. 10 (December 1995): 42–4.

Sidran, Ben. *Black Talk*. Edinburgh: Payback Press, 1995.

Silverman, Kaja. *The Acoustic Mirror: The Female Voice in Psychoanalysis and Cinema (Theories of Representation and Difference)*. Indiana MA: Indiana University Press, 1988.

Simosko, Vladimir, and Barry Tepperman. *Eric Dolphy*. New York: Da Capo Press, 1979.

Smethurst, Reilly. "Say No to Lacanian Musicology: A Review of Misnomers". *International Journal of Zizek Studies* 11, no. 3 (2017). Available at https://zizekstudies.org/index.php/IJZS/article/view/1010/0. (Accessed 21st September 2021).

Smith, Kenneth M. *Desire in Chromatic Harmony: A Psychodynamic Exploration of Fin de Siecle Harmony (Oxford Studies in Music)*. Oxford: Oxford University Press, 2020.

Smith, Kenneth M. *Skryabin, Philosophy and the Music of Desire*. Farnham: Ashgate, 2013.

Smith, Kenneth M., and S. Overy. *Listening to the Unconscious: Adventures in Popular Music and Psychoanalysis*. London: Bloomsbury Academic, 2023.

Solie, Ruth A., ed. *Musicology and Difference: Gender and Sexuality in Music Scholarship*. Los Angeles and London: University of California Press, 1993.

Spellman, A. B. *Four Lives in the Bebop Business*. 4th ed. New York: Limelight Editions, 1994 (orig. 1966).

Spellman, A. B. Liner Notes to *Ornette on Tenor*. CD, Atlantic, 8122 79640-5 [no date] (orig. 1962).

Spitzer, Michael. *Metaphor and Musical Thought*. Chicago: University of Chicago Press, 2004.

Starobinski, Jean. *Les mots sous les mots: les anagrammes de Ferdinand de Saussure*. Paris: Gallimard, 1971.

Starobinski, Jean. *Words Upon Words: The Anagrams of Ferdinand de Saussure*. Translated by Olivia Emmet. New Haven: Yale University Press, 1979.

Bibliography   143

Steel, Lawrence. Liner Notes to *Complete Live at the Hillcrest Club*. CD, Gambit Records 69272, 2007.

Stevens, Catherine and Tim Byron. Review of Sweet Anticipation: Music and the Psychology of Expectation, by David Huron. *Music Perception: An Interdisciplinary Journal* 24, no. 5 (June 2007): 511–14.

Stewart, Dugald. *Philosophical Essays*. Edinburgh: William Creech, 1810.

Strauss, Joseph N. *Introduction to Post-Tonal Theory*. Englewood Cliffs, NJ: Prentice Hall, 1990.

Subotnik, Rose Rosengard. *Developing Variations: Style and Ideology in Western Music*. Minneapolis: University of Minnesota Press, 1991.

Szendy, Peter. *Hits: Philosophy in the Jukebox*. Translated by Will Bishop. New York: Fordham University Press, 2008.

Szendy, Peter. *Listen: A History of Our Ears*. Translated by Charlotte Mandell. New York: Fordham University Press, 2012.

Szendy, Peter. *All Ears: The Aesthetics of Espionage*. Translated by Roland Végső. New York: Fordham University Press, 2017.

Tarrant, Christopher. "Schubert, Music Theory and Lacanian Fantasy". In *Music-Psychoanalysis-Musicology*, edited by Samuel Wilson, 84–99. London: Routledge, 2018.

Taruskin, Richard. "Material Gains: Assessing Susan McClary". *Music and Letters* 90, no. 3 (August 2009): 453–67.

Taylor, Art. *Notes and Tones: Musician-to-Musician Interviews*. New York: Da Capo Press, 1993 (orig. 1977).

Temperley, David. "The Question of Purpose in Music Theory: Description, Suggestion, and Explanation". *Current Musicology* 66 (1999): 66–85.

Tomlinson, Gary. *Music in Renaissance Magic: Toward a Historiography of Others*. Chicago: Chicago University Press, 1993.

Tymoczko, Dmitri. "In Quest of Musical Vectors". Author's website. (March 2016). Available at https://dmitri.mycpanel.princeton.edu/vectors.pdf (Accessed 12th July 2020).

Tymoczko, Dmitri. *The Geometry of Music*. Oxford: Oxford University Press, 2011.

Tymoczko, Dmitri. "The Geometry of Musical Chords". *Science*, no. 313 (July 2006): 72–74.

Tymoczko, Dmitri. "Why Topology?" *Journal of Mathematics and Music* 14, no. 2 (2020). Available at https://www.tandfonline.com/doi/full/10.1080/17459737.2020.1799563. (Accessed 13th June, 2021).

Vickery, Lindsay and Stuart James. "The Enduring Temporal Mystery of Ornette Coleman's Lonely Woman". *Proceedings of the 2015 WA Chapter of MSA Symposium on Music Performance and Analysis* (2016).

Von Hippel, Paul, and David Huron. "Why Do Skips Precede Reversals? The Effect of Tessitura on Melodic Structure". *Music Perception: An Interdisciplinary Journal* 18, no. 1 (Fall, 2000): 59–85.

Walser, Robert. "The Body in the Music: Epistemology and Musical Semiotics". *College Music Symposium* 31 (1991): 117–126.

Warner, W. Lloyd. "American Caste and Class". *American Journal of Sociology* 42, no. 2 (September 1936): 234–237.

Watrous, Peter. "Ornette's Beautiful Difference: The Quartet Re-examined". *The Village Voice Jazz Special* (June 1987).

144 Bibliography

Westendorf, Lynette. *Analyzing Free Jazz*. PhD book, University of Washington, 1994.

Whitehead, Gregory. "Intro: The Squid Piece". Preamble presented at the *Segue Series Reading at the Bowery Poetry Club*, University of Pennsylvania, October 19, 2002. Available at http://www.writing.upenn.edu/pennsound/x/Whitehead.php (Accessed 24th August 2014).

Wiggins, Paula. "Women in Music, Feminist Criticism, and Guerrilla Musicology: Reflections on Recent Polemics". *19th-Century Music* 17, no. 2 (Autumn 1993): 174–92.

Williamon, Aaron, ed. *Musical Excellence: Strategies and Techniques to Enhance Performance*. Oxford: Oxford University Press, 2004.

Williams, Martin. *Jazz Masters in Transition 1959–1969*. London: Collier-Macmillan, 1970.

Williams, Martin. ed. *Jazz Panorama: From the Pages of the Jazz Review*. London: The Jazz Book Club, 1965.

Williams, Martin. Liner Notes to *Free Jazz*. CD, Atlantic Masters 81227 3609-2, 2002 (orig. 1961).

Williams, Martin. Liner Notes to *The Shape of Jazz to Come*. CD, Atlantic Masters 81227 31332 (orig. 1959).

Wilmer, Valerie. *As Serious As Your Life: John Coltrane and Beyond*. London: Cox and Wyman, 1992 (orig. 1977).

Wilmer, Valerie. "Billy Higgins – Drum Love". *Down Beat* (21 March 1968): 26–27, https://www.worldradiohistory.com/Archive-All-Music/DownBeat/60s/68/Downbeat-1968-03-21.pd.

Wilmer, Valerie. "Ed Blackwell: Well-Tempered Drummer". *Down Beat* (3 October 1968):18–19, https://www.worldradiohistory.com/Archive-All-Music/DownBeat/60s/68/Downbeat-1968-10-03

Wilson, Peter Niklas. *Ornette Coleman: His Life and Music*. Berkeley: Berkeley Hills Books, 1999.

Wilson, Samuel. "Does the Psychoanalysis of Music Have a "Subject"?" In *Music-Psychoanalysis-Musicology*, edited by Samuel Wilson, 199–35. London: Routledge, 2018.

Xenakis, Iannis. *Musiques formelles: nouveaux principes formels de composition musicale*. Paris: La revue musicale, editions richardmasse, 1963.

Zbikoswi, Lawrence. "Conceptual Blending, Creativity and Music". *Musicae Scientiae* 22, no.1 (2018): 6–23.

Zbikoswi, Lawrence. *Conceptualising Music: Cognitive Structure, Theory, and Analysis*. Oxford: Oxford University Press, 2002.

Žižek, Slavoj. *Looking Awry: An Introduction to Jacques Lacan through Popular Culture*. Cambridge, MA: MIT Press, 1991.

Žižek, Slavoj. *The Sublime Object of Ideology*. London: Verso, 1989.

Selected Discography

Coleman, Ornette. *Something Else!!!! The Music of Ornette Coleman*. Original studio sessions, prod. Lester Koenig, Contemporary Records, February–March 1958. Reissue prod. Nick Phillips. CD, Original Jazz Classics Remasters 0888072328457, 2011.

Coleman, Ornette. *Tomorrow Is The Question!* Original studio sessions, prod. Lester Koenig, Contemporary Records, March 1959. CD, Original Jazz Classics Remasters OJC20 342-2, 2003.

Bibliography 145

Coleman, Ornette. *The Shape of Jazz to Come*. Original studio sessions, prod. Nesuhi Ertegun, Atlantic Records, May 1959. CD, Atlantic Masters 81227 31332.

Coleman, Ornette. *Change of the Century*. Original studio sessions, Atlantic Records, October 1959. CD, Atlantic Masters 81227 3608-2.

Coleman, Ornette. *The Lenox Jazz School Concert*. Original recording August 1959. CD, FreeFactory 064, 2009.

Coleman, Ornette. *Complete Live at the Hillcrest Club*. Original recording October 1959. CD, Gambit Records 69272, 2007.

Coleman, Ornette. *This is Our Music*. Original studio sessions, Atlantic Records, July–August 1960. CD, Atlantic Masters 81227 3137-2.

Coleman, Ornette. *Free Jazz*. Original studio sessions, prod. Nesuhi Ertegun, Atlantic Records, December 1960. CD, Atlantic Masters 81227 3609-2, 2002.

Coleman, Ornette. *Ornette!* Original studio sessions, prod. Nesuhi Ertegun, Atlantic Records, January 1961. CD, Atlantic, 8122 73714-2, 2003.

Coleman, Ornette. *Ornette on Tenor*. Original studio sessions, prod. Nesuhi Ertegun, Atlantic Records, March 1962. CD, Atlantic, 8122 79640-5.

Coleman, Ornette. *Croydon Concert*. Original recording, August 1965. CD, FreeFactory 061, 2008.

Coleman, Ornette. *At the "Golden Circle", Stockholm, Volume One*. Original recording, prod. Francis Wolff, December 1965. Reissue prod. Michael Cuscuna. CD, Blue Note Records 72435 35518 2 7, 2002.

Coleman, Ornette. *At the "Golden Circle", Stockholm, Volume Two*. Original recording, prod. Francis Wolff, December 1965. Reissue prod. Michael Cuscuna. CD, Blue Note Records 72435 35519 2 6, 2002.

Coleman, Ornette. *The Empty Foxhole*. Original studio sessions prod. Francis Wolff, September 1966. CD, Blue Note Records 28982, 1994.

Coleman, Ornette. *The Music of Ornette Coleman*. Original studio sessions prod. Howard Scott, RCA, 1967. CD, BGO Records BG0CD1049, 2012.

Coleman, Ornette. *The Complete Science Fiction Sessions*. Original studio sessions, prod. James Jordan, Columbia Records, September – October 1971. CD, Columbia/Legacy C2K 63569, 2000.

Coleman, Ornette. *Skies of America*. Original studio sessions, prod. James Jordan, EMI Records, April 1972. CD, BGO Records BG0CD1049, 2012.

Coleman, Ornette. *In All Languages*. Original sessions, Caravan of Dreams, February 1987. CD, Harmolodic/Verve 314 531 915-2.

Noble, Ray, and His Orchestra. "Cherokee". Recorded October 11, 1938. 78rpm, Brunswick 8247.

Parker, Charlie. "Cherokee". Recorded September 1942. Track 12 on *Bird in Time 1940–1947—Selected Recordings and Rare Interviews Vol. 1. ESP-DISK, 2008, compact disc.*

Index

Note: Page numbers in *italics* indicate figures.

Adderley, Julian "Cannonball" 35, 38, 44n26, 121
addition 26–27
algebraic time 21
alto clefs 121
analysis: Hamiltonian 40, 53, 69, 102; known/unknown points 27; and synthesis 26–27, 29, 34, 39; of temporal points 48; of unknown analysands 27–28
antecedent points 62
antinomy 23–24n12
Architecture in Motion 21
Athaliah (Racine) 6–7

Baker, Chet 1
Battiste, Harold 57
bebop 25
Berger, Karl xix
Blackwell, Ed xvii
Bley, Paul xviii
breathing in space 95, 98
Brookmeyer, Bob xviii, 118
Burgoyne, Bernard 13–14, 16, 20

"C.&D." (*Civilization and Its Discontents*) xvi
Cadence magazine 126
change 77–78
Change of the Century, liner notes 55
changes 35, 73
"Cherokee" 82, *83–84*, 85
Cherry, Don xvi, 3, 25, 55, 112
chords 59, *60*, 61; and changes 35–36, 42; diatonic 36; F minor seventh 38–40; A flat major sixth 38–40; and Marsalis 57; and Movements 73, *74*; notes as 73, 80, 124; Ornette on 59; and tonic convergences 37–38; tonic spaces of 35; and triads 59, *60*; and where? 38
chromatic movements 58
Coleman, Ornette xiii, xiv, xv; background xvii–xviii; as composer xx; criticisms of xvii, xviii; and Derrida 65–66; ear of xvi, xviii, 3; *Wire* interview 82
A Collection of the Compositions of Ornette Coleman (Schuller) 85
complete jazz xv
composers, *vs.* improvisers xx
"Congeniality" 99
connections, disavowal of 3–4
continuity 95
convergence: and chords 35; and consequence 39, 41; and discourse 7, 15; and following 7, 127; and movement 125; and qualia 8; and quilting points 7-8, and relations 56, 124; structure of 124; and tonality 8, 44n25; and tonic relations 37; and tonics 33, 41, 42, 45, 61, 124; and transference 15; and Unison 121
convergence tonality 44n25
Creative Music Foundation xix

Db major *46*; in "Invisible" 45–46, *47*
Derrida, Jacques xix, 65
difference 78, 80, 118, 120
direction 29; as angle of inclination 53; as endpoint 53; free 45, 53–55, 78; lack of 25–26, 29; loss of 77; as sense 53
direction effects 62, 98

Index 147

dis-alignments 90–91, 118–19
disconnected space 11
disconnection 3–4, 11, 73
discourse 11–12n12; disconnections from
  3–4; on space 8–9; transferential 14
discourse analysis xviii, 6, 15, 123
discourse of the Other *see Other's
  discourse*
disjoint subsets 73
distance metaphor 43–44n22
division 26–27
Dolphy, Eric 73–74
DownBeat xv, 35, 101, 121
downbeat Ideas 79

effect of situation 69
Ellerbe, Charles xix
Emotion and Meaning in Music (Meyer) 18
emotional bonds 31
Encyclopedists 52, 68
equivalence 48–49
Eros 31
everything 71; and points 70
expectation 18
expositional ideas 95

fear, Lacan on 6–7
feme sole 66–67, 71
Five Spot xviii
following xiii, xvi, 41–42, 62, *63*, 79–80;
  and convergence 27, 41–42; defining 2;
  and direction 26, 29; "go where I go"
  xvi, 1–2, 7, 26, 29, 45, 56, 80, 98, 120,
  123–25, 127; Haden's story of 1–2; and
  leading 2, 32, 62, *63*; and ordered pairs
  9; and retroaction 7; tonic movement 32;
  and unison 120–21
Forte, Allen 9
"Fragment of an Analysis of a Case of
  Hysteria" (Freud) 17–20
free 7, 15, 23, 119
"Free" 55, *56*
free differences 78–81, 118, 126
free interval vectors 58, *59*
free jazz xv
free turning 79
freedom 22, 62, 121–22, 126; and "Law
  Years" xvi"
Freud, Sigmund 13, 15, 17, 31
Freudian groups 31
Freudian identification 17
Freudian transference 17–18
Fuller, Buckminster 40, 101

gains, and losses 77
general conceptions, searches for 50–51
general *vs.* specific theories of music 2–3
geometrical translations 63–64n7
geometry 47
Giordano, John xix
"go where I go" xvi, 1–2, 7, 26, 29, 45, 56,
  80, 98, 120, 123–25, 127
"going anywhere" 80–81
group psychology 31

Haden, Charlie xv, xvi, 1, 14–15, 25, 55,
  112, 120, 123, 127
Hamilton, Andy 105–6
Hamilton, William Rowan 9, 13, 21–22,
  26–27, 29, 33–34, 47–48, 123–24
Hamiltonian vectors 9
harmolodic clefs 112
harmolodic discourses, and transposition 21
A Harmolodic Life (Litwiler) 25
harmolodic movements 74–75
harmolodic reading 112–13, 116
"harmolodic space" xiii
The Harmolodic Theory xv, 101
harmolodics xv, 4, 14, 101, 117, 126; and
  Haden 14–15; and harmolodic thought 15;
  and transference 14–15; and the voice 117
harmonic Ideas 73
harmonic simultaneity 102
harmonic tonics 37–38, 41, 44n27, 73
"hasn't any relation" 96–97
Hausdorff, Felix 10
"having everything" 68, 73, 76–77
Helmholtz, Hermann 101, 103–4
Hentoff, Nat 45, 53, 67, 79, 92–93, 95
Hermann, Imre 13
Higgins, Billy 25, 55, 112
homologies 13

"I Got Rhythm" (Gershwin) xvii
idea 7–8, 71, 76 and relations 77; and a
  tapping foot 92–93
idealisation 31
Idea-names 107–8
Ideas 22, 67–68, 72, 99–100n18, 105–6,
  106–7, 114, 126, 128; and intervals 80;
  Ornettian Ideas 70, 72–73, 93, 114–15;
  and pitches 67–69, 71–72, 106–7,
  114–15
Idea-sounds 114–15, 125
identification 31
identities 10, 12n21, 18–21, 38, 42, 48–50,
  52–55, 115–16, 118–19, 126

148 Index

"in" 71
In All Languages xix
Indian Suite (Noble) 82–83
Inrockuptibles 65
intersection points, and quilting 7
interval vectors 53
intervals 7, 9, 15, 23, 67–69, 124; and
  everything 71, 73; in "Invisible" 45;
  and movement 79–80; Ornettian 69–71,
  73–76, 80; and relations 69; same sound
  of *113*, 115; shifts in 68; from the tonic
  29–30, 32; and transformation 43–44n22
intonational differences 118
invisibility 67–68, 119; and free direction
  53; and relations 50; and transposition 50
"Invisible" 23, 45, 55, *56*, 57, *58*, 124
isolated points 11

Jazz Times magazine 108
Jost, Ekkehard xviii
Jousse, Thierry xix, 65

Kineally, Will 127
knowledge: and Hamilton 29; and identity
  118; Norris on xvii; and Pappus 39; and
  tonic coordinates 38–41; and tonics 38;
  and the unknown 41–42; and where to go
  xvi, 1–2, 7, 26, 29, 33–34, 39–40, 45, 56,
  61–62, 80, 98, 120, 123–25, 127
Koenig, Lester 45

Lacan, Jacques 6
Lacanian Discourse Analysis 5
Lacanian psychoanalysis xiii
language scraps 3
Lavelle, Matt xix
"Law Years" xvi
leading, and "following" 2
Lectures on Quaternions (Hamilton) 26, 48
Lennox School of Jazz xvii–xviii
Lewin, David 43–44n22
listening 2, 95–96
listening for listening 2
Litweiler, John xix, 25, 70
logic 116
London Symphony Orchestra 102, 113
loneliness, and solitude 66
"Lonely Woman" 10, 21–23, 66–67,
  79, 82, 85–86, *87–89,* 90–91, 95,
  99n12, 124
losses, and gains 77
love, and mathematics 13

love conflicts 82–83, 97
love relations 31

McBrowne, Lennie 1
McDowell, Al xix
Made in America xix
"make the changes" xvii
manifestations, and +1 57–58
Marsalis, Ellis 57
Mathematical Collection (Pappus of
  Alexandria) 39
mathematics 13, 92, 95
The Meaning of Meaning (Richards and
  Ogden) 18, 20
meaning shifts 10, 51
meanings, and words 76
Measham, David 102
melodic direction 42, 45, 53
melodic vectors 53–54
metaphor, and transference 19, 24n26
metre 92, 99n8
metrical chains 83–85, 92
metrical feel 85–86
Mill, John Stuart 15, 50–51, 64n10
"Moose the Mooche" (Parker) xvii
Moss, Dave xix
motifs 48, 50
movable points 29, 32, 37, 49, 53, 69
movement 7, 15, 23, 26, 28–29, 33
Movements 73, *74,* 79–80, 124
Movements in Harmolodic Space xvi, 2
Mulligan, Gerry 1
multiplication 26–27
Murphy, Timothy S. 65
music: as cure 4; listening to 95–96;
  Ornette's experiences of 3
music "appreciation" xiii
musical alphabet 113, 116
musical anaylsis 6
musical notes *106–7*, 108, *109–11*, 115
musical timing 92
musical tones 103–4
musical transference 24n26
musical unisons 102

neighbourhood topology 5
neighbourhoods 10–11, 62; tuning
  neighborhoods *104*, 105, 115, 118–19
net duration 93
netted rhythm 92–93, 98
netted time 97
Nix, Bern xix

Index   149

no relation 7
Noble, Ray 82
non-relations 10
non-tempered psyche 118
Norris, Walter xvii, 78

observation 51
Ogden, C. K. 18, 20, 71–72
On the Sensations of Tone (Helmholtz) 101
one note 105, 118
one sound 114–15, 120
one-relation-sounds 114–15
order, and relations 9
ordered pairs 9
ordinal/cardinal relations 27
Ornette! xvi, 58
Ornette, Coleman *see* Coleman, Ornette
Ornette's music 117; and chords 35–36, 59;
   listening to 95–96; Ornette on 5–6, 73;
   and transposition 14
Ornettian chords 35, *106–7,* 108, *109*
Ornettian Movements 79–80
Other's discourse 5–6, 123

parallelisms 14, 20–21, 81n15, 111–13
Parker, Charlie xvii, 25
partial identification 17, 19–21
Peirce, C. S. 18
The Philosophy of Rhetoric (Richards) 19, 76
phrases 72–73
pitch, and tone 104–5
pitch space, and vectors 53, *54*
pitch space neighbourhoods *60,* 64n19
pitch-sole 73, 76, 79
point-effects 62
points 70; isolated 67; and relations 78–79,
   126–28; and transposition 49–50, 62
points of convergence: and following
   41–42; and relations 7; and signifiers 7;
   tonic 8, 34–35, 37; unknown 40
point-sounds 114–15, 125–26
Price, Seth xvi
Prime Time 101–2
"Prime Time for Harmolodics" (Ornette)
   xv, 101, 116, 124–25
producing their own objects 2
proximities, in "Lonely Woman" *87–89,* 90
psychoanalysis: ear of 2; and science 13
psychobiography genre xiii
punctual disunion 121

q1 55
qualia 30, 44n25; and *chroma* 32

quaternions 9, 26–27
quilting xix, 5–8, 15, 33, 123

random overhearing 3
Redman, Dewey 112
relational disUnison 121
relations 4–5, 9–10, 12n21, 23, 97–98;
   disavowed 128; and equivalence 48–49;
   free relations 10, 56–57, 62, 99, 119–21,
   124–25; and harmony 70; and idea
   77; and intervals 69; and invisibility
   50; no relation 7, 81, 96–98, 124–25;
   and order 9, 97; Ornettian 96; and
   partial identification 21; and points of
   convergence 7, 61; and something else
   78–79; of tone 104–5; and *transference*
   9–10, 47–48, 69; and transferential shifts
   20
relation-sounds 114–15, 125–26
respiratory measures 97–98
retroaction 7, 12n19
Richards, I. A. 18–20, 71–72, 76
Rings, Steven 8, 30, 32, 43–44n22, 44n25,
   81n11
Robinson, Abraham 13–14
Rollins, Sonny 96
Roy Noble Orchestra 83
"R.P.D.D" (*The Relation of the Poet to
   Daydreaming*) xvi
Russell's paradox 16–17, 23–24n12

saxophones 104, 116, 118, 121
"scalar multiplication" 84–85
Schenker, Heinrich 30, 33
Schoenberg, Arnold 8
Schuller, Ed xix
Schuller, George xix
Schuller, Gunther xix, 67, 70, 72–73, 82,
   85, *87–89,* 90–91, 93, 95–96, 99–
   100n18, 117
science, and psychoanalysis 13
Science Fiction xvi
"The Scope of Jazz" 67
sensation of tone 101–2, 117
Sertso, Ingrid xix
The Shape of Jazz to Come 25, 67, 85–86
shared spaces 25–26, 29, 33, 41
Shoemaker, Bill 108, 110
signifiers 5, 114; defined 16–17;
   harmolodic 74–75; and identities 52–53;
   phrases as 72; and points of convergence
   7; *see also specific signifiers*
signs 18

150 Index

singular theories 2
situating vectors 7–8, 32–33, 124
situation 8
Skies of America xv, xix, 10, 14, 21–22,
102, *103*, 107, *108*, *110–11*, 113,
119–20; liner notes 101
solitude 4, 7, 66, 76–77, 79–80
solitude relations 10, 99
Something Else!!!! xvii, xix, 23, 45; liner
notes 53, 78–79
something else, and relations 78–79
sound medicine 4
sound names, transferences 114
sounds 114–15
space 5, 8–10, 126
space analysis xviii, xix
"The Sphinx" 93, *94*, 98–99
spread rhythm 92, 95, 97–99, 124
"the squid piece" 3–4
Stewart, Dugald 13, 15–16, 51, 68
Stewart's law 16, 19–20, 22, 52, 68, 126
Stewart's theory of transference 13
subtraction 26–27
synthesis 26–27, 29, 32; and analysis
26–27, 29, 34, 39; interval vectors 32
System of Logic (Mill) 15, 50

"T.&T." (*Totem and Taboo*) xvi
tapping foot 92–93, 95, 97–98,
99–100n18
teleology 40
temporal analogies 47–48
temporal differences 47–48
temporal ideas 97
temporal space 90
temporal vector-relations 70
tenor 19
tension 82–83, 85–86, 95, 97–98, 124–25
"That's it! That's it!" 57
theories of signs 18
Theory of Harmony (Schoenberg) 8
thirds 29, 33–34
time 91–92, 97
Tomorrow is the Question 58
tonal centres 45–46, 119
tonal hearing 8
tonal *qualia* 8, 81n11
tonality: and Ornette's music 34; and
tonics 34
tone 118; and pitch 104–5; Schuller on 117
Tone Dialling xxn2, 59
tonic convergences, and chords 37–38
tonic coordinates 10, 32–33, 38–41

tonic direction 42
tonic relations 35, *36*, 77, 99, 123–25
tonic vectors 31–32, *36–37*, 44n27, 124;
and movable points 32; and situating
vectors 32–33
tonic-directed attention 30
tonics 7, 15, 23, 29, 34–35, 61, 73,
120; defined 30; final tonics 37; and
knowledge 38; and movable points 33;
Ornette's solution 41–42; points of
convergence 8; and scale-steps 30–31;
tonal centres 45; tonal-root transferences
38, 42; tonal tonics 34–38, 41; and
transference 34, 41
topology 10; *see also* neighbourhood
topology
transcriptions xix, xx
transference xvi, xviii, xix, 5, 7, 14;
analogous 22; and completion 18–19;
of context 71–72; defined 15; distance
between points 69; Freudian 17–20;
Hamiltonian 49, 52; and harmolodics
14–15; and identity 19–20; and intervals
68; and metaphor 19, 24n26; of names
51–52, 111–12, 114; Ornettian 35;
Ornettian "laws" 116–17; parallelism/
translation 20–21; and relations 9–10;
Stewart's 49; and tonal orientation 35;
and tonics 34, 41; and transcriptions
21–22; veiling functions of 52
transference class 17
transference of relations 21, 78, 124
transferential shifts 20, 22–23
transformation, and interval 43–44n22
transformational attitude 43–44n22
transitive applications 22, 51, *52*
transitive relationships 44n28
transposition 21, 63–64n7, 125–26; and
the Db major chord 46, *47*; in "Free" 55;
and free relations 62; and the harmolodic
clef 112; and harmolodic discourses 21;
and identity 49; love and music 98; and
Marsalis 57; melodic 49–50; and relation
transference 47–48; and veiling 46–47,
49–50
tuning temperaments 118
"Turnaround" 58
turning 79
Tymoczko, Dmitri 43–44n22

Ughi, Federico xix
unison 7, 10, 15, 22–23, 105, 107, 114–16,
119, 125, 128; harmolodic notions of

108; and musical notes *106–7,* 108, *109–11*; notations of 105–6; Ornettian 121, 125; sensation of 101–2, 117; and the voice 117

unison relations 10, 99, 115–16, 120, 125

unison themes 103, 113, 115

unity 31, 86

univocal applications 52

upbeat Ideas 70–71

vectoral movement 43–44n22

vectoral relations 48, 70

vectors 26–29, 54, 69, 98, 123–24; free interval vectors 58, *59*; free vectors 54–55, 61, 98, 124; and freedom 22; Hamilton's 9, 29, 39, 43–44n22, 49; identities of 54–55; interval 53; inverse 100n19; and quotients 49; tonic vectors 31–32, 69; transfered to points 70–71

vehicles 19, 28, 98, 123–24

vibrations 101

Virgin Beauty xix

voice 117, 125, 128

Wessel, Kenny 59–60

"What Causes Structure to Find a Place in Love?" (Burgoyne) 13

where? 26, 29, 33, 38–39, 61

Whitehead, Gregory 3–4

Williams, Richard 118

The Wire 82, 105–6

words, and meanings 76

"W.R.U." (*Wit and Its Relation to the Unconscious*) xvi, 58, *59*

Printed in the United States
by Baker & Taylor Publisher Services